MARTIAL ARTS MOVIES

MARTIAL ARTS MOVIES

FROM BRUCE LEE TO THE NINJAS 

By Richard Meyers
Amy Harlib
Bill and Karen Palmer

CITADEL PRESS SECAUCUS, NEW JERSEY

First Edition

Published by Citadel Press
A division of Lyle Stuart Inc.
120 Enterprise Ave., Secaucus, N.J. 07094
In Canada: Musson Book Company
A division of General Publishing Co. Limited
Don Mills, Ontario

Queries regarding rights and permissions should be addressed to: Lyle Stuart, 120 Enterprise Avenue, Secaucus, N.J. 07094

Designed by *Paul Chevannes*

Manufactured in the United States of America

Library of Congress Cataloging in Publication Data

Main entry under title:

Martial arts movies.

Filmography: p.
1. Hand-to-hand fighting, in motion pictures.
I. Meyers, Richard.
PN1995.9.H3M37 1985 791.43'09'09355 84-23162
ISBN 0-8065-0950-3

Dedication
To our Masters, Mentors, and Friends

Acknowledgments

A basic premise of film book writing: getting American cinematic material is easier than getting Asian. The cooperation and graciousness of the following were invaluable.

Lou Israel and Zita Siegel of World Northal
Russell Cawthorne of Golden Communications
Rudy De Blasio and Rick Sullivan of Theatre Management Associates
Gary Hertz of New Line Cinema
Michael Wiese, Sharon Stregar, and Lisa Murray of Vestron Video
Laura J. Cameron of Wometco Home Theater
John Pierson of Films Incorporated
Sandra Siegel and all the folks at CFW Enterprises
Miss Choi Suk-kuen of the Hong Kong International Film Festival
Mr. Nobuyoshi Higashi, Director of the International Kokushiryu Goshinho Jujitsu Assoc.
David Owens of the Japan Society
Bill Phillips
Tony Chan
Bill Thompsen
Robert "Indian" Bergman
Video Vault, Broadway, New York, NY
Video Source, Post Road East, Westport, CT
Video Station, Post Road East, Westport, CT
Larry Edelstein
John Gillen
Victor Lim
Laurine White
The Harlib Family
Linda Sampson
Larry Hama
Chris Browne
All artists, martial and otherwise

Contents

Preface

A Note on the Names and Dates

First, the original language titles of Oriental films are often different from the titles Westerners see in the United States. In all cases, we list the original title and then put the U.S. title in parentheses. Sometimes the titles don't change and, in some rare instances, the films haven't been exported yet. In both cases the title is left alone—without parentheses.

Second, Chinese names are tough on Occidental eyes. To prevent further confusion, we have virtually eliminated the hyphens and capitalization changes that are rife in the Far East. For instance, we have changed names like Liu Chia-liang to Liu Chia Liang.

Finally, the dates. In every case we have printed the original language release date, not the date it showed up in America.

The many faces of Bruce Lee.

Introduction

Exhilaration.

That's what the martial arts movie is all about. "To invigorate or stimulate." That's what it means.

We are a writer, a dancer, and two martial artists, but we all found common ground in Chinatown theaters, in exploitation movie houses, and on television—enjoying probably the most misunderstood, most underrated, and most vilified film genre ever projected.

This reputation is not without its basis. At its worst, the martial arts movie is laughable, totally deserving of derision. But at its best, it can supply an audience exhilaration that cannot be found in any other cinema.

In actuality, what we're examining here is Oriental cinema and the American attempts to emulate it. Kungfu movies, judo films, Ninja adventures, karate conflicts, and samurai sagas—all chop, kick, slice, and spin within the Oriental movie arena.

From the animal grace of Bruce Lee through the brutal flailing of Sonny Chiba to the wooden precision of Chuck Norris, martial arts movies are ridiculed or ignored by everyone save the millions who love them. The very same people who gasp in wonder at the Peking Opera deride kungfu movies without realizing that the finest ones are marvelous combinations of opera and ballet. There are those who trumpet the works of John Wayne and John Ford while spurning the kinetic violence of chambara (Japanese "sword-slashers"), without realizing that the historic grandeur of the latter films are just as great as any western.

But enough of this defensiveness. The historic grandeur, the melodramatic emotions, and the impressive choreography only serve to point up the martial arts movies' action. That's what we really love. These are great action movies. These are great superhero movies. They deliver where other unimaginative, overblown, and campy superhero movies fail.

These movies aren't afraid to play their incredible fights straight. These movies don't have to hope that you will believe a man can fly. Men and women actually do fly in these pictures, and without the aid of unconvincing wires or front screen projection. In the Oriental cinema, the actor *is* the stunt man and actually performs all the stunning feats on screen, creating a verisimilitude the likes of which Superman and Batman can't even approach.

That's another thing. The best martial arts movies are period pieces in which people call upon their own greatest abilities to succeed, and not on cars to escape or on guns to win. The heroes of Oriental films are terrific acrobats and martial artists, magnificent athletes who can be literally breathtaking to watch. Their precision and power underline the attributes of the martial arts film.

The history of the Orient and of the martial arts movie is a grand one and this volume is a tour of it. To consider every chop-socky picture would be impossible, not to mention pretty horrible. Unfortunately, American importers seem to seek out the worst the Orient has to offer, while shopping carefully in France, Germany, and other film capitals.

To discourse in extreme detail on how many bad kungfu movies called *Bloody Fingernails* were made in the Philippines for a dollar ninety-eight would serve neither the reader nor the genre. Instead, these pages will tell you just about everything you need to know to enhance your viewing, whether it be in the theaters or in the home. We will tell you what to look for as well as what to watch out for. We will trumpet the best and decry the worst.

From *Enter the Dragon* to *Kungfu Zombies*, get ready. This is the martial arts movie.

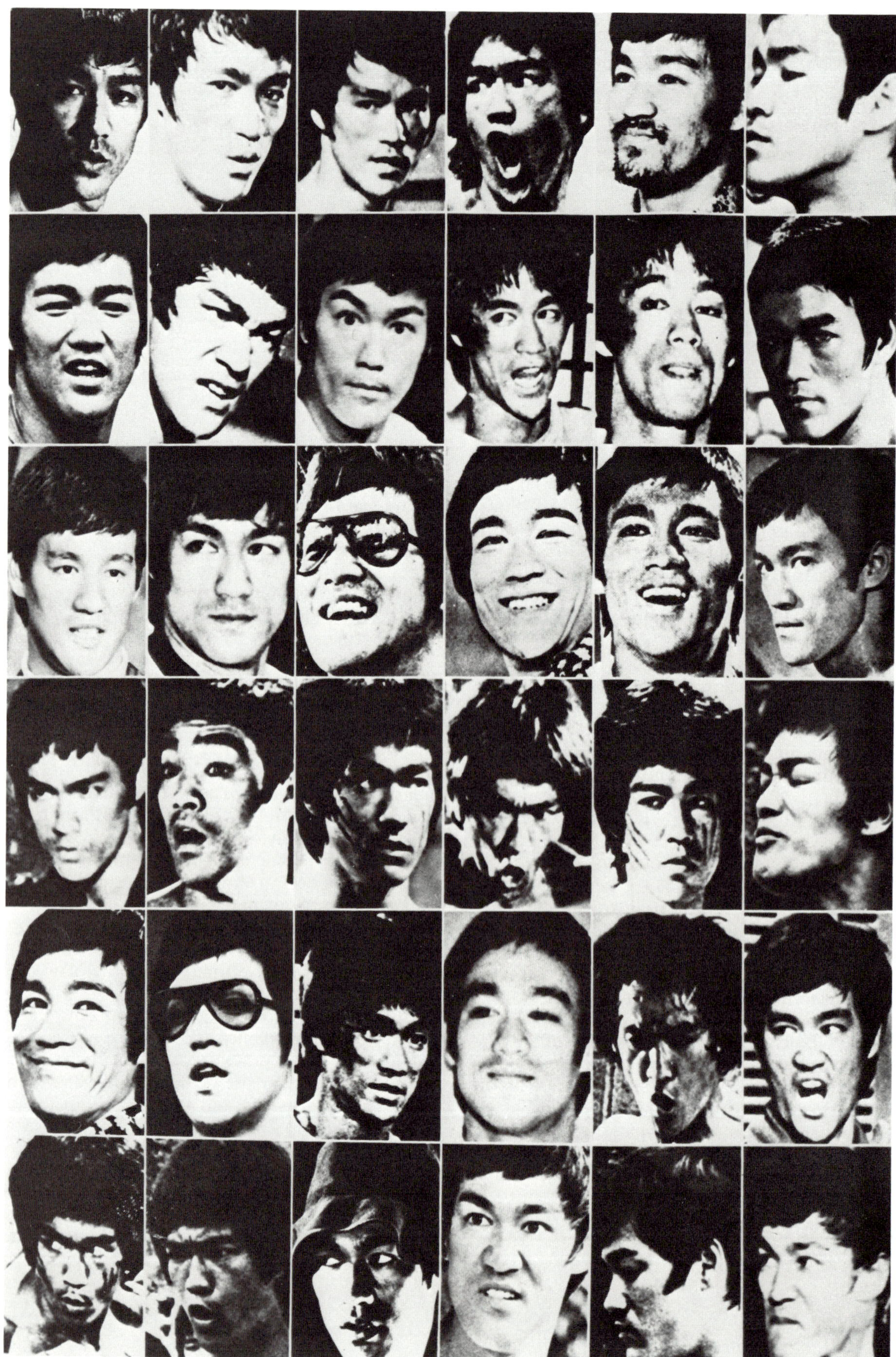

More of the many faces of Bruce Lee.

CHAPTER ONE

"Bruce Lee: The King of Kungfu"

To most of the world, the martial arts movie can be summed up in one name: Bruce Lee. It was he, more than anyone else, who established the power of the genre internationally. It was his superlative martial arts ability and canny filmmaking knowledge which touched audiences everywhere, leaving a mark that cannot be erased.

But it is also Bruce Lee who, through a series of unfortunate occurrences, set a trap for the martial arts film that it is just beginning to escape from. Had Bruce Lee lived, perhaps this trap would never have been sprung. But he did not live and his mysterious, frustrating death marked both the beginning and the end of the martial arts movie genre.

The beginnings for the teacher and filmmaker started November 27, 1940, when Lee Jun Fan was born to Lee Hoi Chuen and his wife Grace in San Francisco. While Orientals always have their family names first, Americans do it the other way around. Since the lad was born in the United States, the hospital needed an Anglicized name. Reportedly, it was the supervising doctor, Mary Glover, who conceived the name Bruce Lee, for the record.

He was born into a family of two older girls, Agnes and Pheobe, and an older brother, Peter. Not too long after Bruce was born, they were joined by another brother, Robert. To them Bruce was known as Lee Yuen Kam, an adaptation of his original name. They were a theatrical family, with Lee Hoi Chuen a renowned actor on both American coasts and in Hong Kong. Just three months after his birth, Bruce joined his father on stage, in a production of *Golden Gate Girl.* Although hardly a triumph, it was a start.

When the family returned to the Orient soon after, Bruce continued his thespian ways while starting a few new distressing ones. He was a thin, small, and somewhat sickly child, prone to nightmares and sleepwalking. Compensation came in the form of energy. He always seemed to be moving, never satisfied with being still. Friends and family remember Bruce as an extremely positive, assured youth; and his assurance became brazen as he matured.

His progress was marked by appearances in Hong Kong movies, starting in 1946, when he was six years old. The director of one of his father's films was impressed by Bruce's attitude and cast him in a small part for the picture *Birth of a Man*, which was also known by the title *The Beginning of a Boy*. Only a year later, Bruce was already starring in films such as *My Son A-Chang* in which he played the title role of a street smart kid trying to get ahead in the sweat-shop world of Hong Kong. His name then was Lung or Siu Lung, which meant "Dragon" or "Little Dragon."

Even at the age of seven, Lee's screen persona was strong. He was a clever, capable, but short-tempered little ruffian who specialized in the scowl, the pout, the stare, and the slow burn. This character served him on the streets as well. Ignoring the lessons of his films and his family, Bruce Lee, in his own words, "went looking for fights."

By the time he hit his teens, he was already well equipped to handle those fights. He was a natural dancer, becoming quite proficient in the cha-cha, and his natural grace lent itself to Wing Chun, the physically economical but brutal martial art he decided to follow. Some nights he would dance. Other nights he would scour the streets for a fight. Already he was showing signs of obsessive behavior.

He would read voraciously, which led to the need for glasses. He would play practical jokes, which only became serious if he were personally challenged by his victim. Oftentimes it was no fun playing with Bruce Lee; his desire to win at all costs was almost consuming. Even when he lost a street fight, he would find a way to make it seem as if he had won. And all the time he exercized and trained—not only wanting to convince himself he was the best, but to actually *be* the best.

The tragedy of his ultimate fate was to be played out on a minor scale in the Hong Kong of 1959. The more famous Bruce Lee became as a teen-age movie actor, the more uncontrollable he became in real life. Things came to a head with the premiere of his most successful film of that time, *The Orphan*. Although Wu Chu Fan was the ostensible

Bruce Lee's first success in America; playing Kato on The Green Hornet.

star, playing a teacher who lost his family in a Japanese air raid, Bruce all but stole the show as Ah Sam, an orphan who survived as a street thief.

Again, all the acting skills which were to lead to his superstardom were well in evidence here. Lee's emotional intensity was powerful. He portrayed frustration beautifully as on-screen schoolmates laughed at his lack of education and his peers were embarrassed by his bad manners. When he finally fights back, threatening his teachers and fellows with a knife during class, it is a cathartic scene, which Lee plays to the hilt, taunting and laughing.

Ah Sam returns to his gang, which masterminds the kidnapping of a rich man's son, but he can't forget the kindness of his teachers. He returns when Wu Chu Fan, playing Ho See Kei, discovers that Ah Sam is his own long lost son, separated from him in the aforementioned air raid. Repentant, Ah Sam leads the police to the gang's hideout and single-handedly saves the kidnapped boy. The film concludes with Lee tearfully begging forgiveness from his father, his teachers, his schoolmates, and his ancestors.

On screen Bruce Lee begged forgiveness. Off screen, he begged from no one, and gave nothing. Things were getting so difficult for his family that Bruce went back to America. The story goes that the Shaw Brothers Studio—the most powerful movie company in Hong Kong—offered him a contract which his mother forbade him to take, all but banishing him to the States, praying that education there would straighten him out.

GO WEST, YOUNG MAN

So, at the moment when Bruce Lee was to gain his greatest success, he was forced to retreat. The exile, self-imposed or not, served its purpose. Bruce Lee was a stranger in a strange land at the age of eighteen, forcing him to work all the harder to excel. At first he enrolled at the Edison High Technical School in Seattle, but moved on to the Uni-

The climactic moment of Bruce Lee's memorable scene in Marlowe, *starring James Garner.*

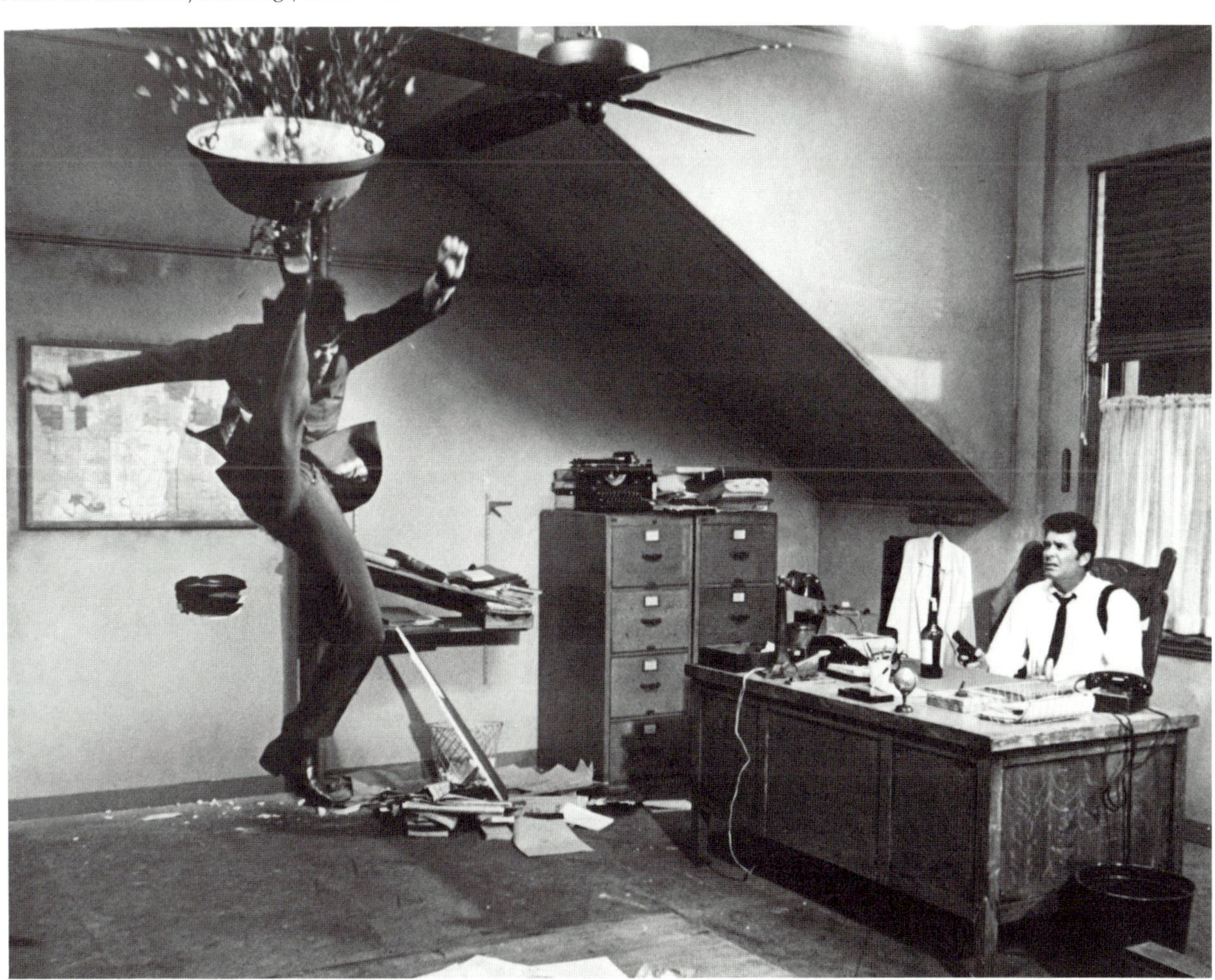

versity of Washington. His energy did not lessen with maturity, but it was directed. Delving deeper and deeper into the martial arts, Lee worked in restaurants for a while, but soon began teaching kungfu.

Kungfu, which is also referred to as wushu (a Chinese version of the words "martial arts"), kung fu, and gung fu, is a method of combat developed in China by Shaolin Temple monks. It is a brilliant method of fighting based on the nature of humanity and the animals that inhabit the earth. It was so effective in its use—and equally effective in developing the student to his or her optimum mental and physical capabilities—that it spread throughout the Orient.

Legend has it being taught in Japan, where it developed into aikido, judo, and karate—the latter a two-stage developement of Tang boxing, which came from the Ryukyu Islands. From there it spread south to become the vicious Thai boxing, and north to Korea where it became the impressive tae kwon do.

Bruce Lee had a foundation of Tai Chi Chuan, which had been taught to him by his father, over which was the effective structure of Wing Chun, taught to him by his master, Yip Man. He thought deeply about his skills and developed them further while attending the University of Washington. Lee's exhaustive research into fighting and self-perfection led to his writing of the book *Chinese Gung-Fu: The Philosophical Art of Self-Defense* in the early sixties. By 1964, the demons that had led him to the streets were now pointing him toward Hollywood.

The year 1964 was an important one in Lee's life. He married Linda Emery, moved to California, and met Ed Parker, Chuck Norris, Bob Wall, and Mike Stone. They were all at the Ed Parker International Karate Championships and became fast friends.

"He did a demonstration there and I won the grand championship in the heavyweight division," Stone remembers. "Afterwards we went out for a Chinese dinner. We became friends and would work out together one day a week. I would work out with him one day, Chuck Norris would work out with him another and so would Joe Lewis." All three men would become influential in the American martial arts movie market.

But it was Bruce Lee who created the market the other men would enter. The man who put Lee's foot in the door was Ed Parker. He had filmed Bruce's performance at the Internationals and showed them to his student, Jay Sebring, who, in turn, showed them to William Dozier, who needed a "Kato" for his *Green Hornet* television show in 1966.

Television producer Dozier was riding high that year with the success of *Batman,* a show that camped up Bob Kane's famous comic-book character. The ABC-TV Network wanted another superhero to follow on the Caped Crusader's heels, and Dozier chose George W. Trendle's popular radio character, the masked master crimefighter known as The Green Hornet. Behind the mask was Britt Reid, created by Trendle as the nephew of John Reid, better known as The Lone Ranger, who was also created by Trendle.

Fortunately for Bruce Lee, Dozier did not eliminate the character of Britt's Oriental manservant and chauffeur. In half-hour episodes which lasted less than a year, Kato piloted the Green Hornet's supercar, "The Black Beauty," through uninspiring battles against organized crime. Dozier eliminated the outlandish villains of the Batman show, but kept the unrealistic approach. The only time the show took off was when Bruce Lee did.

More than the Green Hornet's guns, which shot gas and needles, and his armor-plated, gadget-laden car, what sold the show to it's pre-teen audience was Lee's kungfu. Whenever Kato got out from behind the wheel and started kicking, the show started clicking. But as Mike Stone noted, "They had to restrain Bruce as Kato, because there was a star."

That star was Van Williams, who, although he became a friend and student of Lee's, couldn't convince the powers that be to give Lee more to do. *The Green Hornet* died quickly, but Lee's reputation only grew. By that time he had developed his own form of martial arts, a form commonly referred to as Jeet Kune Do—"The Way of the Intercepting Fist."

Jeet Kune Do was only a name, a label which came to irritate Bruce Lee. At first it was known as Jun Fan Gung Fu. Then it became "Bruce Lee's Tao of Chinese Gung Fu—Using No Way As Way; Having No Limitation As Limitation." It was Lee's unique, simple, effective method of fighting which stressed continual improvement and the joy derived therefrom. "Practice seriously," he said, "but don't seriously practice." In other words, work for the love of it.

By the time *The Green Hornet*'s stinger was removed in 1967, Lee had experienced a variety of setbacks and breakthroughs. His father had died in 1965, but his son Brandon had been born the same year. He attended his father's funeral in Hong Kong, but returned to California to continue pursuing the goal of stardom. His method of direct, practical kungfu attracted a notable following, including many actors, writers, producers, and directors. This led to his being continually tapped for guest-starring roles.

Bruce Lee in the climactic moment of his first film, Fists of Fury. *Notice the man-shaped hole in the wall behind him.*

Bruce Lee prepares for the final fight on the lawn against the Big Boss in Fists of Fury.

Bruce Lee shows what he's made of in The Chinese Connection.

The famous nunchakas appear in Bruce Lee's fists for the first time in The Chinese Connection.

He built up his school's reputation, and therefore his own, in the two years following his stint as Kato. When the entertainment industry was again ready for him, he had three Jeet Kune Do schools, one in Seattle, one in Oakland, and another in Los Angeles. He played a martial arts teacher on an episode of *Ironside,* starring Raymond Burr; he was a technical advisor for the 1969 Matt Helm movie *The Wrecking Crew,* starring Dean Martin; but his most impressive work came in the 1969 movie *Marlowe* and the 1971 TV series *Longstreet.*

The film starred James Garner as author Raymond Chandler's popular hard-boiled private eye, Philip Marlowe. Lee co-starred as a martial arts enforcer of the villain. His is probably the most memorable scene in an otherwise merely decent translation of Chandler's novel *The Little Sister.* To prove his prowess, Lee trashes Marlowe's office with just his arms and legs, culminating in a stunning kick that breaks the ceiling's hanging lamp.

After that, Marlowe's simplistic handling of the deadly character is forced and unrealistic. After taunting Lee with attacks on his manhood while standing on a balcony ledge, Garner merely steps out of the way as Lee delivers a flying kick that takes him over the bannister and down to his death. After the precision of the office attack, this sequence didn't work at all. Many more scoffed at the stupidity of the scene than laughed at the supposed cleverness of the detective.

The two part *Longstreet* episode showcased Lee to better effect. "The Way of the Fist" was written by the series creator, Sterling Silliphant, a fan of Lee's. He had Lee coaching the blind insurance investigator, Mike Longstreet (played by James Franciscus), in self-defense, so the man could trash a bunch of bullies who had mugged him at the outset. In this role, Lee spoke eloquently of the martial arts and the mental serenity necessary to master them.

The two portrayals were perfect bookends—one all flash and the other all substance. While few in the United States were overly impressed, the Orient was buzzing. *The Green Hornet* had premiered there three years after its premiere in the U.S. and Bruce Lee took the opportunity to promote himself to the Chinese audience. Legend has it that a kungfu display during a talk show so impressed Raymond Chow, head of Golden Communications Company Limited—otherwise known as Golden Harvest—that he signed Lee to a contract to do a movie called *The Big Boss,* directed by Lo Wei.

THE BIG TIME

The "legend" was a bit misleading. The truth is that almost every major Hong Kong film company bid for Bruce's participation, but after almost a year Raymond Chow secured the actor/teacher's services to make the movie, on location, in Thailand. To American eyes, this film seems like just another in a long line of cheaply made exploitation pictures featuring a poor man persecuted by the corrupt rich, but it was nearly revolutionary for the Hong Kong movie industry. Up until 1970, almost all of the movies being made there were grand tales of legendary heroes, all promoting the gentle philosophy of Confucius.

Then, seemingly quite suddenly, directors like Chang Cheh, writers like I Kuang, and stars like Wang Yu were tearing up threater screens with violent visions of vengeance. That opened the door for Lo Wei to write and direct *The Big Boss.* Whether Wei collaborated with Bruce Lee on the script or was simply influenced by the actor's intensity is a moot point. *The Big Boss* turned out to reflect many Lee images which would recur throughout his painfully short career.

Lo Wei had started in the film industry as an actor in 1948 and became a director in 1957. He worked steadily through the sixties and joined Raymond Chow on the ground floor of Golden

Harvest. By coincidence or not, for *The Big Boss* he penned a tale of a troubled young man who was unable to avoid fighting. He must leave his family in Hong Kong to toil in Bangkok at an ice factory, and promises his parents not to fight. Therefore, he must hold his prodigious kungfu talents in check while the bosses persecute him and his associates.

But *The Big Boss* is not only a story of class persecution. The Big Boss of the title, played by Han Ying Chieh (who was also the fight coordinator on the film—known in the Orient by the title "martial arts instructor"), is using the ice factory as a front for drug running. When Lee gets too close to the truth, the bosses first try to buy him off, seduce him with women, then try to kill him. They only succeed in killing all his friends, after which he explodes with a barely controlled rage that thrilled audiences.

The scene is now considered a classic. Lee finds the drugs embedded in ice, then finds his friend the same way. He is surrounded by about twenty knife-, club-, and chain-wielding thugs in the eerie, red-lit ice house interior. With a mounting anger clearly etched on his face, he takes the villains apart in a battle that combines dramatic action with nearly cartoon-like violence. Aside from Lee's strong screen presence, the most memorable feature is the moment when a man Lee has hurled through a wall leaves a hole in his exact "man-shape."

From that climactic and cathartic scene, Lee races to the Big Boss's palatial estate to take on the main bad guy and all his minions. It is on the lawn of the mansion where the two antagonists have a knife fight, showcasing two more Lee trademarks—the wounds that inspire Lee on to greater heights of heroism, and the tension-building pauses that add to Lee's acting style. When Lee is cut by the villian's blade, he stops, tastes the blood, and moves forward, always letting the tension build. *The Big Boss* represented the first time moviegoers heard Lee's now trademark animal screeches clearly.

All three main filmmakers—Chow, Wei, and Lee—were happy enough with the results to immediately start work on a follow-up, but none had an inkling as to the first's effect. The trio were already at work on the second movie when word came in. *The Big Boss* was a gigantic success. Made for only one hundred thousand dollars, it made five times that much in Hong Kong alone. Bruce Lee was now, officially, a star.

The next film was to improve on the first at least one hundred percent. The basic structure was still there; a consummate martial artist is persecuted by bigots and snobs who also happen to be insidious villains. The martial artist takes on the superior forces of the villains and wins, but at a terrible cost. In *The Big Boss,* it was his freedom. At the finale, Lee was arrested by Thai police. In *Fist of Fury,* he would pay with his life.

The Chinese made movies the way some people make cars; on an assembly line. With such a gigantic population to supply, Oriental filmmakers in the early seventies could wrap up a normal production in seventy-two hours, a "big budget extravaganza" in a week. *Fist of Fury* premiered in Hong Kong less than five months after *The Big Boss,* but proved to be at least twice the picture.

The production values of the second film made the first look even tackier than it was. It cost twice as much, but made twice as much as well. Again, Lo Wei is credited as director and writer, although it is said that prolific screenwriter I Kuang had a hand in the script. Whoever the author was, this time everything was in place; the cinematography, the costumes, the choreography, all were impressive to any eyes, Occidental or Oriental.

Here, Lee seems to be more in control than ever; it is his performance and skill that holds the movie together. This was no easy task, considering that when the audience first sees him, he is so overcome by grief at the death of his martial arts school master ("sifu") that he leaps into his sifu's grave, onto his sifu's coffin, clawing and crying. From there on, Lee's body became an extension of his mind.

Set in the Shanghai of the late twenties, the film depicts a society in which the Chinese are all but spit upon by Japanese rulers. The racism has become so manifest that a rival Japanese martial arts school has poisoned Lee's sifu. It appears that almost every waking moment of the Japanese rivals was used to persecute Lee's school and its students. Lee, playing a fighter named Chen, has a much shorter fuse this time. He has promised no one to hold back. Using a series of disguises, including that of a rickshaw puller and, in a delightful turn, of a grinning, mincing phone repairman, Lee discovers the murderers and takes them apart.

The mood of the picture is set by Lee smashing a "No Dogs or Chinese" sign outside a Shanghai park with a *Marlowe*-type kick. From there he wades through the Japanese school, taking out all the students, the sword master, a brawny Russian fighter (played by Jeet Kune Do student Robert Baker), and, finally, the head of the school. It is this series of bouts that makes up the heart of the action.

Lee is nothing short of masterful in each. Although Han Ying Chieh is again credited as martial arts instructor, Lee's approach is plainly evident throughout. When fighting the Russian, he

The incredible leap that ends The Chinese Connection, *Bruce Lee's second and, some say, finest film.*

Bruce Lee shows Chinese waiters the joy of Jeet Kune Do in Return of the Dragon.

is caught in a leg scissors but bites the man in order to escape. Then his arms swirl stroboscopically in front of the confused opponent. Finally he faces his main adversary with the infamous nunchakas—the small clubs joined by a short length of chain which Lee made famous.

Supposedly Lee learned the particular nunchaka skill with his star student Daniel Inosanto. However he learned it, he had chosen a particularly impressive, esoteric weapon to dazzle viewers with. To see Lee swirl and spin the sticks with ridiculous ease was to experience pure enchantment. The moment of the character Chen's greatest triumph was the moment of Lee's ascension to superstardom. He had gone from being a suprahuman fighter to being a superhero.

Lo Wei himself played the Chinese policeman caught between his loyalty to his people and his Japanese masters. It is his sad duty to bring Chen in for the murders of the Japanese school fighters. Lee, barechested and brazen, gives himself up to the cop, but not to the mob of rifle-toting Japanese outside. *Fist of Fury* ends by freeze-framing on a tremendous leap by Lee seemingly right into his persecutors' bullets—defiant to the end.

Bruce Lee directs then unknown karate champion Chuck Norris for the American's entrance in Return of the Dragon.

To say the Oriental audience went crazy would be an understatement. Unlike the screen heroes before him, Lee did not turn the other cheek, Lee did not remain humble and unassuming. He stood up and shouted, "I'm Chinese and I'm proud of it!" Not only that, but he had much to be proud of. His acting and especially his fighting skill were supreme, leaving other action actors miles behind. Lee was as fast, as precise, and as good as he looked.

And Lee knew it. No more would he listen to either Chow or Wei. Creating his own Concord Productions, he struck a deal with Golden Harvest to co-produce his next film, which would star, be directed by, written by, and choreographed by Bruce Lee. He had said all he could say on the themes of his first two movies. He wanted to explore other directions, in waters Lo Wei did not want to navigate. As a result, *Way of the Dragon* opened in Hong Kong just nine months after *Fist of Fury.*

Essentially, this is Bruce Lee's last film. It is the only film he controlled completely and the only film in which his approach was primary. In it he played an unassuming but fiercely patriotic and surprisingly clever young martial artist, Tang Lung, who travels to Rome to help relatives run a Chinese restaurant. Although the first part of

Chuck Norris on the left, Bruce Lee on the right. This is the exceptional fight scene which climaxed Return of the Dragon.

the movie chronicles largely humorous "stranger in a strange land" confrontations with the English/Italian language and Western ways, Lee slowly strips his character, Tang Lung, of his surface naïvete to reveal a supremely capable hero beneath.

It starts slowly. First he shows the other restaurant employees the superiority of "Chinese boxing" over other styles in the alley behind the restaurant. But when racketeers arrive looking for protection money, the lessons become more pointed. Lee is taken back behind the bistro by the gangster's hoods to "be taught a lesson." Instead he teaches them a lesson in a nicely structured fight which culminates with the appearance of the nunchakas.

Probably the sharpest moment here is when the hoods' leader manages to grab a nunchaka. At first he seems to think that he will be imbued with some sort of magical power simply by the possession of it, but then winds up knocking himself out with it. All this is achieved silently, and is a mark of Lee's skill as an action director.

The next major step forward *Way of the Dragon* takes is in allowing the appearance of guns. Guns sound the death knell of kungfu movies because no matter how skillful one is, no martial artist can fight a bullet. Bruce Lee confronts that problem in this movie, set in modern times, by having his character make wooden darts which he hurls into his enemies' gun hands. It is the most unlikely technique in the picture, but at least Lee attempted to deal with this particularly sticky genre drawback.

Tang Lung repeatedly puts down the gang boss's takeover attempts, so the boss decides to fight fire with fire—by calling in a Japanese and two American martial artists. The two former enforcers, played by Wang Ing Sik and Bob Wall, pretty much take care of the restaurant employees. The final American is flown in especially for Tang Lung.

He is Chuck Norris, seven-time Karate Champion, playing Tang's ultimate Anglo enemy. The two face each other in the Colosseum and fight with all the graciousness and solemnity of honor-bound samurai warriors. Lee, the director/writer, even manages to infuse this somber scene with small humorous touches, mostly supplied by a mute kitten witness to the fight. He also creates a high point when he comes away from a clinch with a handful of Norris's bushy chest hair—which Lee blows off his hand defiantly.

Norris's character is winning at first, bloodying Lee's face. But Lee tastes the blood, spits it out, and carries on. Finally, it is Lee who triumphs, but not before a subtle, magnificent silent exchange between the two fighters. Norris almost smiles. Lee shakes his head. The two have communicated, and the audience clearly sees it. Then Tang Lung breaks his enemy's neck.

The movie ends with a confusing union of images. First, Lung drapes his enemy's shirt and belt over the fallen man's corpse and kneels beside it in silence—a strong, effective moment. Then it turns out that the restaurant manager has betrayed his help by siding with the gangster and stabbing his own employees. The police arrive to take the villains away before Lee can rip them apart.

Another change in Lee's approach is the ending. He is not arrested or killed. Instead, it looks as if he will settle down with the romantic lead, played in all three Lee films by Nora Miao, only to suddenly pack up and go.

"In this world of guns and knives," is the last line—"wherever Tang Lung may go, he will always travel on his own."

And travel Bruce Lee did. All the way back to America.

ENTER THE DRAGON

There is a respected producer in Hollywood named Fred Weintraub who fell in love with Chinese movies. He loved the last ten minutes, when the hero would take on an army of crooks and defeat them all barehanded. He was certain a hugely successful American movie could be made in this image.

"I went to Hong Kong and saw Bruce's films," he recalls, "and brought one back to show Ted Ashley (then chairman of the board at Warner Brothers). If it wasn't for Ted Ashley, the movie would have never gotten made. I had half the money but everybody else had turned me down—including other executives at Warners. But Ted asked me what I needed, then said, 'Go ahead.' "

What he went ahead with was a movie called *Enter the Dragon*—a movie many think is the greatest martial arts movie ever made. And, in a way, despite all its shortcomings, it is. More on that later, but first things first. Weintraub and coproducer Paul Heller cut a deal with Lee's Concord Productions, then worked with Lee and screenwriter Michael Allin on the script. Robert Clouse was chosen as director because, in Weintraub's words, "Nobody else wanted to direct the picture except him."

The story was simplicity itself. In fact, it was James Bond by way of Fu Manchu. An unnamed espionage agency asks a Shaolin Temple teacher named Lee to compete at a martial arts tournament in order to infiltrate an island off Hong Kong lorded over by a Shaolin renegade named Mr. Han. Lee goes to the island in the company of Williams, a cocky black fighter, and Roper, a gambler—both of whom are in trouble with the law.

Once on the island, they face the evil Han, an Oriental with a fake, interchangeable hand, a small army of guards, and a combination inner sanctum and museum. All three men discover his drug-pushing and white slavery operation, Williams paying for the knowedge with his life. Roper and Lee fight the minions with the help of freed slaves. Lee faces and defeats Han in the name of his family and the Shaolin Temple.

To put it mildly, the script was fairly lame. The dialogue and situations seemed second-hand—all borrowed from 007 adventures. Han is little more than Dr. No. He even has a white long-haired cat like Bond's main nemesis, Ernst Stavros Blofeld. The only place the movie excels—in fact, the only place the movie is unique—is in its martial arts. And that was the territory of one Bruce Lee.

Getting the project started, however, was no easy task. John Saxon, an actor who had been toiling in unspectacular "B" pictures since the mid-fifties, shared equal billing with Lee by playing Roper. A man named Rockney Tarkinton was cast as Williams.

"Jim Kelly was a last-minute replacement," Weintraub explains. "He came on the night before the picture was to start. At the last minute Tarkinton said I was taking advantage of him. I disagreed and that was the end of that. At two o'clock in the morning I went to see Kelly and said, 'You're hired.' "

Weintraub had Saxon, he had Kelly, he had Hong Kong film veteran character actor Shih Kien as Han, Bob Wall and Yang Sze as Han's most prominent bodyguards, and he even had Angela Mao as Lee's sister, who commits suicide rather than be raped by Han's minions. What he didn't have, at first, was Bruce Lee.

"For the first three weeks, we shot around him," Weintraub maintains. "Linda Lee, his wife, was the one who kept things going when he wouldn't show up on the set. He was nervous. It was his first big film. He was scared. And he was fighting with Raymond Chow at that time. He was fighting with me, too, but not as much. It was just that he was so nervous. On the first day, he had a facial twitch. We needed twenty-seven takes. Then he

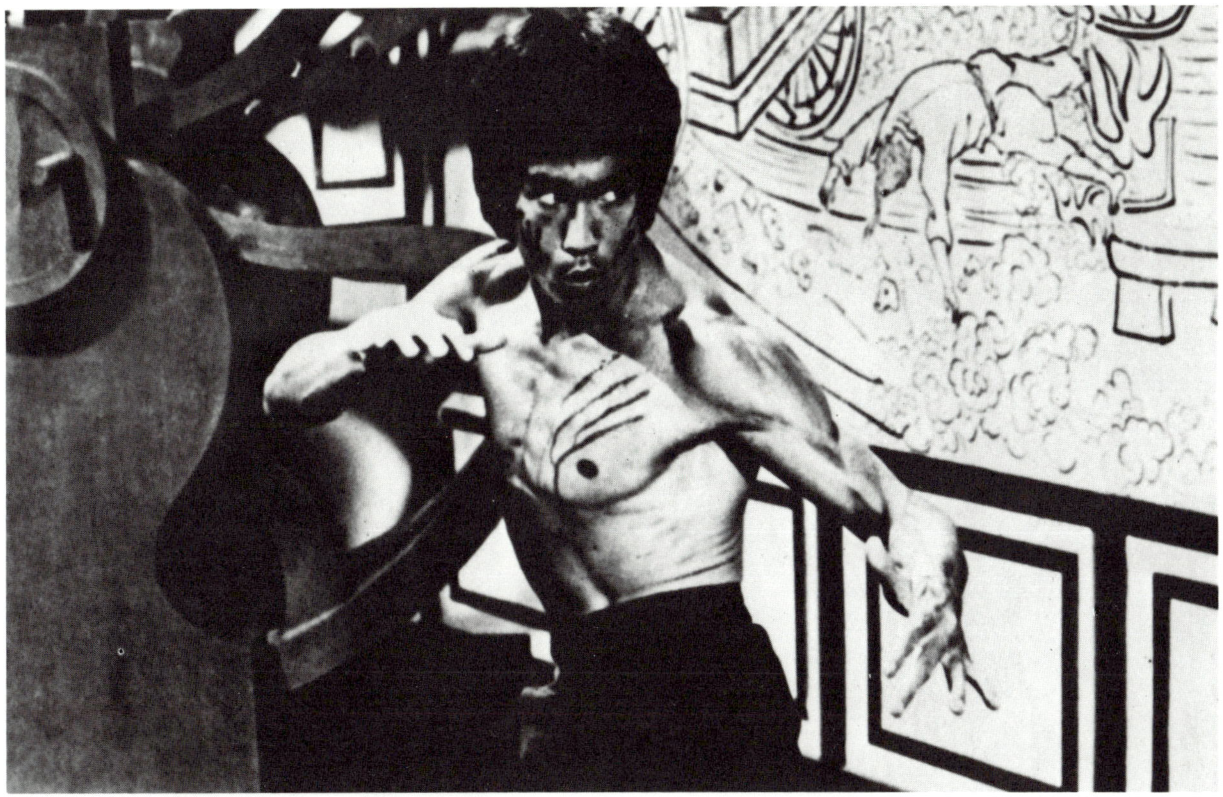

Bruce Lee, the panther-like stalker of evil, about to corner Mr. Han at the end of Enter the Dragon.

Bruce Lee finally relaxed on the set of Enter the Dragon *with co-star John Saxon.*

John Saxon beats on Bolo (Yang Sze) during an important bout in Enter the Dragon.

The other side of Bruce Lee's mercurial personality: whimsical, mischievous, and clever. From Enter the Dragon.

Bruce Lee at his animal best in Enter the Dragon.

A hand in hair, an arm lock, and this Han minion is no match for Bruce Lee in Enter the Dragon.

settled down and we made the film."

Lee's contribution was telling. What the film's detractors don't seem to realize is that if *Enter the Dragon*'s plot wasn't so pedestrian, Bruce Lee's first major international appearance would not have had the impact it did. This was Lee's showcase, and its every fault only served to bolster Lee's participation. He was truly the best thing about the movie. In those terms, it could not have been a better vehicle for him.

Enter the Dragon is a fantasy, and every device used to make the fantasy palatable worked in the film's favor. When first given the assignment to infiltrate Han's island by a Mr. Braithwaite, Lee again brings up the sticky subject of guns. Why not just blow Han's head off, he asks. Braithwaite explains that Han is so fearful of assassination that he doesn't allow guns on the island. A neat way to eliminate a most pressing genre problem.

Michael Allin's dialogue seemed extremely aware of the plot's shortcomings. At one point William's says to Han, "Man, you come right out of a comic book." It is touches like these, in addition to the rest of the semi-Confucian by way of Spider-Man conversations, that make the non-fight scenes palatable.

Bruce Lee starred, essentially as himself, and supervised all the martial arts. However, he also gave the entire film a heart most aren't aware of. "I don't think anyone else knows this," Weintraub reveals, "but when *Enter the Dragon* was finished,

The famous nunchakas make their appearance in Enter the Dragon.

Enter the Dragon*'s Mr. Han has a hand made of blades.*

Bruce Lee was also well versed in stick fighting in Enter the Dragon.

I completely reedited it. When it was initially done, it was a linear story that started in the United States. But Bruce went back and did the Shaolin Temple sequence. That was his. He did that without me and I loved it. I took that and opened the film with it. Then I went onto the boat and did flashbacks which everybody thought I was crazy to do."

Although it at first seems that Bruce Lee played little more than an Oriental James Bond in the picture, he finally faces Han with the line, "You have shamed my family and the Shaolin Temple." The martial arts influence has come full circle. He is not destroying Han in the name of espionage but in the name of his Chinese ancestors. It is only Bruce Lee's participation and contribution that makes *Enter the Dragon* successful. It served Bruce Lee beautifully and will always be remembered by most of the world as Lee's greatest and *the* greatest.

Bruce Lee takes care of Mr. Han's leg at the end of Enter the Dragon.

LITTLE GRASSHOPPER

Countering the success of this movie, Lee suffered a major setback in the television arena. It's name was *Kung Fu*. "Once we started *Enter the Dragon*," the producer recollects, "everybody thought Bruce was going to be something and started sending me scripts in the middle of shooting. There was a man at Warner Brothers named Dick Moore who understood the market, so we worked up a script with Ed Spielman and Howard Friedlander and showed it to Bruce. We tried to do it as a movie first."

Kung Fu the movie took place in the High Sierras of 1868 and is concerned with the coolie laborers building the Transcontinental Railroad. Among them is Caine, a half-breed Chinese. Almost immediately the movie flashes back to Caine's training by Shaolin Temple monks, culminating in a final test that has him in a booby-trapped hall blocked by a red-hot cauldron. He escapes the corridor by lifting the cauldron with his forearms, which leaves tattoos of a dragon on one arm and a tiger on the other.

From there Caine travels to Peking where his blind sifu, Po, stumbles into a royal guard. He's shot for his mistake, and Caine kills the guards and, of all people, the prince. He escapes to America and gets a job on the railroad. From there, the script degenerates into a western *The Big Boss,* but with one added twist. After Caine leads the coolies in a revolt against their corrupt masters, another Shaolin monk appears to challenge him. It seems the temple was destroyed as retribution for Caine's act, and the monk wants revenge. Caine kills him, bows farewell, and disappears down the road.

"Tom Kuhn, who was in charge of Warner Television at the time, said, 'Why don't we try this as a series?' " Weintraub relates. "I said, 'Great. Bruce would be perfect.' We designed the series for Bruce."

There is one story that relates that Bruce Lee ultimately turned down the offer to star in the series, thinking he wasn't ready yet. Weintraub doesn't remember it that way. "When he didn't get the part," the producer says, "I was stunned. Bruce was heartbroken, and I couldn't blame him."

The executive who actually turned Bruce Lee down doesn't remember it that way either. "Ted Ashley wanted Bruce," he says, "but the network wanted someone like William Smith [a brawny American actor known for villainous roles and totally wrong for the part]. We felt that casting David Carradine made for a good compromise. To tell you the truth, I didn't think Lee's English was strong enough yet."

This executive also remembers a personal visit during which Lee proved his kungfu prowess by touching the television man's nose with the tip of his foot. It wasn't enough. Carradine got the part in the series, which ultimately succeeded because of *Enter the Dragon.*

It would seem that Bruce Lee had the last laugh. He returned to Hong Kong to a tumultuous reception. It was months before *Enter the Dragon* would premiere, but just the very fact that he had starred in an international film after having attained Oriental star status from his first three movies put him in the catbird seat. Weintraub and he were already discussing a second American movie, for which he would receive a million dollars. He supposedly was on the verge of signing a contract with the Shaw Brothers studio to do a period piece; photos to the effect were taken.

But first he had a project to do. A project that went under the title *Game of Death.* Initially it seemed to be a sequel to *Way of the Dragon.* Tang Lung was to travel to Korea where he must fight his way up a pagoda, facing a different type of martial artist on each level. Bruce Lee filmed three fight scenes, one with Daniel Inosanto, one with Kareem Abdul Jabbar, and one with a hapkido fighter, Chi Hon Joi. He was frightfully thin and wan in these scenes, and, except for a few in-

Kareem Abdul Jabbar, the famous basketball player, laughs with Lee on the set of the incomplete Game of Death.

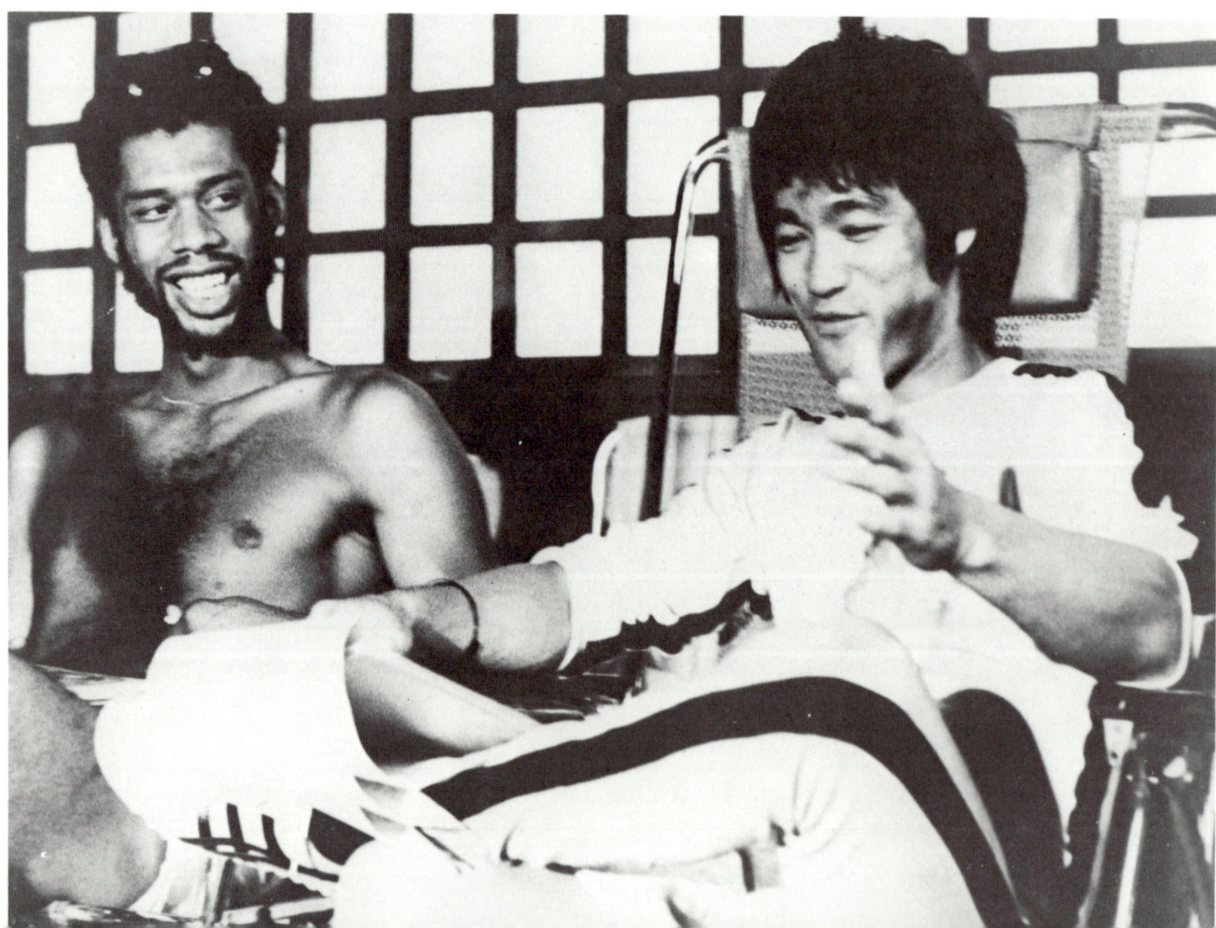

Bruce Lee, teacher, martial artist, filmmaker.

stances, the sequences had a rough, unfinished look to the choreography.

THE KING IS DEAD

On July 20, 1973, Bruce Lee died. He was found in the apartment of Betty Ting Pei, an actress. His death was attributed to a cerebral hemorrhage or brain aneurism. None of his fans could believe it, and the hysteria that followed was equally hard to believe. Stories circulated that he was murdered by envious kungfu masters utilizing the "Death Touch," or poisoned by envious film studio personnel. There were tales of his involvement with gangsters and drug pushers. In short, no one could believe that their superhero had died naturally. He had to have been killed by a supervillain.

Enter the Dragon premiered in the United States in the summer of 1973. It opened in Hong Kong that October. In the meantime a small distributing company called National General had secured the rights to present Lee's earlier films to the American public. Bruce Lee's voice was dubbed and the Chinese titles were translated. *The Big Boss* was to be called *The Chinese Connection* and *Fist of Fury* was to be called *Fists of Fury*.

But somehow, somewhere, the U.S. distributors switched the titles. Now *The Big Boss* was *Fists of Fury* and *Fist of Fury* was *The Chinese Connection*. That's how American audiences saw the features and that's how American audiences know them. By the wrong titles. But, like it or not, that's

Kareem Abdul Jabbar on the Game of Death *set, with the diminutive Lee (5'7") making up the difference.*

From the left, Mike Stone, James Coburn, Chuck Norris, and Bruce Lee in a photo taken in America during the mid-sixties, when Lee was still seeking stardom

what they are to English-speaking Bruce Lee fans. Soon after, *Way of the Dragon* came to U.S. shores as *Return of the Dragon*—promoted as a sequel to *Enter the Dragon,* although made before.

Bruce Lee was the most successful Chinese star in the world a month after he was already dead. But even more than ten years later, people disbelieve the official cause of his death. Many maintain that drugs had to be part of his downfall. While it is impossible to say for certain that Bruce Lee did not use drugs, Fred Weintraub is definite in his opinion.

"Let me tell you that Bruce would never put anything into his body that would hurt him," he maintains. "I had him examined at UCLA the week before he died. He was in great shape. He had an aneurism. That happens to people under the age of thirty-five."

Mike Stone echoes Weintraub's sentiments. "I've met several people with Bruce's intensity and, interestingly enough, those people died quite young. But the unique thing about Bruce was that his belief in himself and the intensity with which he did things was always at a peak. He had a tremendous faith in himself and a belief in his ability."

A prime example of the infamy that took place after Bruce Lee's death. That's not Bruce Lee. That's the inferior Bruce Li.

Sadly, the Chinese film industry could not let their hero go. They chose to remember him by mounting literally dozens of quickie, rip-off productions that proportedly showed the king back in action or told his life story. Even the best of these films were dreadful. A Western equivalent would be to have Hollywood make a bunch of *Dirty Larry* movies starring Clint Westwood over the next decade.

Eastern filmmakers recruited Ho Tsung Tao, a tall young Oriental with good martial arts skills, to become "Bruce Li" in a series of forgettable adventures titled such things as *Bruce Lee Superdragon* (1974), *Goodbye Bruce Lee—His Last Game of Death* (1975), *Exit the Dragon, Enter the Tiger* (1976), *Fist of Fury II* (1976), *Bruce Lee the Invincible* (1977), and *Bruce Lee's Secret* (1977).

These movies are quite funny, both in terms of content and conception. One never knows when a Bruce Lee clone will appear behind trademark sunglasses (as in *Exit the Dragon*, when the "real" Bruce Lee asks Bruce Li to solve his murder if he just so happens to get killed in the near future) or when mountain gorillas will rise on their hind legs and fight with kungfu (as in *The Invincible*).

Following hot on Bruce Li's heels was Bruce Le, originally named Huang Kin Lung. At least Li is a decent performer; an actor who has been able to shake his Lee clone mantle in recent years to act in better, more honorable productions. Le is not and has not. Le is a decent martial artist, but not a decent actor. He is a wooden screen presence, sinking any scene in which he isn't swinging his fists. In addition, he seems intent on toiling in the exploitive garbage, trading on his vague physical resemblance to the original.

The directors and writers of these travesties manage to sink anything the star can't. Quite possibly the most interesting exploitation came with *I Love You, Bruce Lee,* known in America as *Bruce Lee: His Last Days, His Last Nights* (1975). This was reportedly Betty Ting Pei's own statement as to her alleged lover's fate. She was given credit as both star and co-writer of this trashy farce, which featured Li Hsiu Hsien as a Bruce Lee who gave forewarnings of his coming aneurism by gripping his head and collapsing in the middle of scenes.

This is the saddest pornography imaginable, made all the sadder by being a Shaw Brothers production. While that company can put out exceptional period pieces, their modern-day love, crime, and horror films were, until very recently, execrable. *I Love You Bruce Lee* was no exception. Ting Pei was constantly in the nude and the movie portrayed Lee as an immature rapist. For the record, Betty tells a sympathetic bartender her life story after the hate of Bruce Lee fans forces her to disguise herself and leave town. The bartender beats up some thugs at the finale and tells them to respect Bruce Lee's memory. Which is far more than this film did.

Ho Tsung Tao, otherwise known as Bruce Li, readies himself for yet another inferior exploitation—in this case, the movie Dynamo.

However, the worst was yet to come. Word leaked out that Golden Harvest had in its possession one hundred and one minutes of film Bruce Lee had completed before his death. Using that footage, they were going to complete *Game of Death.* They hired Robert Clouse to direct "some" new footage and set the premiere for 1978.

The result was probably the worst exploitation of all, basically because it was the film with the most talent behind it. After a wonderful credit sequence designed by John Christopher Strong III, in which clips of Bruce Lee from his other films appeared in and on floating games of chance, the plot unfolded to disbelieving eyes. Rather than following Lee's original scenario, *Game of Death* was now about Bruce Lee himself, fighting off the corrupt desires of an insane actor's agent!

The one hundred and one minutes of film turned out to be less than ten, which showed the real Bruce Lee fighting the aforementioned men, while the other ninety *Game of Death* minutes featured snatches of film from his other movies, but mostly pathetically transparent doubling by Kim Tai Chung and Chen Yao Po, among others.

Viewing the picture is a schizophrenic experience, what with Kim in one shot, Chen in the next, and fading clips of Bruce Lee in a third. The single most unbelievable moment comes in a dressing room where director Clouse films a mir-

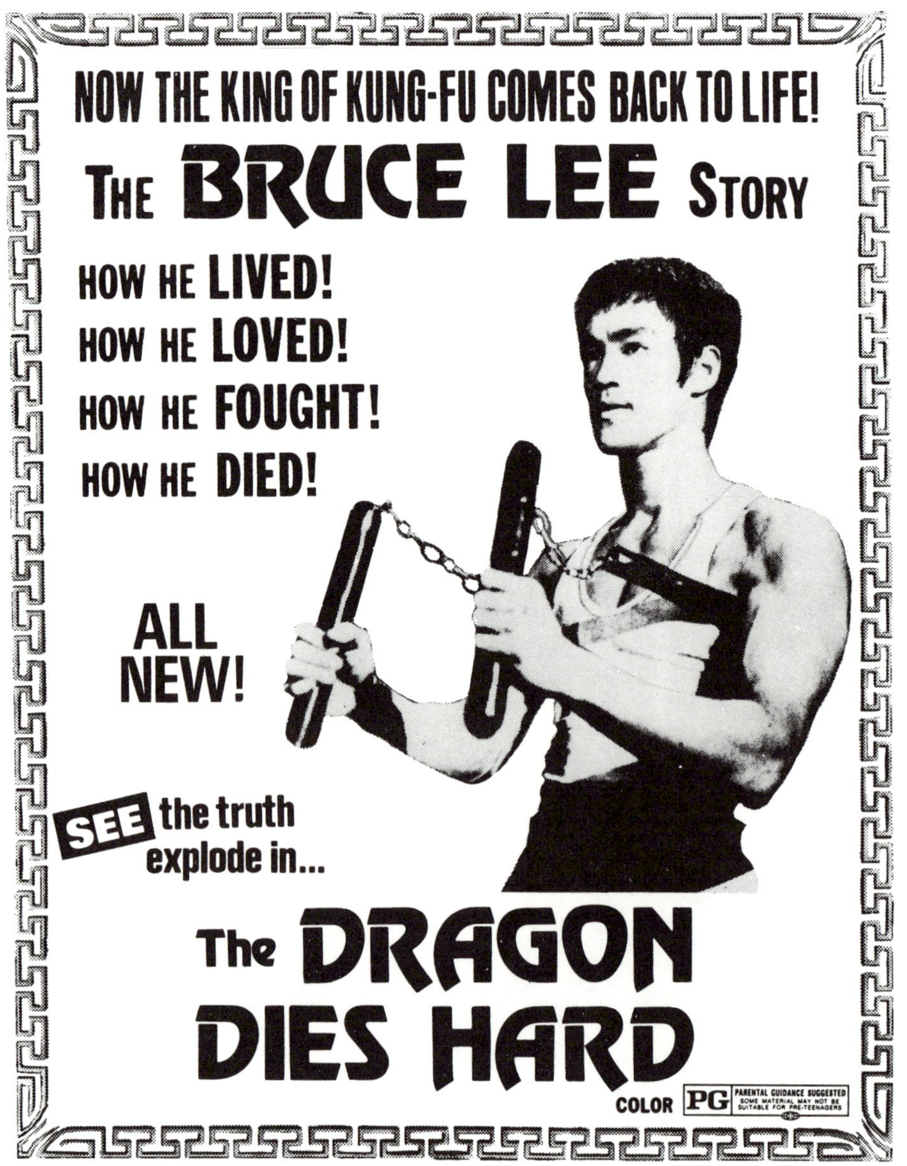

More false advertising promoting one of the worst of the Bruce Lee exploitations.

ror on which a photo of Bruce Lee's head has been pasted and the stand-in positioned so his shoulders seem to come from the photo's neck!

The stand-ins play a character named Billy Lo who incurs the wrath of syndicate head and theatrical agent Dr. Rand, played by Dean Jagger. On Rand's side is bodyguard Steiner, played by Hugh O'Brian, and Stick the hitman, played by Mel Novak. On Billy's side is girlfriend Ann, played by Colleen Camp, and United Press International reporter Jim Marshall, played by Gig Young. Ann is kidnapped by the bad guys, Billy rescues her and then fights his way up the various levels of Rand's restaurant to kill all the villains.

This is one bad movie. Markedly better was 1981's *Tower of Death,* known in the U.S. as *Game of Death II.* Directed by Ng See-Yuen, who also directed *Bruce Lee, the True Story* (U.S. title: *Bruce Lee, the Man and the Myth—1976),* it now starred Kim Tai Chung in the leading role of Bobby Lo, the brother of Billy Lo, the lead of *Game of Death.* This time the actual Bruce Lee footage came from scenes edited out of *Enter the Dragon,* with all new dialogue dubbed in.

The real Bruce Lee appears in only the first half hour, playing Billy, who is mysteriously killed, allowing Bobby to investigate. Instead of trampling Lee's memory by trying to fool audiences, Kim is given a series of eight, increasingly more ambitious fights until he reaches the top of the pagoda, where he has an excellent battle with Huang Cheng Li.

In a bunch of dreadful movies, *Tower of Death,* a.k.a. *Game of Death II,* reigns supreme. Which, of course, isn't saying much. Many fans thought that *Game of Death* would be Lee's ultimate martial arts statement had he lived. Given that Lee wanted to continue making movies, that theory is doubtful. For Lee to have shot his entire wad on his fifth movie would have been foolish. Besides, he had yet to realize his potential as a filmmaker. But there is little doubt that Bruce Lee's fully realized version of *Game of Death* would have been far superior to what we are left with.

At the present time there is Bruce Li, Bruce Le, Bruce Liang, Bruce Leong, Bruce Lei, Bruce Rhe, Dragon Lee, Rocky Lee, Bronson Lee, Conan Lee, and Jet Lee (among others) to contend with. There are also scores of movies with the words "Enter," "Fist," "Fury," "Dragon," "Connection," "Game," and "Death" in their titles. Is this the legacy Bruce Lee has left us?

"Bruce Lee proved that someone from the ghetto or upstate New York, or Malibu, or wherever, would accept a Chinese as a hero," Mike Stone contends. "He proved that through his ability. Bruce set a standard of performance that hasn't been met. I don't think there's anyone who comes close to him in terms of ability or charisma yet. As a result, no U.S. filmmaker feels comfortable making martial arts films. In many cases, we've taken a few paces back since his death."

That is probably the reason almost no Westerner outside the exploitation filmmakers have touched kungfu films, despite the success of *Enter the Dragon.* In truth, English-speaking filmmakers just aren't that good at this kind of high-flying, highly emotional form of heroic moviemaking. The great majority of directors and writers seem to need to camp up their superheroes, to not take any of them seriously, be they Superman, Flash Gordon, James Bond, or Bruce Lee. So what remains are people tearing at his legend with inferior product, misdirection, or outright deception.

Fred Weintraub puts the question of Bruce Lee in perspective. "I miss Bruce. I liked him. We fought, but it was never personal. It was for the film, for art's sake. He knew I cared and that was all that counted. He knew, in a funny kind of way, that I was the only one who cared enough to get him into the international market. Nobody wanted him. In the history of show business, there had never been an international Chinese star, especially not one who was five foot seven and not gorgeous.

"Bruce stood tall. Bruce is martial arts. He made the form work. No matter who you see doing martial arts, you always compare him to Bruce Lee. Say 'cowboy' and you think 'John Wayne.' Say 'martial arts' and the name that pops to mind is Bruce Lee. That makes him one of the few giants in show business. That's the mark of his influence and his genius."

Bruce Li in Bruce Lee-inspired action, from the movie Dynamo.

Bruce Li is not a bad fighter, but his Bruce Lee impersonation hurt his reputation. Here he holds his own against veteran villain Li Hai Sheng in The Three Avengers.

Bruce Le is actually Huang Kin Lung and Cobra *was one of his better films.*

A double exploitation! Not only does this film tread on Bruce Lee's memory, it has a Jackie Chan impersonator as well.

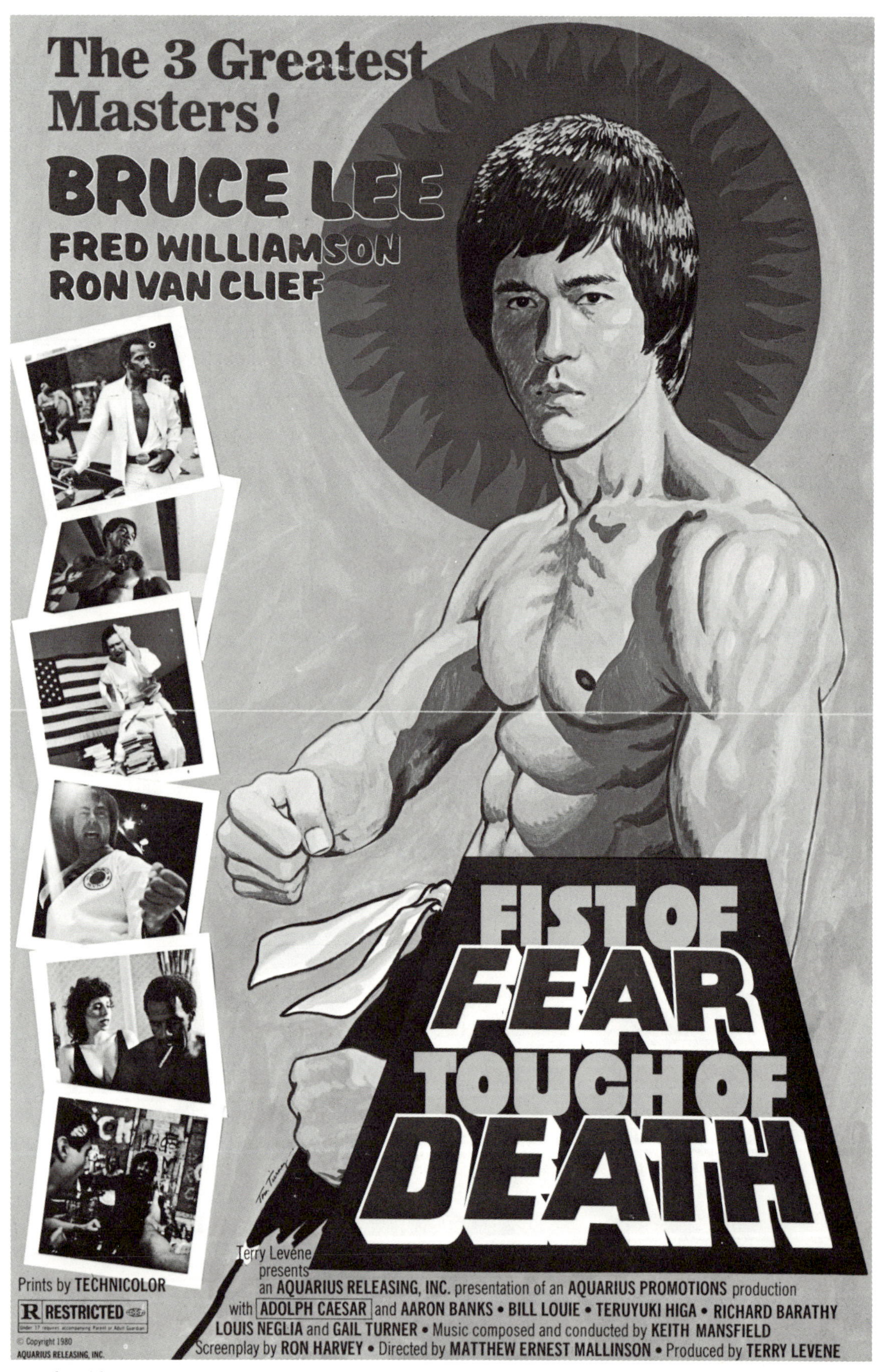

Another film at the bottom of the barrel.

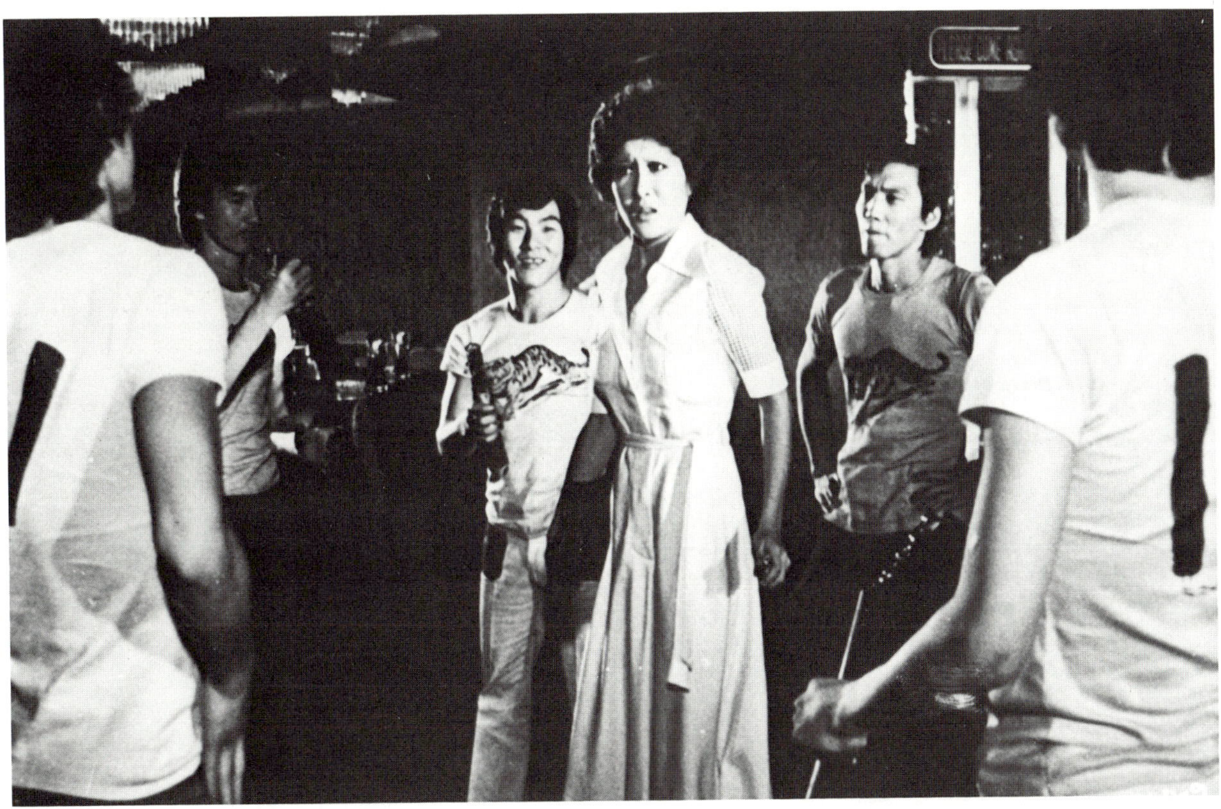

Bruce Lee died in Betty Ting Pei's apartment. Sadly the actress decided to tell her own cinematic story in the dreadful Bruce Lee: His Last Days, His Last Nights.

At least Li Hsiu Hsien (left) didn't change his name to Bruce Dragon or some such to portray the king of kungfu in Bruce Lee: His Last Days, His Last Nights.

Bruce Lee: His Last Days, His Last Nights *was low on kungfu and high on this sort of scene, as Betty Ting Pei fools around with Li Hsiu Hsien.*

BRONSON LEE, CHAMPION starring TADASHI YAMASHITA as Bronson Lee and MASAFUMI SUZUKI • directed by YUKIO NODA produced by MARTIN SATO and LUKE IMAGAWA • from NEW LINE CINEMA

CHAPTER TWO

China: The Source

"The problem with kungfu," Fred Weintraub says. "is that it is fantasy. Once someone shoots someone else, everybody understands it. That's reality. But when somebody does fantastic martial arts, that's fantasy. You never see that in life. You never see that on the news. What you see is people shot and run over. When you're working in martial arts, you're working in fantasy. You're working with ballet."

Truer words were seldom spoken. And fewer people were better equipped to deal with the balletic fantasy of kungfu than the Chinese. We're talking about a history here that goes all the way back to at least 2500 B.C. From that period to the present the annals of the Chinese are rich in mythology, legend, and lore. It is these legends that make up the bulk of the best martial arts films. It is this rich tradition that Bruce Lee was planning to tap—and thereby introduce to an international audience—before he died.

Instead, money-hungry distributors invaded the Orient in the early seventies buying up the cheapest movies they could find to take advantage of the voracious Western martial arts market. Almost all of these films were chaotic garbage which hinted at almost nothing of China's fascinating culture. It is doubly unfortunate in that one of the very first kungfu films seen in the United States, even before the bulk of Bruce Lee movies, was a 1972 classy Shaw Brothers production of director Chang Cheh's *King Boxer*, known in America as *Five Fingers of Death*.

Lo Lieh played the naïve lead in the picture, successfully shucking his reputation for playing villains. It was, again, about the struggle against the Japanese—using a martial arts tournament as background—but one done with richness, style, and pomp. It did extremely well in Western markets, which, again, made it all the more unfortunate that distributors chose to foist inferior product on American eyes in the post-Bruce Lee period.

But China is used to invasions of every kind, not to mention revolutions, insurrections, intrigue, and war. First, there was the ANCIENT period, dating roughly from 2500 to 207 B.C. At the very beginnings of this Oriental civilization there were already great legends. Fu Hsi the Hunter, Shen Nung the Farmer, and, most importantly, Huang Ti, bringer of fire and music.

Lo Lieh, a long-time Hong Kong screen villain, led the Chinese invasion of America with Five Fingers of Death.

There were almost no kungfu films made about this time period. In fact, there have been fewer than a dozen marital arts movies made about the entire ancient era. And most of those concerned the CHOU and CH'IN DYNASTIES, starting around 1100 B.C. Already Chinese history was full of complexities, complications, rivalries, and conflicts. There was much in this period to make movies about. But before the really juicy stuff could occur, China had to settle in.

Most of this settling in took place in the HAN DYNASTY, which stretched about four hundred years from 200 B.C. to 200 A.D. By that time a certain ruling logic was in effect. A certain member of a family became emperor and other members of the same family succeeded that person when he died. It sounds simple, but it was fraught with dangers. The Chinese had *big* families and the infighting to become emperor was ornate and often deadly.

Craziness wasn't restricted to the royal family. Constant wars were being waged to take over China from both the outside and the inside. Different families wanted to create different dynasties and different Orientals wanted to create different Chinas. As has been said—lots to make movies about. Even so, one could count the number of kungfu movies made about this period on the fingers of one hand (and have two digets left over).

However these few films were extremely mystical. They were fantasies both in form and content, featuring gods, demi-gods, wizards, witches, devils and demons. Thankfully, all these folk had swords and knew how to use them. Meanwhile, back in the real world, Chinese government was becoming more structured at the end of the Han Dynasty. The central government was located at the capital with a chancellor, an imperial chancellor, and a commander-in-chief advising the emperor.

Out in the field, as it were, were nine ministers of state, each supported by a staff of directors and minions. In addition there was the Department of Agriculture and Revenue, and the Lesser Treasury. Throughout this organization were various officials, secretariats, and even eunuchs. None of these people were immune to the emotions that is the stuff of great motion pictures. Emotions such as lust, greed, pride, and envy.

As the population grew, the needs for greater government controls became obvious. The emperor gave parts of the country to his relatives as kingdoms. Agencies and armies were everywhere, especially in light of warring nomads in Central Asia—called the Hsiung-nu—who kept attacking from the north. As 200 A.D. neared, things just got worse and worse. China was divided and dynasties came and went with alarming frequency.

Because of this, the period from about 250 A.D. to 600 A.D. was known as THE SIX DYNASTIES. Now *there* was a mess. Almost no filmmakers touch that time period, but it was important because both Taoism and Confucianism were weakening. Although the former promoted simplicity and the latter ethics and education, both were reinterpreted, like all religions, to fit the times. And the times were turbulent.

In their stead came Buddhism, an Indian religion founded on enlightenment and an elimination of suffering by eliminating desire. This led the way to the SUI and T'ANG DYNASTIES (approximately 600 to 1000 A.D.), which were the stuff of at least a dozen films. The Sui Dynasty reunited a Northern and Southern China, but collapsed from overextending itself. The T'ang Dynasty saw the creation of the Shaolin Temple, and, thereby, officially marked the start of kungfu.

As usual Lo Lieh is outnumbered on the handsome Chinese set. But not to worry. He doesn't need a knife. He's got the Five Fingers of Death.

BLOOD FEUDS

Now we're talking. To make things even more interesting, outside the temple walls all sorts of court intrigues were going down, resulting in many lives being ruined or ended. Several emperors were truly perverse and depraved, creating all sorts of situations the Shaolin Temple monks could fight in (see chart for the kinds of kingfu that were created).

Life went on as usual in the royal court, with everyone stabbing everyone else in the back. Everyone jockeyed for power, including the courtesans and concubines. One, Empress Wu, was so good at power games that she rose from being just one of an emperor's women to deposing the rightful heir to become Empress herself. None of this happened—not the reunifications or deposings—without all manner of bloody confrontations.

Empress Wu managed to hold on until she was eighty years old, then handed the empire over to a rightful heir, but he was poisoned by his wife who tried to become Empress herself. She, however, was outclassed by Wu's daughter, who got her brother to the throne and tried to run the country through him. She, in turn, was foiled by her brother's rightful heir, who took over by a coup

In Five Fingers of Death*'s wake came inferior works like this.*

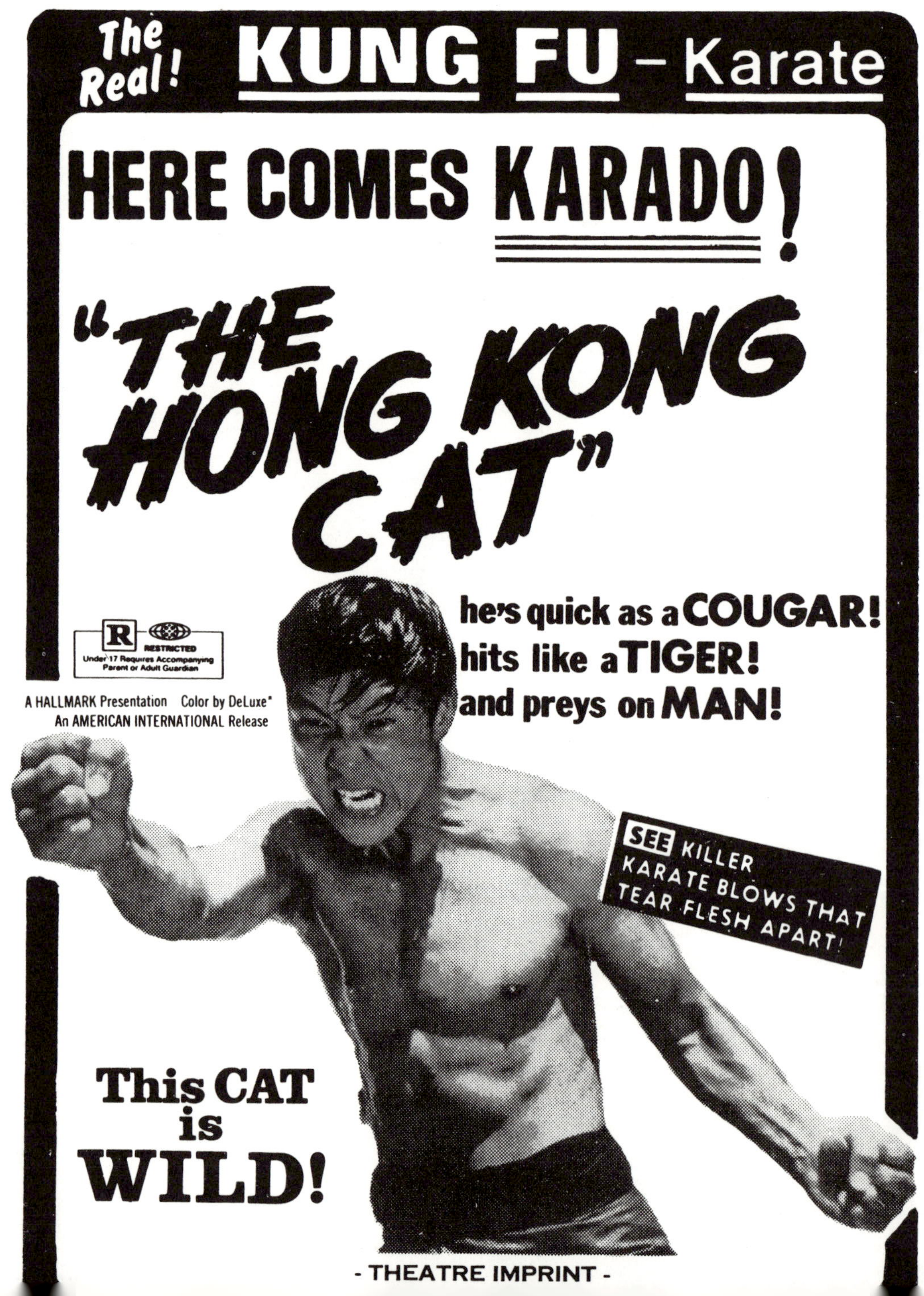

resulting in her "suicide."

Strangely, although Western filmmakers would no doubt make mini-series and soap operas out of this rich tapestry of intrigue, modern kungfu movie makers concentrated on the legends of the Monkey King—the most heroic and beloved character in the Peking Opera canon. Things improved noticeably (at least as depicted in modern-day cinema) with the coming of the following era, the SUNG DYNASTY.

This lasted almost three hundred years, in which the battles came out of the back rooms and onto the battlefields. Two dozen corking-good martial arts epics were made concerning this turbulent period, featuring some spectacular meldings of the supernatural and Shaolin teachings. This dynasty started on an auspicious note.

The Sungs united a deeply fractured China known as the TEN KINGDOMS into a Northern Sung and a Southern Sung. The Northern consolidated and instituted reforms which didn't quite take. The Southern had a sophisticated political structure which led to legal problems and clerical corruption. Overpopulation didn't help things either. Already the Chinese people numbered in the millions.

The Chinese made historicals such as this tale of Marco Polo's exploration.

And then there was Genghis Khan. He led a horde of Mongolians who decided to take over China. The Northern Sung made a deal with the Mongols, and for the next forty years waited until the time was right to take out Southern Sung. Genghis's sons, Mangu and Khublai, marched down in 1250. By 1268 Mangu was dead and Khublai was attacking. By 1280 the Mongols controlled the entire Chinese empire.

Thus began the YUAN DYNASTY, a less-than-one-hundred-year reign marked by resistance fighters and espionage. About half a dozen movies have been made about this period to date; it was not a happy time in Chinese history. Most Orientals are deeply concerned about their pride—their "face"—and this era marked a great loss of face.

All that changed in the mid-1300s. Bad government led to rebellion. The Mongols were pushed north and the MING DYNASTY started in the south. Now here was a dynasty modern-day Oriental movie producers could get their teeth into. Over a hundred and fifty films are set in this roughly three-hundred-year period, dealing with all the ingredients that make history interesting.

There were clan intrigues, gang battles, threatening Western Mongolians, threatening Far Eastern Manchurians, threatening Japanese, and internal warlord conspiracies. Things came to a head in the mid 1600s when the Manchus combined with bandit leaders to take over China and institute the CH'ING DYNASTY. This was yet another roughly three-hundred-year reign that made the stuff of another hundred and fifty films or so.

This was a period of great change in which magnificent fighters were created to survive those changes. It marked the destruction of the Shaolin Temple, forcing the surviving monks to create new kungfu forms so that they could take revenge. It was also a time of remarkable foreign contacts. The early Ch'ing emperors had relations with Russia, Tibet, Turkey, Nepal, Burma, Thailand, Vietnam and Korea. They even had some trouble with Rome and Christianity.

Then drugs entered the scene. In the early 1800s, the British East India Company sent opium to China. Once introduced it could not be gotten rid of. A booming smuggling trade sprang up and the demand was so great that it even strained national silver supplies. The leaders in Peking and the walled city of Canton wanted opium out. England wanted the silver opium brought. In 1841 the British attacked.

By 1846 China was open to the British, the French, and the Americans. Anti-foreign feelings swelled in Chinese hearts, leading to some very nasty goings-on—what with British heads impaled on spikes and all. The central areas of anti-Anglo feelings were in Kwangtung and Canton. Pirates and bandits were everywhere, taking white people's heads. In 1857 the British and French occupied Canton and started moving toward Peking. The Russians joined them.

Fighting the Japanese is a greatly overworked theme in Chinese movies, and this movie overworks everything.

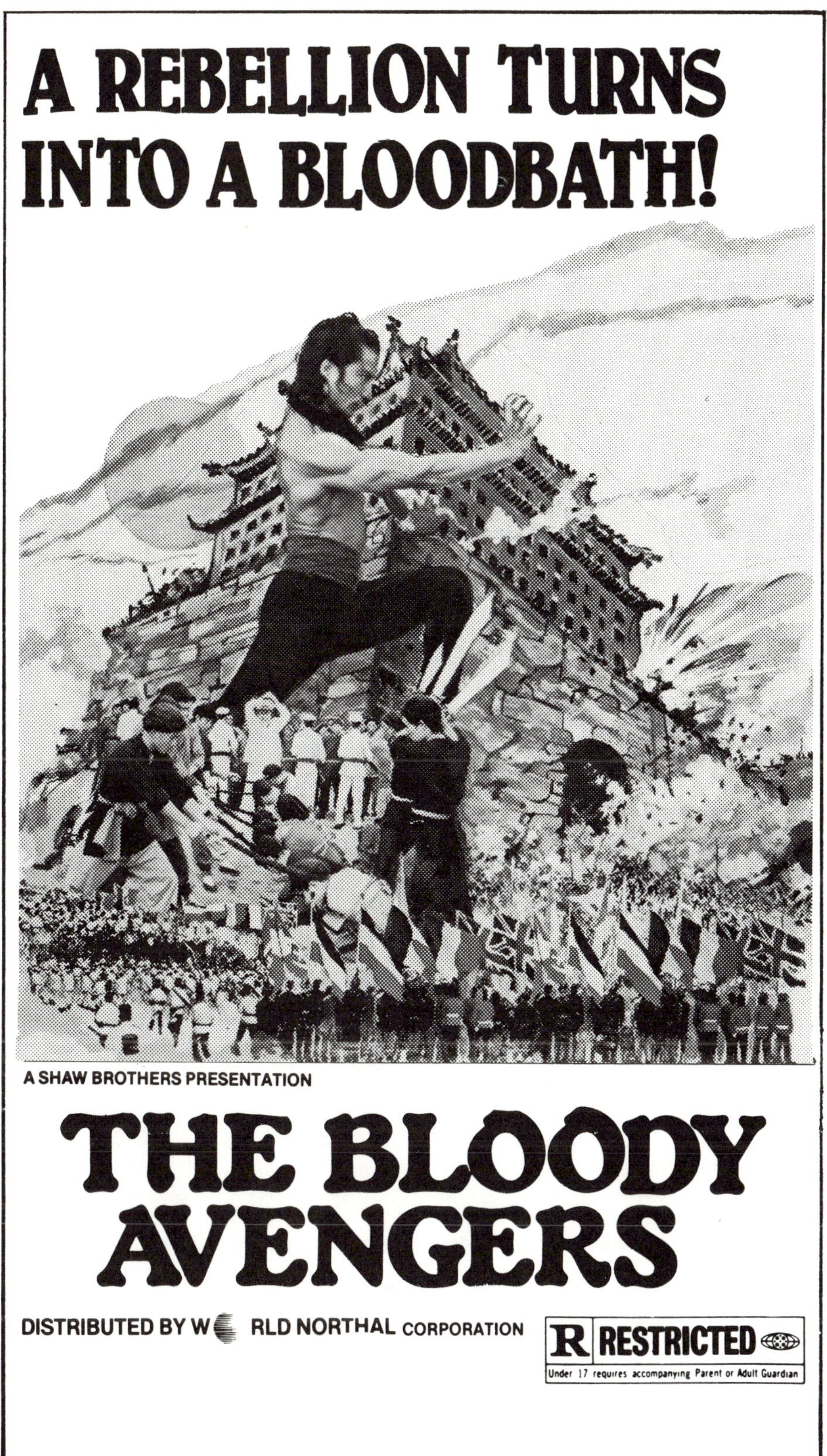

A REBELLION TURNS INTO A BLOODBATH!
A SHAW BROTHERS PRESENTATION
THE BLOODY AVENGERS
DISTRIBUTED BY WORLD NORTHAL CORPORATION
R RESTRICTED
Under 17 requires accompanying Parent or Adult Guardian

The Boxer Rebellion was a vital part of Chinese history. A part this film chronicles with a cast of hundreds.

By 1860, things had come to a boil. There were Taiping rebellions and Muslim rebellions, marking political and religious unrest. The more confusing things became, the more widespread was corruption. All the outlying areas—Nepal, Burma, and the like—were falling under British control. Meanwhile Japan was getting into the act, coming into conflict with China over the sovereignty of Korea.

Things got so bad between China and the foreigners that the government leased Hong Kong to the British for ninety-nine years to serve as an import-export way station. It was basically a liaison between the fractious powers.

KUNGFU REVOLUTION

Things boiled over in 1900. This was the justly famous BOXER REBELLION. This was an absolutely vital martial arts movie period, since this anti-foreign movement consisted of zealous followers of the "Righteous and Harmonious Fists"—what they considered to be an invulnerable form of kungfu!

They fought, according to their slogan, for "support of the Ch'ing and extermination of foreigners." On June twentieth it became full-scale declared war on all foreigners. It was Chinese boxing versus guns. Kungfu lost. By 1901, China was

THE MOST
EXCITING
KUNG FU
ADVENTURE
EVER FILMED!
In COLOR
ACTION PACKED SCENES THAT
WILL LEAVE YOU LIMP
SHANGHAI
CONNECTION
KARATE KING
R
• A PACIFIC GROVE FILMS RELEASE

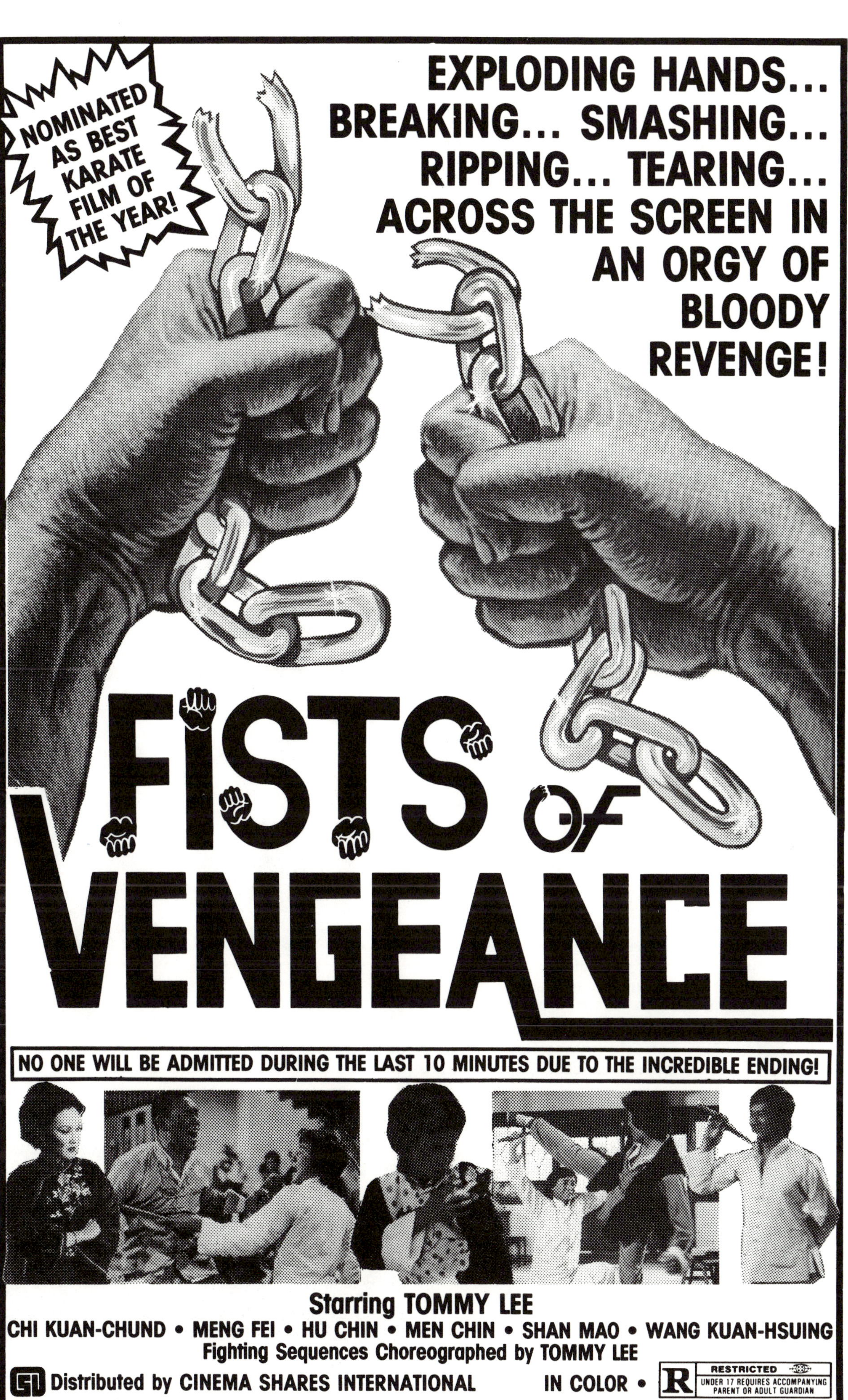
NOMINATED
AS BEST
KARATE
FILM OF
THE YEAR!
EXPLODING HANDS...
BREAKING... SMASHING...
RIPPING... TEARING...
ACROSS THE SCREEN IN
AN ORGY OF
BLOODY
REVENGE!
FISTS OF
VENGEANCE
NO ONE WILL BE ADMITTED DURING THE LAST 10 MINUTES DUE TO THE INCREDIBLE ENDING!
Starring TOMMY LEE
CHI KUAN-CHUND • MENG FEI • HU CHIN • MEN CHIN • SHAN MAO • WANG KUAN-HSUING
Fighting Sequences Choreographed by TOMMY LEE
CSI Distributed by CINEMA SHARES INTERNATIONAL
IN COLOR •
R RESTRICTED
UNDER 17 REQUIRES ACCOMPANYING PARENT OR ADULT GUARDIAN

no longer free and the populace was humiliated.

For the next decade China suffered under various foreign rule and had to be content with frothing at the mouth on the sidelines of international affairs. By 1911, it was all too much to take. Civil wars, Japanese invaders, and foreign influence all led to the development of THE REPUBLIC, starting in 1912. Although initially conceived as a democracy, China just didn't seem capable of sustaining it.

The National Assembly, another name for parliament, was created, mostly populated by former revolutionaries. But just because they were revolutionaries didn't mean they were any less insidious than their royal predecessors. Dirty deeds and assassinations were the order of the day. One Yuan Shih-k'ai took over, making the parliament appoint him president and then disbanding the parliament. By the beginning of World War One, Yuan's government was a dictatorship.

Yuan died in 1916 and the government battled amongst themselves to see what sort of country China would become, Imperial or Democratic. When the smoke cleared there was the Nationalist Party and the Communist Party. By 1922, most of the influencing nations agreed to allow China to find its own way, and from there on in, it became a battle between Chinese regions—mostly north and south.

All this history was rich fodder for modern filmmakers. China's story was full of "no-win" scenarios. There were many times during its eras when both sides of an issue were "right," allowing producers to picture all kinds of heroes, Ming, Ching, Manchu, or Shaolin. The thirties were equally rich in stories. The Nationalists had established a new order which lasted from 1928 to 1937, even though they warred with the Communists most of the time.

What brought them both together was an outside enemy: the Japanese. For years the Japanese ravaged China, committing atrocities the Chinese still can't quite get over. This is an absolutely vital aspect of Chinese kungfu movies: hatred of the Japanese. It wasn't until very recently that a Japanese was pictured in a favorable light in a Chinese movie. For the most part, they are pictured as the worst kind of cowardly, arrogant, dishonest, foul creatures imaginable.

By 1939, things had stalemated somewhat. The Allies threw in some five hundred million dollars to aid China in her fight. Sadly the fight wasn't just with the Japanese. It also continued between the Communists and the Nationalists. On December 7, 1941, it all changed. Japan bombed Pearl Harbor. America was angry now. That didn't help the Nationalists. As World War Two dragged on, bringing with it poverty and inflation, the reigning Nationalist government fell completely out of favor.

Once the World War ended, Chinese civil war began and raged until 1949. It was Chiang Kai-shek versus Mao Tse-tung, and Mao won for the Communists. October 1, 1949, marked the establishment of the People's Republic of China.

In terms of martial arts movies, that's where it ends. Great Britain had acquired Hong Kong from China in 1898 with a ninety-nine year lease. The story of Chinese kungfu movies actually becomes a story of Hong Kong kungfu movies. The People's Republic didn't make a bona fide martial arts epic

Chinese movies at their stupidest. Men in ape suits jump two knife-wielding girls and everybody does kungfu.

until 1981.

Kungfu movies set in modern-day China reflect the concerns of the areas they are filmed in. That means mostly Hong Kong with a bit of Taiwan and the Philippines thrown in for good measure. All three areas are pretty depressed in terms of economy and quality of life, so modern-day martial arts movies are usually fairly squalid affairs filled with ugly pessimism.

Nevertheless, the period between 1912 and the present is the richest in terms of kungfu material. At least two hundred kungfu films are set during this era—everything from superheroic adventures to madcap comedies to sizzling crime tales. This is where we can begin. Now that we've established where all the martial arts movies' stories come from, we can get down to the history of the kungfu films themselves.

CHINESE MARTIAL ARTS CHART

Different kinds of kungfu are as varied as the characters who populate the martial arts film genre. To list them all would be impractical and, considering the way new "fictional" kinds of kungfu are created in various movies, darn near impossible.

Listed below are the most prevalent forms of real kungfu presented on the silver screen. All are extremely difficult to learn, so watching a master practitioner in a movie is almost always a delight.

Even more delightful is watching how two masters of two different forms fight each other and how the hero must adapt or adjust his style to defeat a seemingly invulnerable opponent. Such is the stuff of great kungfu confrontations.

CHOY LI-FUT: Cantonese name for a popular Southern style which relies on a strong stance. Its best known techniques are "back fist," downward scraping arm swings, and "knuckle fist." It is also a style that utilizes weapons. When you see someone using things called the "Eighteen Staff," the "Baat Gwa Lance," or the "Willow Leaf Double Swords," you'll know the fighters are proponents of Choy Li-fut.

DRUNKEN STYLE: An extremely popular, versatile, adaptable style which calls for astonishing ability, strength, and control because it seems to involve no strength or control. A student of the Drunken style wobbles, weaves, and just generally imitates the actions of a drunkard. This student may even fall down, but watch it—it is just a ruse to draw an opponent into a lightning foot or hand. This style's popularity also rests on its adaptability to other styles; there can be a drunken version of almost any martial art. The art derives from legend, so listen for references to "The Eight Immortals" or "The Eight Drunken Fairies."

EAGLE CLAW: A vicious but graceful art derived from the movements of the eagle. The emphasis here is on quick eyes and fingers twisted into a claw position to strike at an opponent's pressure points.

THE FIVE ANIMAL STYLES OF
THE SHAOLIN TEMPLE:

1) CRANE—The hands become beaks, and one-legged stances are standard. The Crane fighter goes for the nerves and pressure points.

2) DRAGON—The most esoteric of the five animal styles; it needs the most power to perform. The object here is not to slash or break but to crush.

3) LEOPARD—Believe it or not, the foreknuckles of the hands are the primary striking area of this style.

4) SNAKE—A wonderfully cinematic "sneaky" style in which the arms and fingers turn into a snake, with all the dangerous "snake bites" that suggests.

5) TIGER—Rip and tear, rip and tear. A slashing, scratching style.

HSING-I: One of the three "internal" systems. The other two are Tai Chi and Pa-kua. The visible clues to these techniques involve soft, circular motions and regulated breathing patterns. But these three are actually methods of concentrating power. When a fighter pauses to do a strange sort of breathing, you can bet he's utilizing one of the three internal systems of China.

HUNG GAR: One of the most popular Southern styles because it combines the best from several other styles. One of the great kungfu movies, *Executioners from Shaolin* (U.S. title: *Executioners of Death*), was all about the development of this technique—the combination of the Shaolin Tiger and Shaolin Crane styles. Since this development took place in the eighteenth century, many films set in the time shortly after that period utilize Hung Gar extensively. No wonder, since it is a dazzling form to watch.

MONKEY: Another extremely filmable style which imitates the movements and fighting strategy of the simians. Although a strong technique, it is most often unmistakably pictured as a mincing style with the proponent screwing up his face in a monkey impression and making monkey sounds. The style has five main forms—"Lost Monkey," which utilizes surprise attacks; "Tall Monkey," which uses swinging arms for distance; "Stone Monkey," which is the powerful attack; "Wood Monkey," which is used to deceive the opponent; and "Drunken Monkey," the monkey version of the aforementioned art.

PHOENIX EYE: Another esoteric but popular cinematic style since it uses the single or double foreknuckle. When the foreknuckles come up on screen, Pheonix Eye is unmistakable.

PRAYING MANTIS: A great-sounding martial art which has a Southern style, but the Northern form is prevalent in films. Both forms are referred to in three ways, as "Seven Star," "Eight Steps," or "Six Harmonies." Listen for one of those, and watch for the hooklike hand and its grasping, clawing, and sudden punches.

SHUAI CHIAO: Did someone on screen just grab his opponent's arms, legs, shoulders, or other limbs to throw him, while also using indefinable kicks, blocks, and blows? Well, he's probably using this unusual form of wrestling.

TAN TUI: An exhausting but watchable form characterized by low kicking techniques. A sure sign of Tan Tui is the swift transition of high and low stances.

WHITE CRANE: Not from the Shaolin Temple, but from Tibet, this is a style based on the movements not just of cranes, but of apes as well. It's tough to distinquish regular Crane styles unless they are openly labeled White Crane, Tibetan White Crane, and even sometimes by White Lama Crane or Lama Crane.

WING CHUN: The most powerful-looking form of Chinese kungfu besides Jeet Kune Do (which isn't really a form). This is a direct Southern style that emphasizes simultaneous defense and attack with multiple straight punches at close range.

THE FIGHTING BEGINS

There seems to be a slight disagreement concerning which was the first Chinese martial arts movie. The Hong Kong International Film Festival lists it as 1920's *Thief in the Car.* The late lamented *Martial Arts Movies* Magazine listed it as *Monkey Fights Golden Leopard* in an article by James Seetoo. This was a 1926 silent film about the Monkey King, taken from a famous Chinese novel entitled *Journey to the West.*

However, most English-speaking fans of the genre consider it to be 1929's *The Burning of the Red Lotus Temple.* It hardly makes any difference, really, since the thirties and forties were rife with nebulous martial arts-influenced films made in Shanghai and Hong Kong.

These movies were little more than filmed stage plays, all sharing an artificiality that reduced the effect of whatever kungfu was included. Usually this kungfu was either faked by actors who were laboriously choreographed and then filmed move by move, or was shown as amazing feats accomplished with wires and pulleys.

Even so, the films from 1920 to 1949 are interesting in terms of how they relate to the later movies. Also for how their colorful titles compare to their somewhat staid presentation. For instance, there was 1927's *How Wu Song Killed His Sister-in-Law,* 1933's *Bloody Fights,* 1939's *Hu Weiqian Smashes the Engine Room,* and 1948's *How Fan Shiyu Took a 10,000 Mile Journey for Vengeance.*

The reason movies were being made at all was that Hong Kong and Shanghai were Westernized. That is, they were more modern and less restricted than their mainland Chinese comrades. These areas were also overpopulated and stricken with all manner of social ills that progress can create. Therefore they were in far more need of mass media entertainment. Up until 1949, this entertainment was highly stylized theater and cinema, mostly based on ancient traditions.

But then a director named Hu Peng heard about a master of martial arts named Huang Fei Hong. Born in 1847, died in 1924, Huang Fei Hong was the son of one of the famous Ten Tigers of Kwangtung (a group around which several movies have been made). Other than the fact that he practiced medicine, was expert in many forms of kungfu, and excelled at a sport/contest called "lion dancing," not much is known about the fellow.

Hu Peng rectified all that by starting a marathon film series which comprised an incredible eighty-five feature films over a twenty-year period. 1949's *The Story of Huang Fei-Hong Parts One and Two* was only the beginning of a phenomenon which was to become the foundation of the modern kungfu film.

Up until then, most movie martial arts feats were totally ludicrous and completely inaccurate (a problem which still afflicts most bad kungfu movies; namely most of the ones that appeared in the U.S. immediately after Bruce Lee died). Men leaped higher than trees, women flew through the air for hundreds of yards, and fighters did endless somersaults.

The actors in the Huang Fei Hong movies insisted on realism in the all-important action scenes. For the first time, kungfu was the heart of the film, not just a peripheral ingredient. So the need for accuracy became vital in order to honestly portray the leading character's life. It also didn't hurt that the lead actor was so similar to the character he played.

Kwan Tak Hing was the name of that actor, and his similarities to the actual Huang are telling. Born in 1906 and still thriving when he made his movies, Kwan was an actor in Cantonese opera, but more importantly, was an accomplished lion dancer and spectacular martial artist. He was initially well versed in Hung boxing, which goes several steps farther than Hung Gar. Instead of melding two forms, Hung Fist, as it is also called, melded all five Shaolin styles with the Horse, Elephant, Lion, and Monkey techniques. From there, Kwan became a master of the White Crane style.

As the films progressed over the decades, he became skilled in almost all the areas Huang himself excelled at. Huang seemed dedicated to mastering the most esoteric, difficult skills, such as the "Iron Wire," "Five Forms," and "Tiger Vanquishing" Fists as well as the impressive "Shadowless Kick," which actor Kwan seemed to delight in displaying throughout the film series. Kwan himself was the creator of what is now known as the Omni-Directional Gangrou Fist.

So director Hu had the character and the actor. And while the honorable legend of Huang and charming personality of Kwan were vital, it took more than those to make the film series a success. First, these were pictures about a beloved personage in fairly recent, happier times, so they became a nostalgic preserver of particular Cantonese pastimes such as "vying for firecrackers."

This was another sport/contest in which fireworks shot a bunch of red sticks into the air which teams would fight for when they came down. Whichever team held the most firecrackers at the finish was the winner. Being champion was a matter of great pride for many martial arts schools. Of even greater importance was being the winner of the various "lion dancing" competitions.

Here is a hallmark of Cantonese life. Beneath ornate costumes of the colorful Chinese lion, martial artists vie for what is called "lucky money." Not only is the acquisition important, but how the prize is gained is equally telling. It is the skill of the dancers beneath the costume which imbues the rippling lion body and heavy, puppet-like head of the outfit with character. Maneuvering this lion in competition with other lion-dancers can call for the greatest skill a martial artist possesses.

In this area Kwan was a master, making the many Huang movies that involved lion dancing a visual delight. But the nucleus of the Huang Fei-Hong films was the martial arts. These pictures reintroduced the Chinese to the joys of watching realistic kungfu exquisitely performed by masters. The real thing, in this case, was far more impressive than the artificial, theatrical kind of feats portrayed in years past.

For the record: there were five basic Kwangtung schools of kungfu teaching—the Hong School, the Liu, the Cai, the Li, and the Mo. They taught the ten major fist forms based on the movements of the crane, elephant, horse, monkey, leopard, lion, snake, tiger, and tiger cub. In addition, there was training utilizing the eighteen legendary weapons of China, which included staffs, spears, and swords. From there the possibilities become endless. The Huang Fei Hong movies made use of many of these possibilities, in addition to showcasing the subtler, but just as important, concept of "wu de"—which means "martial virtue."

Up until that time, the Oriental action films concentrated on savage tales of vengeance, characterized by a plot that had rival martial arts schools in conflict with one another because of pride or greed. This tried-and-true plot is still being overused today, but the Huang Fei Hong movies introduced an expert martial artist who used kungfu for health and self-defense only. He was a chivalrous, considerate saint of a man who was always patient, humble, and on the underdog's side.

Wu Yixiao, a Cantonese opera writer, scripted the first four films, but Wang Feng is generally credited as being the main influence on the series, since he wrote as well as directed many of the most popular. But this was truly a partnership between the actors and the crew. Kwan choreographed most of his own battles with his main opponent, Shih Kien (best known as the evil Han in *Enter the Dragon*). Together, they created stunning bouts which remain the series' highpoints.

Almost every major modern kungfu director was influenced by or actually worked on these motion pictures. The best of them, like 1955's *Huang Fei Hong Vied for the Firecrackers at Huadi* and 1956's *How Huang Fei Hong Vanquished the Twelve Lions,* not only displayed great martial arts but Huang's wisdom, courage, restraint, morality, and intelligence as well.

Although there were some other martial arts films during the fifties and sixties, the Huang Fei Hong movies practically monopolized the market. By 1956, twenty-five of the year's twenty-nine kungfu pictures featured the hero. These films were in the cinemas practically every month, and there were some years when the only martial arts movies were the Haung Fei Hong ones.

About the only other film series that was any kind of competition at all concerned the character Fang Shih Yu, an eighteenth-century, fiery-tempered master swordsmen and bare-handed fighter who was trained at the Shaolin Temple. There

The Tiger Jump *was the original name of this inexpensive movie obviously filmed in the Philippines. It came to American theaters with the strange title of* Hard as a Dragon.

編·導·演

雷成功

李司祺

李影

周江
陳嶺威
唐廸
陳舜
邱明
孟浪
麥鎮鷹
凌霄

聯合主演

成功影業(香港)公司

SUCCESS FILM COMPANY PRODUCTION

were about sixteen films concerning this legendary young man over the same two decades the Huang movies reigned, but his character was to flourish while Huang's languished—once other moviemakers discovered the joys of the kungfu film.

The reasons why the genre didn't explode sooner were many and varied. First, it is not easy to create good martial artists. It takes years of dedication to perform kungfu well on screen, no matter whether you are a martial arts student, a Peking Opera alumnus, a gymnast, an acrobat, or an actor. And if you don't perform kungfu well it is painfully evident to the audience. A bad martial arts actor looks like a clumsy fool.

Second, the Hong Kong film industry wasn't sophisticated enough during the fifties and sixties to mount the extravaganzas which were soon to explode throughout the Orient. About the only man who seemed to know what to do with a camera was King Hu, a lush epic filmmaker who toiled in Taiwan. He is probably the best action filmmaker the East has so far seen, but far from the best moviemaker.

This is not as fine a distinction as it might first appear. The "film" aspect of entertainment is technical. The "movie" aspect is emotional. King Hu's films, which include the recently rereleased *A Touch of Zen* (1966), are sumptuous, grand affairs which concentrate far more on character interaction and cinematic technique than they do on martial arts. Nothing wrong with that certainly, but this is a martial arts movie book.

To Hu, kungfu was a dance and was treated as such. There's hardly any action in *A Touch of Zen* but plenty of mood and symbolism—not to mention three distinct endings—within its three-hour running time. King Hu showed what could be done cinematically with what Chinese movie industry people had to work with, but essentially his films were magnificent visual elaborations of legends and stage plays. By the 1970s, the audience was ready for action and a few folk were ready to give it to them—with a vengeance.

CHAPTER THREE

Hong Kong: Wushu Warriors

The first hint of things to come was in 1967. There had been years of Huang Fei Hong films, but also other movies like 1964's *The Young Swordsman.* Swordplay movies had been a regular staple in Chinese cinema since the beginning, ranging in quality from predictable to awful. They were also marked by a ponderous artificiality. So audiences weren't expecting anything special when the lights went down and the screen lit up with *The One-Armed Swordsman.*

No one was prepared for what they saw. People stared in amazement as a supreme swordsman is saved from a murderous attack by his servant, who dies in his master's place. The swordsman takes the servant's son, Fong Kong, as his own, teaching him everything he knows. Years later, the swordsman is ready to retire, and plans to turn his martial arts school over to Fong. All the attention Fong has received has turned the swordsman's daughter bitter and hateful. With two male students, she plans her revenge.

The trio confront the confused Fong, and, in the ensuing fight, the daughter hacks Fong's right arm off herself. Blood pouring out of his shoulder, Fong falls into the arms of a girl named Shiu Min, who slowly nurses him back to health. But by that time the situation has only grown worse. A rival martial arts school, led by the "Long-Armed Devil," wants to destroy the elder swordsman's school utterly.

They find the one-armed man and the girl. He manages to fight them off but is again badly beaten in the process. Bloody, exhausted, despondent, Fong is inspired by his woman's love. It is she who tells him to start again. Laboriously, he learns to master the One-Armed Sword.

But time stands still for no one, one-armed or not. The villain kills the two men who conspired with the evil daughter and holds the girl as captive. Fong rescues her, instigating a series of bloody retributions. Fong goes to join his master, but is confronted by the villain's henchmen. He wipes them out.

He returns to his master's school to find the elder swordsman wounded and his students killed. Completely alone, Fong marches into the Long-Armed Devil's headquarters and massacres everyone. With the screen littered with bodies, Fong Kong sets off to settle down with his woman.

The audience was not the same when the lights came up. They had viewed a cathartic experience.

After years of Confucian morality and bloodless, unconvincing, stagy fights, *The One-Armed Swordsman* showed them a tortured anti-hero who thought nothing of slaughtering his enemies. And after all the abuse he had taken, the viewers went along with the slaughter—in fact, cheered it.

And the slaughter was realistic. None of this swinging a sword and having the opponent fall down. Here, things were chopped off, blood spurted, and victims fell writhing. Suddenly producer Runme Shaw, director Chang Cheh, writer I Kuang, and star Wang Yu had the first million-dollar-grossing movie in Hong Kong history.

A sequel was called for and made. Not surprisingly, it was called *The Return of the One-Armed Swordsman* and premiered in 1969. The production team was the same, as was the film's point of view. Fong Kong is living peacefully in the country with his wife. An invitation to a dueling contest arrives, which Fong declines. Then the Eight Demon Swordsmen capture all the contestants, demanding an arm from each. As if that nastiness weren't enough, they kidnap Fong's wife. Now that was a mistake. That gets the One-Armed Swordsman angry. From there on, it is slaughter time.

The filmmakers had found a formula: Take a quiet, unassuming hero, heap incredible abuse on him, then have him fight back with equally incredible rage and bloodlust. But more than that, Cheh and Kuang liberally littered the film with sensitive touches and telling actor's moments—which build audience sympathy for the put-upon, otherwise noble hero. They also set striking backgrounds for the action, such as the snowy woods where Fong's arm is chopped off.

Naturally, in a realistic movie, none of this could have been possible. The arm could not have been so easily and cleanly hacked off, Fong would have fallen, screaming, to the ground instead of stumbling away, and he would have died within

Is this the face of a movie series superstar? Kwan Tak Hing is no James Bond, but the Chinese kungfu "Jimmy Stewart" appeared in over eighty movies.

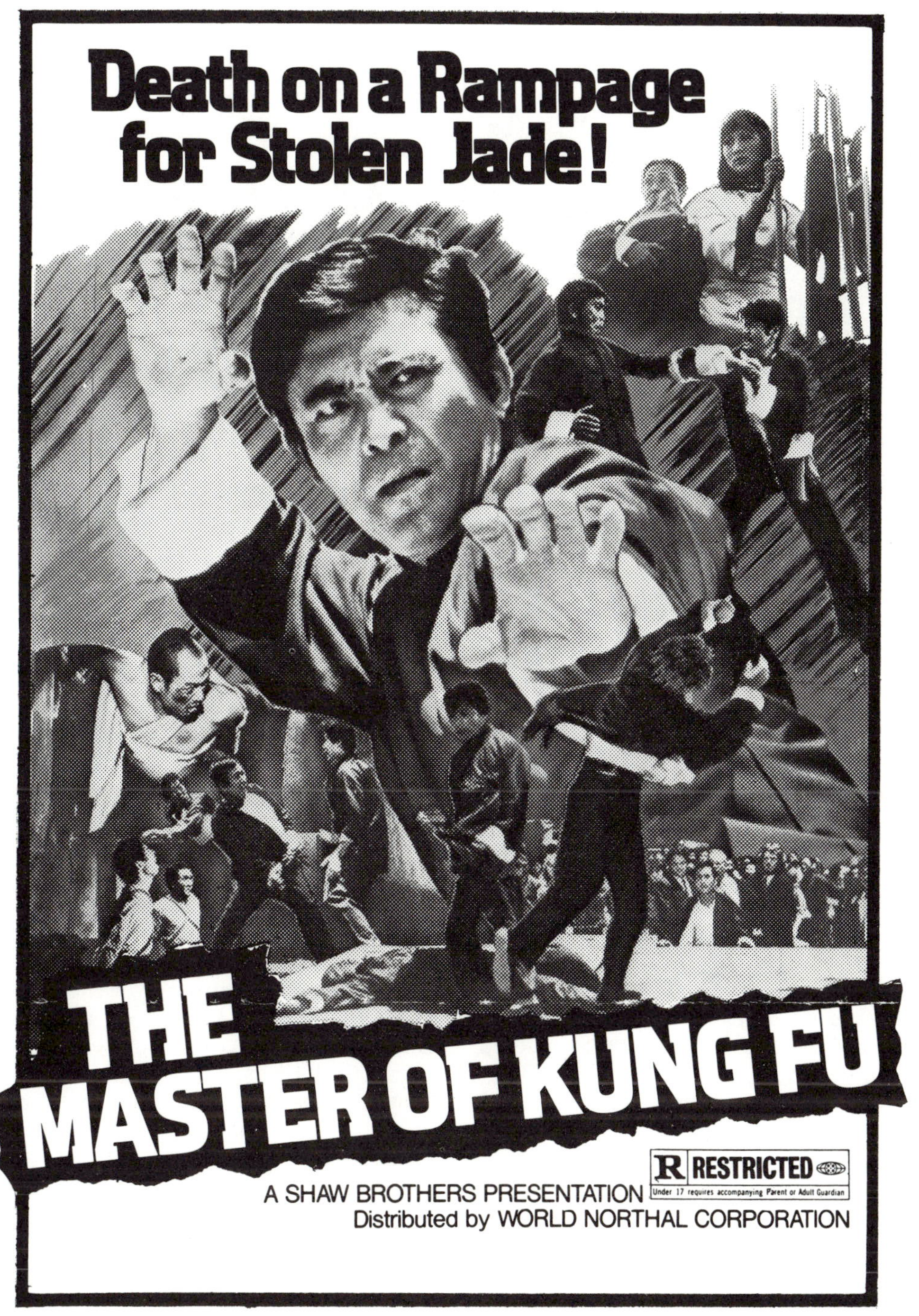

Death on a Rampage for Stolen Jade!
THE MASTER OF KUNG FU
R RESTRICTED
Under 17 requires accompanying Parent or Adult Guardian
A SHAW BROTHERS PRESENTATION
Distributed by WORLD NORTHAL CORPORATION

Kwan Tak Hing wasn't the only man to play the famous Huang Fei Hong character. Ku Feng, one of the great Chinese supporting actors, here starred as the beloved martial artist.

minutes from the shock and loss of blood. But taken as a superhero film, it works, and works beautifully.

Not content with this extreme statement of their theme, the same team goes even further with 1968's *Golden Swallow,* which is a sequel to one of King Hu's films called *Come Drink With Me.* Both were about a swordswoman named Cheng Pei Pei, but the Shaw Brothers Studio production cast Wang Yu as the white-garbed swordsman Silver Roc, who is a walking, two-armed death machine.

Here the writer, director, and star went for

Although he's already wounded, Jimmy Wang Yu is about to lose an arm in order to become The One-Armed Boxer.

broke, mounting riveting scenes of wholesale mayhem, marked by an extremism that bordered on the supernatural. Silver Roc takes on the Dragon Gang with sword and darts, with traps and weapons of all kinds complicating matters until Silver Roc stands, mortally wounded, blood all over his white outfit, defiant to the end.

The name of the game here was hysteria. Wang Yu, a small, unimpressive-looking actor played an obsessed man in all his films, and the fans loved it. It was an image Yu himself promoted, and cemented in 1970 by writing, directing, and starring in *The Chinese Boxer.* In this, Wang Yu added his own particular stamp: intense hatred of the Japanese.

Wang Yu plays Lei, the top martial artist in his school until a bunch of Japanese karate killers murder everyone. They would have killed Lei as well had they known he was not dead. He was merely wounded, lying amidst the dead. So while the Japanese terrorize the town, Lei goes to a cave and tortuously learns the Iron Palm technique. He weights himself, burns his arms, and suffers mightily among the eerie confines of the macabrely decorated interior of the cave.

At the start of his career, audiences were curious as to how Wang Yu would top himself in succeeding films. The carnage of the last seemed insurmountable. That is, until Yu showed up again. In *The Chinese Boxer* Lei builds up audience participation through his training as well as the astonishingly heinous violence of the occupying Japanese, until the two forces smash into each other.

Eyes are gouged out, knives are plunged into chests, limbs are shattered, until Lei is mortally wounded through trickery. Even so, he bounces around the room and wipes out the final Japanese martial arts fighter. Once again, Wang Yu, now the filmmaker himself, had exhausted and exhilarated his audience.

Curiously, Wang Yu's cinematic hatred of the Japanese began the year he completed his best film—a Japanese co-production featuring the famous blind swordsman of Japan, Zatoichi. Directed by Kimiyoshi Yasuda, a master stylist of samurai movies, it had a poetic realism and sociological undercurrent the Chinese couldn't get close to.

Zatoichi and the One-Armed Swordsman (Japanese title: *Zatoichi Meets His Equal*) was about blindness of all kinds, not just the leading character's lack of sight. Fong is traveling through Japan and becomes the astonished witness to a mass murder during a funeral procession. He saves a single child and escapes, only to be accused of the killings and hunted down. Zatoichi, as always played by Shintaro Katsu, finds, and then allies himself with, Fong, to reveal the real killers and mete out justice.

This plot synopsis cannot convey the visual power of this nearly unique combination of Japanese and Chinese martial arts movies. The images and action of this ninety-four minute movie seem unsurpassable, and it also seems quite clear that Wang Yu learned much from it. Upon returning to Hong Kong, he left the Shaw Brothers Studio before his contract was up to pursue his own goals.

The immediate result of his departure were the last two films he made which could be called great. The first appeared to be a combination of two previous films; it was called *The One-Armed Boxer* (1971). Again, extremism was the watchword here. He does *The Chinese Boxer* several times better by having his character face, not just the Japanese, but fighters from all over the Orient!

This is a wild tournament film that has Yu losing an arm in an early bout but learning the Iron Arm from a wise sifu so that he can return and do each of the other fighters one better with just one arm. He takes out a whole series of martial artists, who range from the barely plausible to the totally ridiculous. Of course, there's the trademark karate man, but also Koreans, twins from Thailand, Mongolian lamas who can actually pump themselves up, and an Indian mystic who walks on his hands.

The One-Armed Boxer marked the start of Yu's degeneration. Although still entertaining, this movie crossed the line from superheroism to ludicrous farce. The actor played his scenes straight, but those scenes were stupid. His last roaring shout was *Beach of the War Gods*, Wang Yu's ultimate statement. He plays Hsaio Feng, a legendary fighter intent on preventing Japanese pirates from destroying a small Chinese coastal village in the last days of the Ming Dynasty.

The film is full of characters and fights, but Wang saves the best for last. It is an unrestrained twenty-minute battle in which Feng lays low the whole crew of Japanese pirates. The second-to-final shot shows him standing amid the bodies on the beach as a slightly late group of Chinese soldiers approach. The final shot shows him slowly dropping dead amidst the corpses as the army marches by.

Now, is this the face of a superstar? It's Jimmy Wang Yu, who was the biggest thing in the Orient before Bruce Lee, in Tattooed Dragon.

It's hard for the action film lover not to appreciate such grand visions and extreme statements. However, it seemed as if Wang Yu had nothing else to say after those first few films. Had he died, like Bruce Lee, his reputation and fame would have grown. But since he lived on to make a long list of uninspiring and, in some cases, dreadful movies, his contribution to the genre is tarnished.

In 1972 he made a series of mediocre films with Lo Wei as director. Wei could not do with Yu what he had been able to do with Bruce Lee. Wang Yu was nowhere near the skilled stylist Lee was. Yu's expertise was not in the martial arts, really. It was in the dramatic, cinematic use of his limited kungfu ability. He could make fight scenes look good. That is, until a truly great martial artist, such as Bruce Lee, showed up.

These new films, made just months after Yu's

Jimmy Wang Yu may not be that handsome, but he knows how to express himself, as he does here to someone's face in Tattooed Dragon.

greatest triumphs, were tacky-looking, small-scale adventures. He no longer seemed interested in, or even capable of, mounting a grand production. *A Man Called Tiger* was one in which Yu played a modern-day fighter who appears to join a crime boss until he can get some incriminating evidence for a cop played by Lo Wei. The ending had a bunch of thugs pulling axes on him. He gets his leg sliced up, but manages to hurl the bad guy off a Hong Kong skyscraper.

The Tattooed Dragon was more like the Wang Yu of old, but only in that he's persecuted, badly wounded, and taunted until the very end, when he wipes his enemies out. Still, the climax involved only a few people, and the battle took place in a claustrophobic tea house.

In 1974, an attempt was made to assure him an international following (he was one of the first to be declared "The New Bruce Lee!") with *The Man from Hong Kong*, a British production directed by Brian Trenchard Smith. For this film he was dubbed Jimmy Wang Yu, and the monicker stuck. He has been known by that name ever since.

Although well meaning, decently made, and featuring George Lazenby as the villain, this modern-day espionage/crime thriller did not impress audiences who had seen what Bruce Lee could do. It was back to the Orient for Jimmy Wang Yu, and to reams of pale copies of his past groundbreakers.

LET THE BLOOD FLOW

The same fate was not to befall Chang Cheh. He was too experienced to let youthful enthusiasm overwhelm him. He was almost fifty years old at the time, and had been toiling in the Oriental film industry since 1947. He had been working for Shaw Brothers for ten years. When Wang Yu left the studio, the contract director seemed to realize that the day of the non-martial arts actor in action films was over. He started looking for stars who matched the charisma, attitude, and handsomeness of Bruce Lee. As it turned out, no one man could match Lee's popularity. In this case, it took two.

They were David Chiang and Ti Lung. Their first major effort came in a bleak, intense 1970 drama *Vengeance.* Many consider it Cheh's best piece of "serious" kungfu cinema. There is no doubt that his and scriptwriter I Kuang's juggling of ancient (represented by the Ti Lung character's involvement with a Peking Opera troupe) and modern images made for some of the director's most impressive relevant visual statements. As his career was to progress, his visuals would become more and more cartoonish.

But trying to pigeonhole Chang Cheh is difficult, considering he has made about a hundred movies in the last twenty-two years. His period of greatest fluctuation came in the years immediately after Wang Yu's departure. He made historical action films with Lung and Chiang as well as modern sagas featuring that duo and another young newcomer named Chen Kuan Tai. All three deserve attention.

David Chiang was born the year Chang Cheh started in films, 1947. His parents were both actors, so he made his initial appearances in child roles. He grew to be a slight, short young man, but he was quick and accurate in the martial arts. He started as a stuntman for movies, but graduated to acting when Cheh discovered him.

In the early years he specialized in wily, con-artist characters—perfectly matched with Ti Lung's matinee-idol attitude and looks. He is sometimes known to U.S. fans as "Rover," the street-thief character he played in *The Savage Five* (released in America in 1979). In the later years he played what parts he could, but was never completely convincing as a supreme kungfu master because of his size and slight build.

Ti Lung, on the other hand, is probably the most majestic of all kungfu movie stars. He has matured into a regal personage; a versatile actor with a staunch respect for, and a seemingly effortless ability at, the martial arts. This ability derived from studying karate, hung gar, tae kwon do, and

These crooks have several axes to grind with Jimmy Wang Yu (right) in A Man Called Tiger.

Although Jimmy Wang Yu's martial arts expertise is way below Bruce Lee's, he certainly knew how to jump in A Man Called Tiger.

Mantis Fist since 1961. His screen presence was honed by a year-long Shaw Studio course that sharpened his acting and fighting skills.

Both Chiang and he seemed to be naturals, and played off each other well. In the early films, Lung was often cast as the regulation hero with Chiang as the anti-hero. It was this sort of part which best suited Lung and has followed him throughout his continuing career, a career that includes over seventy martial arts movies. No one ever said the Shaw Studios didn't put their actors to work.

Chen Kuan Tai was the third wheel on this Chang Cheh bicycle, and didn't stay riding with the duo for long. Unlike the other two, he was known as a martial artist before his film career, winning the 1969 light-heavyweight championship at the East-Asian Tournament in Singapore. He started learning Monkey style kungfu when he was eight and displayed how powerful the art could be in several films. Unlike other screen Monkey stylists, he never resorted to prancing monkey impersonations.

While Ti Lung was featured in Wang Yu's *Return of the One-Armed Swordsman,* Kuan Tai was in *The Chinese Boxer* as well as *Huang Fei Hong Bravely Crushing the Fire Formation*—the last Huang movie of the early seventies. He achieved stardom with Chang Cheh's *Boxer from Shantung* (U.S. title: *Killer from Shantung*—1972) in which he played a naïve martial artist in the corrupt, danger-fraught city of Shanghai on the eve of the Sino-Japanese war.

The most notable film the trio made together under Cheh's direction was *Blood Brothers* (U.S. title: *Dynasty of Blood*—1973), one of the director's more ambitious attempts at combining martial arts action with a meaningful story. The story was about the dangers of power and friendship. It is set in the mid-nineteenth century during the Taiping Rebellion and is based on actual people and events.

Chiang and Kuan Tai are highwaymen until Lung convinces them to join the Imperial Army. As Lung excels, his absolute power begins to corrupt him absolutely. He has an affair with the Kuan Tai character's wife, then has Kuan Tai killed. Chiang takes revenge for his dead friend on his ex-friend, then willingly gives himself up and is executed.

The film well represents the Shaw Brothers movie of the early seventies. The brothers, Run Run and Runme, own a gigantic studio with sound stages, standing exterior sets, and a costume warehouse. Sets and costumes are meticulously designed in intricate detail, covering a cross-section of Chinese history. They have a school on the premises, complete with dormatories. In this, what is called "Movietown," they are able to film massive productions with sweep and pageantry.

They also have a waterfront, where Chang Cheh filmed *Deadly Duo,* another early seventies kungfu adventure that represents a regular Chiang/Lung team-up. This featured the pair as noble heroes of the Yuan Dynasty, trying to save their prince from the Mongol hordes. Naturally, Lung is nobler than crafty Chiang, but it is Chiang who gives up his life in the finale to save Lung and the prince.

After the excitement of his first four films, Jimmy Wang Yu did variations on them for the rest of his career. Here he does a follow-up to The One-Armed Boxer.

Deadly Duo was also a good example of what was wrong and what was right about Cheh's early kungfu output. Although the film was full of interesting characters and esoteric weapons—Lung had a battle-ax, Chiang a steel whip, and the villains were Fire, Earth, and Tree Men—time between fights crawled like a snail. In one particularly ludicrous scene, the main heroes' associates discuss crossing a treacherous drawbridge at length before each in turn tries it and falls to his death.

The ending, however, is worth the price of admission. Chiang and Lung chop away at the Mongol hordes until Lung is safely at sea with the prince on a raft while Chiang stands, dead, on the wharf, blocking the surviving Mongols. To Paraphrase the final line by the Mongol general: "If the Chinese have other warriors of this quality, we're in deep trouble."

In 1972, David Chiang was given the distinction of playing *The New One-Armed Swordsman,* who must avenge Ti Lung's character's death inside the Tiger Fort. This One-Armed Swordsman was named Lei Li, and he supposedly chopped off his own arm when defeated in a fight, but no one was fooled. Chiang's intensity was not the alienated, obsessive kind Wang Yu's was, and while Chang Cheh puts in some wonderfully clever visuals and handles the bloody battle scenes exceptionally, these proposed new adventures did not take off.

Where Chang Cheh distinguished himself from the directors who followed was in his use of blood. He has never shirked from its use while those around him sought a cleaner, less ugly format with which to display their martial arts expertise. Chang has also been fortunate in his ability to scout and promote talent in both his actors and martial arts instructors.

He broke the mold in 1972 with *The Water Margin* (U.S. title: *Seven Blows of the Dragon*), in which he introduced a protracted-fight-scene filming style that has remained vital to this very day. Although crude at that time, this movie marked the end of the razzle-dazzle editing style which made non-martial artists look decent in fight scenes. Although the camera work can still be eye-straining, from this feature on the best kungfu battles were filmed without technical "juice."

The Water Margin/Seven Blows of the Dragon was based on the classic novel by Shi Nai-an called *Outlaws of the Marshes,* written in the fourteenth century. It concerned the 108 Mountain Brothers—a famous band of righteous mercenaries in the eleventh century (Sung Dynasty) who fight bad guys where they find them. It, and the sequel, *All Men Are Brothers,* gave Chang Cheh a chance to film kungfu fights just for their own sake.

But he truly found his niche in 1975 with *Five Shaolin Masters* (U.S. title: *Five Masters of Death*), the fourth in Cheh's Shaolin series. As far as critics were concerned, this movie marked the start of Cheh's decline. As far as this book is concerned, it marked the start of his finest martial arts movies. Indeed, he no longer seemed to be looking for relevant images. Now he seemed intent on producing one hundred percent superhero entertainment. He seemed to stop taking his movies' histrionics seriously, and got down to some serious mayhem.

CHANG'S GANG

Five Masters of Death was based on the famous story of the Shaolin Temple's destruction and the survival/vengeance of its escaping students. It followed *Heroes Two* (U.S.: *Bloody Fists*), *Shaolin Martial Arts,* and *Men from the Monastery* (U.S.: *Disciples of Death*)—all 1974. In these preceding films, Cheh introduced Chi Kuan Chun, a dark-skinned actor with high cheekbones and a ferret face, as well as Fu Sheng, a lively acrobat/martial artist who was in the first class of the studio's newly conceived project—The Shaw Training Center for Young Actors and Actresses.

The 1975 Shaolin movie teamed Ti Lung and David Chiang with Chun and Sheng, then added a cute-looking fellow named Meng Fei to fill out the Five. Together they take on early eighteenth-century enemies led by actor Wang Lung Wei—a brutish, mustached presence who was to become one of the most versatile villains in the kungfu genre.

Here is a telling distinction of martial arts movies. Wang Lung Wei is not a versatile actor. He is a versatile fighter. It is his particular skill that he can make defeats by everyone from Fu Sheng to David Chiang look believeable. When Wang Lung Wei is ultimately defeated, whether it be by a hundred-and-fifty-pound lad or a hulking muscleman, the beaten fighter makes it work.

To beat him this time, Fu Sheng and Chi Kuan Chun learned the Shaolin animal styles, Meng Fei learned the "rolling" style (a form of wrestling that looks artificial on screen—David Chiang did it in *Seven Blows of the Dragon*), Ti Lung became master of the staff pole, and Chiang used the steel whip with deadly accuracy (he hurls the sharpened point through two men at once during the climactic free-for-all).

Only Sheng, Chiang, and Lung survive at the fadeout, but this film's success was to lead to many other Shaolin movies made by Chang Cheh over the next two years. At this time he got the first of two brainstorms. That was to give Fu Sheng

SIX FEET OF
SILVER DEATH!
ONE MAN...ONE WEAPON...
ONE HELL OF A MOVIE
BLOOD
OF THE
DRAGON

Blood of the Dragon *pales in comparison to Jimmy Wang Yu's previous classic* Beach of the War Gods, *the fame of which this film is based on.*

STARRING
WANG YU

MUSIC BY
FLOOD

Directed by KAO PAO SHU Produced by PARK VENGEE

Associate Producer
LEON WALTERS

Executive Producer
MICHAEL THEVIS

In charge of Production
WILLIAM DIEHL, JR.

Advertising and Publicity by MICHAEL PARVER ASSOCIATES, INC.

Music recorded at the SOUND PIT, Atlanta, Ga. Color by METROCOLOR R RESTRICTED

A Harnell Independent Productions Release

his due. In a very short time, this personable actor had won over audiences with his boyish, impish, charm. Even when playing a straight character, he had a wit and prickly style unmatched by any other action star working.

Cheh secured Fu Sheng's future by starring him in *The Chinatown Kid* (1977) and the *Brave Archer* series (1978–79). The former film was probably one of the best modern-day martial arts movies made. In it Sheng plays an impoverished troublemaker who is forced to flee the Orient for San Francisco. There he slaves in a Chinese restaurant, meeting up with a quiet student (Sun Chien).

Because he is such a good martial artist, he runs afoul of two warring street gangs, led by muscular Lo Meng on one side and sophisticated Kuo Chui on the other. All Sheng's character wants to do is be good, so when Sun Chien's character becomes addicted to the drugs supplied by the gang, Sheng sees the error of his ways. Although a successful and rich member of the gang, he attacks, killing all his enemies, but dying himself.

The Chinatown Kid was more realistic than most modern-day chop-socky pictures and the filmmakers pull off one of their cleverest symbols in the form of a digital watch. It represents the brave new American world to Sheng's character, and his actions all revolve around attaining and sustaining the watch. At the end, as he's dying, he offers it to Chien . . . who doesn't take it. The whole business is obvious, but extremely effective.

Sheng proved his mettle in period pieces directly afterward with *The Brave Archer* (U.S.: *Kung Fu Warlords*), in which he played a Sung Dynasty hero named Kuo Tsing, who did precious little archery. But Chang Cheh dazzled audiences with his sunny, brightly colored scenes of astonishing mayhem. This stuff went far beyond the Bruce Lee style of hurling around grossly inferior martial artists. These were duels between fighters of at least equal ability, in sumptuous period costumes on exact, intricately detailed period sets.

Following quickly came *The Brave Archer Part II* (U.S.: *Kung Fu Warlords Part II*), *Brave Archer Part III* (U.S.: *Blast of the Iron Palm*), and *Brave Archer and His Mate.* All promoted Chang Cheh's interest in extremely complicated plots that involved liberal doses of stunning fight scenes in which characters routinely flipped, kicked, chopped, and leaped with the greatest of ease. His films required exceptional acrobats and athletes. Although all the actors did almost all their own stunts, these sequences can be literally unbelievable to Western eyes.

But Eastern audiences loved it, which led to Chang Cheh's second brainstorm. Taking the "team" concept of *Five Masters of Death,* why not film a series of lively kungfu movies all starring the same actors in basically the same roles? Thus gave rise to Chang Cheh's Teams. The first team was David Chiang, Ti Lung, Chen Kuan Tai, Fu Sheng, and Chi Kuan Chun—even though those five rarely all played in the same film.

He introduced his second team in the preceding Fu Sheng starring vehicles. The first team had split up to work with other directors and other studios, so the second team premiered on it's own with *The Five Venoms* (U.S.: *Five Deadly Venoms*—1978). In the fifteenth century, a dying teacher taught five masked students the deadliest forms of kungfu known—Snake, Centipede, Lizard, Toad, and Scorpion. None of the students knew each other at the time, but now several had teamed to become criminals. The teacher tells his last student, who knows a bit of all five arts, to find the students and stop their crimes.

From this simple premise, Cheh extracted martial arts extremism. The villains practice esoteric, nasty killing styles. They defeat each other with a solid gold, knife-lined casket, pins in noses, knives in ears, as well as their own unbelievable skills. In the finale, when the venoms fight, the heroes literally walk up the walls and stand there. It is all done with bold, unapologetic style.

The second team, formally introduced: Kuo Chui was always the main hero, and always played a street-smart supreme fighter who hid behind a guise of a beggar or a transient or a criminal. Chiang Sheng is known by fans as "cutie-pie," and indeed he is—just as small and thin as David Chiang, but almost always playing the acrobatic partner to Chui. Sun Chien was the kicker; sometimes hero, sometimes villain. Lo Meng is the thick-headed muscleman, and Lu Feng is almost always the insidious traitor who lures heroes into his traps.

Chang Cheh also used a variety of regular actors in secondary roles, but these five were the main unit for at least ten adventures that were unique in their extremism. The tone was set by their second movie, *Crippled Avengers* (U.S.: *Mortal Combat*—1978). Chen Kuan Tai played a Ming Dynasty kungfu master driven mad by his wife's death and son's disfigurement. Some of his enemies chopped off the boy's forearms and the mother's legs.

Years later, Kuan Tai has taught his son (Lu Feng) Tiger style and replaced his limbs with metal arms that can elongate and shoot darts. From then on, the wealthy man cripples whoever he doesn't like. He blinds a trinket salesman (Kuo Chui), deafens a blacksmith (Lo Meng), chops the feet off a passerby (Sun Chien), and makes retarded a hero who wants to avenge them (Chiang Sheng), by

Angela Mao Ying herself, the first major female kungfu star, as she appeared in the violent When Tae Kwon Do Strikes.

Angela Mao Ying in action, showing the power she became known for, in When Tae Kwon Do Strikes.

tightening a steel band around his skull.

The four unite, find the retarded hero's teacher, and learn new kungfu techniques. The disfigured man is given metal feet. The crippled masters return to town during a birthday party for their oppressor—which many of the country's great, but wicked, kungfu masters attend. The four wipe them all out, a climactic moment coming when Sun Chien puts his metal foot into the chest of one of them.

The Chiang Sheng character is killed by the metal arm's darts, but the others survive to take their vengeance on their insane tormentor. There is hardly a believable second in this adventure, but as a martial arts movie, it works. As does such following adventures as *The Daredevils* (1978), an early Republic of China conflict in which street performers revenge themselves on a corrupt general (about the only second team film in which the Kuo Chui character dies), and *The Kid with the Golden Arm* (1979).

Here Kuo Chui plays a Drunken style master who aids a hero-laden escort service trying to get a wagon of gold to a famine area during the Ming Dynasty. The ax-, sword-, spear-, and winejug-carrying heroes face masters of the Iron Palm (which here leaves a black imprint that slowly kills the victim), the Iron Fan (a gigantic, sword-edged, steel war fan), the Iron Head (really, a man with a steel forehead shield), and the infamous Kid with the Golden Arm himself—a master of an art which makes him invulnerable to blades.

To see any of the Chang Cheh movies of this

Huang Ing Sik, the villain of When Tae Kwon Do Strikes, *was to become one of the legendary screen bad guys of Chinese cinema.*

period is not to believe them, but to enjoy them for the kungfu craziness and exuberant bloodiness. The director started searching out new talent while teaming his second team with Fu Sheng and Ti Lung for *Ten Tigers of Kwantung* (1979), a Cheh mess which juggled two stories through flashbacks, involved Huang Fei Hong's father and cousins, and had a man's head kicked off at the climax.

That out of his system, he took the second team through *The Spearmen of Death* (1980) and *Masked Avengers* (1981). Kuo Chui fought spear-topped flags in the former and tridents in the latter, both about eight feet long. The two films were baroque and bloody.

The final complete second team movie was *House of Traps* (1981), which pushed all Chang Cheh's concepts to the razor's edge. In the Sung Dynasty, an evil man hides incriminating evidence in a death-filled pagoda and hires kungfu criminals to guard it. Kuo Chui is the "Black Fox," a tarnished knight-errant who signs on as a guard but actually intends to secure the evidence for honorable Judge Pao (an actual Sung Dynasty lawman made famous in literature along with Judge Dee).

But first his associates must be slaughtered by the house of traps' spike-growing floors, spear-hurling walls, ax-swinging supports, arrow-shooting panels, and, most incredibly, razor-lined stairs which take off toes and parts of feet. The Black Fox masters them all, wondering at the fadeout at the evil that greed causes.

Huang Ing Sik (left) shows his poor opponent what Tae Kwon Do is all about. This is really When Tae Kwon Do Strikes.

CHANG'S MASTERPIECE

The second team was no more. Kuo Chui, Chiang Sheng, and Ku Feng left the Shaw Brothers Studio. Sun Chien remained behind, but for some reason he was never given much to do in any of Cheh's pictures even though he showed himself to be an accomplished leg fighter. Only Lo Meng, the strongman, remained, and he was the only second unit "regular" who appeared in the director's most grandiose, possibly best structured, certainly bloodiest, superhero saga.

Five Element Ninja (U.S.: *Super Ninjas*—1982) starred Chien Tien Chi as a virtuous member of a kungfu clan attacked by the most insidious power for evil the martial arts world has ever known: the Japanese Ninja. The film can be divided into four sections. Section one: The virtuous clan is challenged by an evil clan who have hired Ninjas to do their dirty work. The good guys go to the five prearranged contest locations only to be massacred by the Ninjas who work within the five elements.

The sun Ninjas use golden shields to blind their victims, the wood Ninjas use camouflage, the water Ninjas come shooting out of a river, the fire Ninjas deal fiery death, and the earth Ninjas burrow underground. With all their main fighters dead, the good clan rallies around their leader, expecting an attack at any moment. Unfortunately, a sympathetic clan member (Lo Meng) takes in a supposedly abused young woman (Chen Pei Hsi) who is actually a Ninja spy.

Section two: The Ninjas attack, using their spy for information. She also wounds Lo Meng, but it doesn't stop him from fighting like a man pos-

Angela Mao Ying as she appeared in Stoner, *one of the first inferior movies she made after a string of winners.*

sessed, only to be speared to the smoking door of the locked house where the Ninjas burn the clan leader alive. The Ninjas then turn on their employers, killing the other clan, to become the masters of the martial arts world themselves.

Section three: Chien's character, Hsaio, escapes to find an old sifu who knows all the Ninja tricks. Hsaio joins this teacher's other three students to be laboriously taught new forms of kungfu while voice-over narration traces the Ninja arts (Ninjutsu) back to 200 A.D. After that they traveled to Japan during the Tang Dynasty, which is where this sifu had to go to learn them.

Section four: Revenge! The four students, complete with metal axes that have more hidden weaponry than Batman's Utility Belt, face the five elemental Ninja on the same sites where their Chinese associates were executed, and do the bad guys one better. They reflect the sun back at the golden-garbed Ninjas and hurl the villains onto a cliff face. The wood and water Ninjas are also dispatched, while the poles sprout flags which sweep away the flame and smoke of the fire Ninjas.

Finally the four take on the supreme Ninja, who is the earth fighter. He erupts out of the ground time and again, slashing with his knife-covered boots, until the hero forces the knives into his own chest to hold the villain still while his co-fighters literally tear the bad guy in half. The last freeze-framed image is of the surviving good guys smashing the Ninja emblem, which has been cut into a boulder, to pieces.

After this elaborate phantasmagoria, Chang Cheh seemed to step back for awhile. Like Wang Yu before him, he seemed to have gone just as far as he could go in one direction. His second team

編劇 倪匡　導演 張徹

主演 劉丹 陳星 馮淬帆

合演 鄭雷 王光裕 劉剛 唐炎燦 游龍 楊斯 胡威 金淇珠 陳鳳鎮 楊澤霖 陳全 劉家榮 黃培基 吳池欽 鮑嘉文 雷龍 梁尚雲 鄧炳照 岑潛波 李超俊

SHAW SB SCOPE

Ti Lung (left) and David Chiang (second from right) show their youthful style in The Deadly Duo.

had dispersed and the director really didn't have a third team. Although he had many young actors to choose from, most of them didn't want to be tied down to one director or one kind of film. By the early eighties, the Hong Kong film industry had exploded with new concepts and new possibilities, both in the technical and creative areas.

Chang Cheh seemed to figure that since he had been essentially doing fantasies for the last few years, why not go all the way? His next few films were flat-out, old-fashioned supernatural kungfu adventures with ghost children, avenging spirits, and demi-gods who could fight on water and in the air. *Attack of the God of Joy* (1983) and *The Nine Demons* (1984) were "anything goes" pictures, with explosions, colored lights, and horrors bursting in at any moment.

Interestingly, his second team's first independent feature was *The Hero Defeating Japs* (1983), a decent Ninja film that guest-starred Ti Lung and Shoji Kurata, a man who has made his living playing evil Japanese martial artists in Chinese films. Kuo Chui (who also directed), Chiang Sheng, and Lu Feng were in place as the heroes who fight Ming Dynasty Ninja invaders to protect a book called *Summary of Fighting Skills.* Although the movie had fine kungfu and a workable plot, it was inferior to their previous master's wild, scarlet-soaked visions.

THE MASTER OF MARTIAL ARTS

"Forgive man and forebear. Never forget humility and kindness. That's the way real kungfu should be."—*Challenge of the Masters* (1976)

Once Bruce Lee, Wang Yu, and Chang Cheh started their early seventies film careers, the basic stories of all kungfu movies were established, as were their shortcomings. The difference between a good martial arts movie and a bad one was how carefully the filmmakers paid attention to details.

A sure death knell for these pictures was a totally unrealistic kungfu technique (such as shooting through the air like Superman), ridiculous plot developments, or such camera tricks as editing out individual frames to make a fight scene seem faster (it also makes a fight scene seem to lurch).

The challenge of the martial arts movie is to make the same tired plots seem fresh and important. The other trick is to make the well-worn kungfu seem new and amazing. In the seventies there were a few men who could do this. But there was only one man who did it strictly in the area

The Five Masters of Death: *(from left) Meng Fei, Alexander Fu Sheng, Ti Lung, David Chiang, and Chi Kuan Chun discuss their groundbreaking movie.*

of Chinese Wushu. The others sought, wisely, to broaden the genre, to make it understandable to a world-wide audience.

But only Liu Chia Liang seeks to make the greatest movies about the ancient arts of China without dilution or distortion. He exaggerates, he enlarges, certainly, but to him, kungfu is the thing. And it shows. He is without doubt, and without peer, the finest pure martial arts movie maker.

Liu Chia Liang has lived up to the promise that is inherent in his family. His father was Liu Chan, who learned kungfu from Lin Shih Yung, who, in turn, learned it from the real Huang Fei-Hong. As fate would have it, Liu Chan often played his own teacher in the Huang Fei-Hong movies. Liu Chan also taught his small son kungfu, starting him at the age of eight.

It wasn't long before Liu Chia Liang was featured in the Huang movies, learning as much about filmmaking as he did about martial arts. In 1965, when he was twenty-one years old, he joined the Shaw Studio after having served as martial arts instructor on two films (*South Dragon, North Phoenix*—1963, and *The Jade Bow*—1965), along with a gentleman named Tang Chia. Chia was to start directing fine, traditional martial arts movies in the eighties, but in the mid-sixties he remained teamed with Liang and assigned to the Chang Cheh unit.

The duo choreographed movies with Wang Yu (*Golden Swallow*), Ti Lung, David Chiang (*Deadly Duo*), and Fu Sheng (*Five Masters of Death*), among others. In some cases, the actors never looked better. While he advised them on-set, Liang also trained many of the actors offset as their sifu. Finally, in 1975, he was given his chance to direct. Tang Chia went to other directors and Kuo Chui, Chiang Sheng and Lu Feng took over the choreography on Chang Cheh's pictures.

Liu Chia Liang's very first movie was a groundbreaker and boxoffice success. *The Spiritual Boxer* (1975) was not only the first of what was to become Chinese "new wave" kungfu comedies, but a direct satire of martial arts films as well. Taking place before the Boxer Rebellion, it featured a drunken master and his student trying to convince a village that they are masters of Spiritual kungfu, which makes them invulnerable to any weapon.

But when the master is too drunk to convince the residents that they should hire him to protect the town from bandits, his student takes over, *faking* all the feats of strength and invulnerability—and neatly lampooning such feats in previous serious kungfu films. The student is too successful. The townspeople hire him and the criminals attack. And, although he isn't a Spiritual boxer,

Ti Lung (right) shows what The Five Masters of Death *was all about: great fight scenes with esoteric weapons.*

David Chiang blocks the tonfa blows, ready to lash back with a steel whip, in Five Masters of Death.

he is versed enough in the martial arts that, when his master calls out different forms—Dragon, Tiger, and Snake among them—he is able to utilize each to vanquish the foes.

Not only was the subject matter special, but Liu Chia Liang's presentation was special as well. He had learned much on the Huang Fei Hong and Chang Cheh sets. His filming of the elaborate, complex martial arts was clear, fluid, and concise. Somehow, through a unique combination of actor and camera choreography, the specific techniques of kungfu were plainly displayed to the audience, even though the fighters were lightning quick.

In addition, his leading actor was personable. Rather than relying on an established Shaw star (both Ti Lung and Chen Kuan Tai are featured only in the prologue), Liang used Yung Wang Yu, one of his own students. The difference between Yung Wang Yu and Jimmy Wang Yu is the difference between day and night. If Jimmy could be considered the Chinese Bruce Dern, then Yung could be the Chinese Richard Pryor—a sprightly, clever, smiling survivor.

If *Spiritual Boxer* made him a director to watch out for, Liang's next film, *Challenge of the Masters* (1976), established his reputation for making a traditional concept seem brand new. In this case, it was the Huang Fei Hong movies. Liang had seen them all and figured it was about time someone made movies about the character's youth—the all-important genesis of the ultimate Confucian hero. What made the man so saintly?

The film started on a striking note—one which would be repeated throughout the director's career. The credits played over a stark scene, obviously filmed on a huge soundstage. There had been no attempt to make the environment realistic. It was a huge white expanse with two towers of Chinese characters (lettering) around which two fighters practiced their moves. The fighters were Chen Kuan Tai, portraying Huang's teacher Lu Ah Tsai, and Liu Chia Hui, the adopted brother of the director, playing Huang Fei Hong.

This second film was a family affair with all three brothers playing featured roles. In addition to Hui as the star, the director played the villain, and the third brother, Liu Chia Yung, played the policeman who dies trying to capture the crook. (Remember, the Chinese use their family name

Chen Kuan-Tai matured into one of the strongest of kungfu actors. Here he's discovered the "umbrella skeleton of death"—his one hope against The Flying Guillotine.

first. Liu Chia is their family name; Hui, Liang, and Yung are their surnames.)

The director didn't falter. *Challenge of the Masters* was a well-paced, involving thriller. It starts with Huang's father's martial arts school being defeated in the "vying for firecracker" competition by a rival school, which cheated—thanks to the advice of a visiting kungfu master, who also happens to be a wanted criminal. The Huang Chi Ying (Huang Fei Hong's father) school is badly abused and humiliated by the rival school's vicious tactics, but the sifu still refuses to teach his son the martial arts.

Enter a traveling officer who befriends Huang Fei Hong and introduces him to his father's sifu. After the boy goes off with his father's blessing to train for two years with the master, the cop corners the fugitive. In the ensuing fight within a bamboo forest, the killer uses steel shoe caps to weaken the policeman, then finishes him off with his deadly spear.

When Huang hears of his friend's death, he prevents the sifu from taking vengeance because he wants to do it himself. He throws himself into learning with even more dedication and in the ensuing scenes a strong bond develops between teacher and student—a recurring theme in Liu Chia Liang's movies. In Chang Cheh's films, the sifu is a means to an end. He's just there to give Sun Chien metal feet. In Liang's movies, relationships, not violence, are important.

Huang spars with his teacher until he becomes skilled enough to take the smoking pipe from his sifu's hand. Then he returns to town on the eve of the "vying for firecrackers" contest. He faces the criminal in the same bamboo woods where the cop was killed, but remembers what his sifu taught him: "Forgiveness, forebearance, kindness, and humility."

He defeats the killer but refuses to finish him off. And then he almost singlehandedly prevents the rival school from using the metal slats they had secreted on themselves to unjustly win another firecracker contest. But when he and the other students refuse to beat them silly, the rival school realizes the error of their ways. Although this somewhat cloying ending would not have worked at all in another director's hands, Liang almost pulls it off.

Any audience doubts, however, were erased by his following feature; *Executioners from Shaolin* (U.S.: *Executioners of Death*—1977). This starts where Chang Cheh's *Men from the Monastery* leaves off; the massacre of Shaolin students and the escape of one Hung Hsi Kuan, played in *both* films by Chen Kuan-Tai. Just to let viewers know he wasn't fooling around this time, Liang kills off his brother's, Hui's, character in the opening slaughter.

He wasn't kidding about other things, either. This new movie is a genuine Shaolin epic, but one where the filmmaker is trying to make the audience understand why. In previous works, directors knew that the audience was already familiar with the Shaolin story. Therefore they simply had the actors play staunch Shaolin heroes without texture or edges. In other words, they were representations, not real people. Liang was going for the real people here.

In terms of martial arts, the movie is about the creation of Hung Gar, otherwise known as Hung Fist or Hung Family boxing. It is the story of the Hung family. During his escape from Manchu persecuters, Hung Hsi Kuan meets Fang Yung Chun (played by Lily Li), who is a Crane fighter. They fall in love and marry as fugitives, constantly sparring. But unlike Western movies, they don't fight verbally, they fight physically—testing each other's skill.

They have a son, and Hung spends ten years training for the fateful, inevitable revenge against Pai Mei, the White Browed Hermit (Lo Lieh), who killed the Shaolin sifu. Hung then fights up the steps to the Hermit's Temple and is soundly defeated by Pei Mei, just barely escaping with his life.

He returns home to train further, using a fascinating brass statue filled with moving metal balls which simulate the flow of Pai Mei's internal power. The dreaded hermit had developed a skill that allowed him to be impervious except for one single spot. Hung trains for seven additional years

Alexander Fu Sheng's breakthrough role was that of Na Cha the Great, *a demi-god of ancient Chinese times.*

Director Chang Cheh made his best modern-day kungfu movie with Fu Sheng starring as the Chinatown Kid.

until he hits the right ball at the right time in the right place. He goes back to face Pae Mei again, only to discover, to his horror, that the Hermit has also been studying. Now he can move his vulnerable spot *around*.

Hung hits what should have been the right spot and Pai just smiles, breaks his legs, and kills him. By this time, Chinese audiences were reeling in their seats. They weren't used to this sort of thing. Sure, heroes had died before, but not this ignominiously . . . not after they had married and seen their son grow up.

That son had grown up to be Hung Wen Ting, played by Yung Wang Yu. Unlike his father, he listens to his mother's advice. She had begged her husband to learn her Crane style in addition to his Tiger style, but he would not. Wen Ting was raised with the Crane style and now learns the Tiger from his father's old manuals. It is he who almost casually enters Pai Mei's lair and kills him with the newly created Hung Family Fist.

Executioners of Shaolin was ambitious and audacious, and even though the White Hermit's techniques were unrealistic and the reasons for Hung's failure and Wen Ting's success weren't that clear, the movie succeeded grandly on an emotional level. The scenes of the family practicing their skills on each other were very funny and combined well with the outlandish realism of the serious fight scenes.

But Liu Chia Liang wasn't about to let up. His next movie was the impressive milestone *The Thirty-Sixth Chamber of Shaolin.*

MASTER KILLER

The American title for *The Thirty-Sixth Chamber* was *Master Killer* (1978), and it was the film that most impressed non-Oriental martial arts lovers since Bruce Lee's death. Up until then, most kungfu movies forced the audience to accept the hero's mastery of his art at face value. Although there were training sequences in Chang Cheh and Wang Yu movies, they were terse setups, showing the student at the very beginning and the very end of the process. What Liang had in mind here was a movie about the process itself.

Master Killer starred Liu Chia Hui as Liu Yu Te, the reluctant revolutionary who was to become the famous real-life Shaolin monk, San-te. After Yu Te's family has been killed by Manchu assassins, the wounded, exhausted young man seeks shelter in the Temple, vowing to learn kungfu and take revenge.

What follows is a protracted set of training sequences, taking up almost a full hour of the film's 116-minute running time. Yu Te is taught the meaning of many things at the Temple, having to discover much about himself before he even enters the first of thirty-five chambers. He learns balance, lightness, and intelligence before he is subjected to the tortures that pass for training.

To build up his arms, he carries water in heavy buckets, but knives are attached to his forearms so that if he lowers his limbs he will stab himself in the sides. He must hit a gigantic bell with a sledgehammer that has a twelve-foot-long handle—to strengthen his wrists. He must smash hanging weights with his head to build his skull strength. He must endure and master all of that and more before he actually starts to learn to fight.

Then he must become skilled with his hands, feet, and weapons. To the surprise of his teachers, he excels in all thirty-five chambers within five years and is offered the sifu-ship of any one of them. That is, until another high-ranking monk, played by Li Hai Sheng (another well-known genre villain), suggests that they fight. If the newly dubbed San Te can defeat his "Butterfly double-swords" style, then he can choose his chamber.

All Fu Sheng wanted to do in Chinatown Kid *was get a digital watch. And he'd do whatever he had to to get it.*

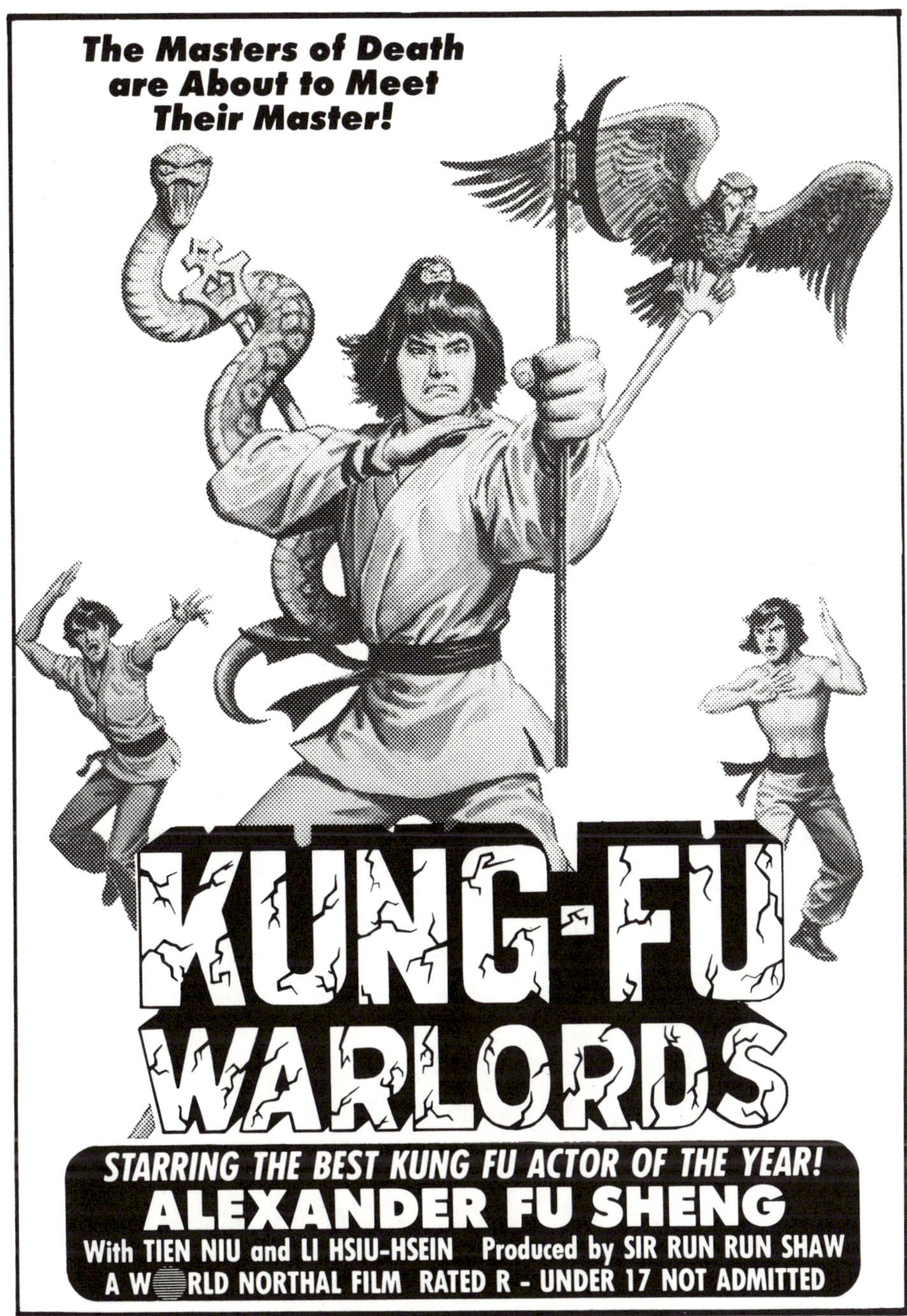

The Masters of Death
are About to Meet
Their Master!
KUNG-FU
WARLORDS
STARRING THE BEST KUNG FU ACTOR OF THE YEAR!
ALEXANDER FU SHENG
With TIEN NIU and LI HSIU-HSEIN Produced by SIR RUN RUN SHAW
A WORLD NORTHAL FILM RATED R - UNDER 17 NOT ADMITTED

San Te is soundly defeated in his first two tries. Wandering in the bamboo forest nearby, he invents the three-sectional staff—three thin wooden poles approximately two feet long, each joined by a short length of chain. With this he defeats the two short swords of his opponent and is allowed to choose his chamber. Instead, he suggests instituting a thirty-sixth chamber, a place where other young men can be trained to resist Manchu treachery.

The remainder of the movie moves San Te out of the Temple, where he takes revenge on his family's killers, and recruits the first thirty-sixth chamber students. Many Western viewers wonder why so much emphasis is placed on incidental characters during these climactic sequences. But Eastern audiences know that each of these men San Te comes across are actually famous historic characters—including some who had been portrayed in previous Liang films.

Master Killer was an amazing movie. It was the training sequences that made it fascinating and involving. It also secured Liu Chia Hui's stardom.

LIKE "RETURN OF THE DRAGON" AND "SHOGUN" ROLLED INTO ONE!!!

INCREDIBLE ADVENTURE!

EXPLOSIVE ACTION!

BY POPULAR DEMAND!
THE AMAZING EXCITEMENT OF PART I CONTINUES!

PLUS! Dozens of MAGICAL KUNG FU tricks you've never seen before!!!

KUNG-FU WARLORDS PART II

A WORLD NORTHAL FILM

Starring **ALEXANDER FU SHENG**

ESTHER • LI HSUI-HSIEN • LI YI-MIN • KUO CHUE

Produced by RUNME SHAW • Directed by CHANG CHEN

SB A SHAW BROTHERS PRESENTATION

RATED R—UNDER 17 NOT ADMITTED

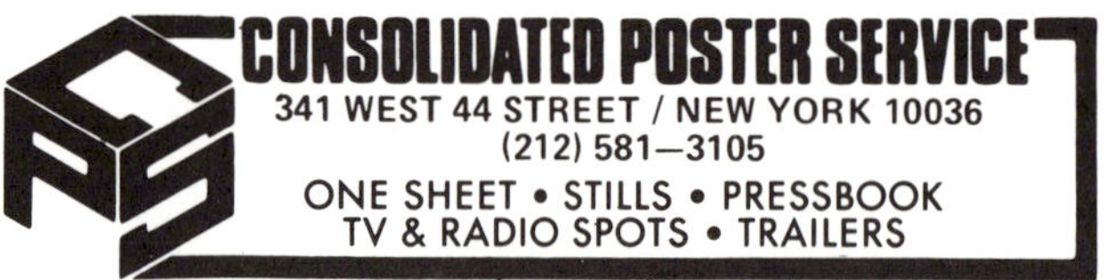

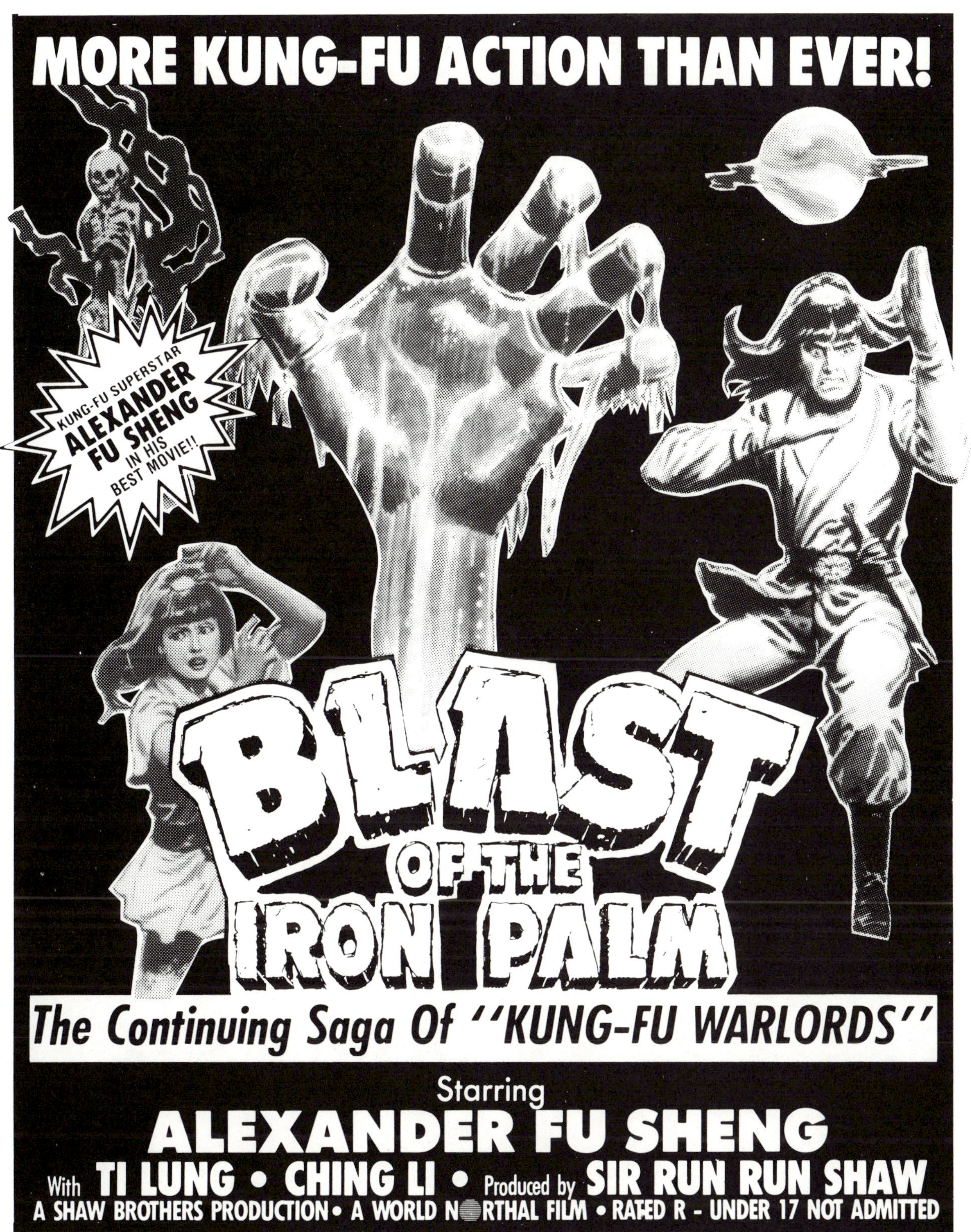
MORE KUNG-FU ACTION THAN EVER!
KUNG-FU SUPERSTAR ALEXANDER FU SHENG IN HIS BEST MOVIE!!
BLAST OF THE IRON PALM
The Continuing Saga Of ''KUNG-FU WARLORDS''
Starring
ALEXANDER FU SHENG
With TI LUNG • CHING LI • Produced by SIR RUN RUN SHAW
A SHAW BROTHERS PRODUCTION • A WORLD NORTHAL FILM • RATED R - UNDER 17 NOT ADMITTED

Although wiry, baby-faced, and—when playing a Shaolin monk—bald, Hui had the internal power and acting talents to become famous. Presently he ranks as one of the Orient's two top attractions (the second will be considered shortly).

After the power and influence of his first four films, Liu Chia Liang took something of a breather. Rather than take on another genre-shaking subject, he pulled an interesting switch with *Shaolin Mantis* (U.S.: *Deadly Mantis*—1978). It marked David Chiang's only appearance in a Liu Chia Liang film. His very presence marks this movie as a change of pace. In it Chiang plays Wei Feng, a Ching Dynasty official who investigates a suspected family of revolutionaries.

His presence there leads to a romance with the head of the household's granddaughter, played by Huang Hsing Hsiu, resulting in marriage. Only then does he discover the proof of the family's treachery and fights his way out with the help of his newlywed wife. She dies during their escape, leading Feng to develop the Mantis Fist so that he can go back and practically disembowel the grandfather, played by Liu Chia Yung.

Although up until that moment the film was the usually entertaining Liang mix of character development and precise, dazzling martial arts, he distinguishes the film with its ending. Although soundly cheered by the Imperial Court, Feng is poisoned by his own father for helping the traiterous Chings suppress the Chinese people. Liang had neatly and surprisingly skewered another genre tradition by pointing out the yin-yang aspect of Chinese history. In this movie, David Chiang played a heroic *villain*.

The director did it again the following year with *Heroes of the East* (U.S.: *Challenge of the Ninja*). Here was a kungfu movie in which no one was seriously hurt, let alone killed. And still, it is a thunderously good martial arts movie. Lui Chia Hui (with hair this time) played Ho Tao, a wealthy

Ti Lung defeats all comers in Seven Blows of the Dragon, *another breakthrough by director Chang Cheh.*

young modern man who marries a Japanese girl in an arranged ceremony. The couple's only problem is that they differ in terms of which country's martial arts are superior.

The wife, Kun Tse (Yuko Mizuno), is so stubborn, she won't accept her husband's continual martial arts superiority. Finally she resorts to Ninjutsu to win. Tao firmly condemns what he considers this "art of cheating." Sadly, the woman can't accept the basic inferiority of the Japanese martial arts and runs back home to be consoled by her teacher (Shoji Kurata).

When Tao writes a baiting letter suggested by his servant, the Japanese family misunderstands and sends their best fighters to challenge the Chinaman. From here on it's one long bout, with each of the Japanese confronting Tao on each successive day.

At first he defeats a samurai swordsman with a Chinese sword, then he goes up against a spear man, a karate fighter, a "tonfa" pro (T.J. Hooker uses the tonfa instead of a nightstick on his ABC-TV cop show), a nunchaka user, and an Okinawian sai expert (the sai is like a small trident with the center spike three times the length of the others) before facing Kurata's Ninja skills.

But remember, Ninjutsu is an extension of Chinese arts. At the end, Tao has his wife back and defeats all the fighters—but also gains their respect through his adherence to the Confucian ways of Huang Fei Hong. Audiences were delighted by Liu Chia Liang's ability to extend the kungfu genre beyond its traditional limitations.

But they didn't seem to realize that this was a Chinese movie which featured sympathetic, non-insidious Japanese. Although they were the bad guys of the piece, their villainy came from misunderstanding and a lack of communication—a problem they rectify at the picture's close. Under the guise of a kungfu movie, Liu Chia Liang had made a very important film. One, no doubt, that was instrumental in making him and his brothers stars in Japan as well.

The director's next film was a step back in his progress, inasmuch as it was a sequel to his first film, which added nothing to his reputation. Even so, *The Spiritual Boxer Part II* (1979) was an enjoyable martial arts/comedy showcase for the star, Yung Wang Yu. Still, other directors had gone much further with the comedy concept Liang introduced in *The Spiritual Boxer*, so this follow-up was not the inspiration his past films had been.

Dirty Ho (1979), however, was. Although many Westerners were put off by the title that seemed borrowed from *Dirty Harry* (1971), this Ching Dynasty period piece should have been called *The Eleventh Prince*, since it concerned Emperor

David Chiang tried for international stardom with this lively horror kungfu movie. Not surprisingly, neither he nor the film was taken seriously.

Kang's eleventh son's attempts to keep from being killed by the fourth son, who thinks the favored man will be deemed heir. This eleventh son, Wang Ching Chin, is played by Liu Chia Hui, but he is not the Dirty Ho of the title.

That distinction belongs to Ho Chih, as played by Yung Wang Yu, a street-thief and con artist who first comes upon the incognito prince in a brothel (many period Chinese brothels were on boats floating in the bay, as is this one). They compete with each other for the affection of the girls, revealing the disguised prince's desire to keep people from realizing what a master martial artist he is.

Throughout the first half of the movie, he keeps subtly utilizing his skills so no one can tell he is using them. He sees Ho as a perfect front, and cleverly manipulates things so that Ho might always be at his side, shielding him from the deadly machinations of General Liang (Lo Lieh), who has been hired by the fourth son to do away with Ching Chin.

They will never rest until they uncover the hidden deadly art of the past!
The LOST KUNGFU SECRET
THE ANCIENT KEY TO DEATH!
Starring GARTH LO ● HELIOS BOLD
SEWOL TI and introducing ARAUJO as
THE MASTER" ● Directed by REGAS LIEW
AN ede films inc. production
R
RESTRICTED
UNDER 17 REQUIRES ACCOMPANYING PARENT OR ADULT GUARDIAN

After leaving his partnership with Ti Lung, David Chiang toiled in films like this one—where he is listed as "Garth Lo."

Although this appears, at first glance, to be just another kungfu movie, director Liang uses this almost sitcom situation to mount some of the most dazzling kungfu scenes he has ever conceived. Dazzling because they are so clever and subtle. The first of three highpoints comes when the supposedly cowering prince uses a female entertainer (Hui Ying Hung) as his "bodyguard" against an enraged Ho. He kicks, twists, and pushes the girl's limbs from behind to deflect Ho's blows, without Ho's knowing they were his and not the girl's actions.

The second, and best—ranking as one of the best martial arts sequences ever—is Hui's "secret" bout with a wine connoisseur, played by the wonderful Wang Lung Wei. As the seemingly civil, polite gourmet serves the prince wine in a public place, he is actually trying to kill him. What makes the scene all the more wonderful is that the wines are named for different kungfu styles, and the battlers—the prince, the connoisseur, and his waiter—use the style of the served wine as offense and defense. To cap it off, no one else in the place is aware the pitched battle is going on. It is a marvelous display of subtle, masterful martial arts.

The finale is close in effect to that central scene. After fighting off the general's minions, the pair (the prince and Ho) must face the general himself before Ching Chin can reach the royal court, his father, and thirteen brothers. Unfortunately, the general has two aides with him and the eleventh prince has been wounded in the leg so bad that he can't stand. What follows is an amazing fight in which Ho becomes the prince's support as they frantically fight the evil trio, all of whom are using different weapons.

The sheer virtuosity of this scene is impossible to relate in words. The only sad note—an interesting one—is the film's ending. After all they had been through together, the prince hurls Ho away as he enters the royal court; the gigantic double regal doors slam closed as Ho falls backwards in a freeze frame. They were never truly partners after all. The prince had been using him all along.

Dirty Ho revealed another facet of Liang's achievement. It was in this picture that the director's ability to impart character and personality *simply through movement* became clear. Although Liang had already shown how interested he was in character and story development through images and dialogue, here he openly demonstrates his choreographic genius. A viewer can tell what a character is like simply by the way he does his kungfu. Liang adds and subtracts subtle flourishes of movement to achieve this effect. It is wonderful.

Ti Lung, after leaving his partnership with David Chiang, became the most majestic of kungfu stars. Here he plays the leader of the Ten Tigers of Kwangtung.

Fu Sheng, playing his customary hothead, spars with Lu Feng during Ten Tigers of Kwangtung.

Liang put his own face on the line in *Mad Monkey Kung Fu* (1979). Although he had been featured in *Challenge of the Masters*, here he was playing a major role. It was that of a turn-of-the-century (twentieth) street performer, who, with his sister (Hui Ying Hung), travel from town to town performing Monkey style kungfu. This film was another of Liang's "treading in place" movies, with a gimmicky story that only exists to showcase Monkey stylings.

Lo Lieh plays a cliché, a lustful, evil rich man who frames Liang's character, Chen Po, for rape, then breaks the man's hands and takes his sister as concubine. The sister is killed when she discovers the frame-up while Chen Po teams up with a pickpocket (Hsaio Ho) to take revenge. It was a good movie, far superior to the hundreds of poor kungfu pictures the majority of inferior Chinese filmmakers were doing, but somehow the audience had come to expect more from Liu Chia Liang.

He tried to give it to them with *Return to the Thirty-Sixth Chamber* (U.S.: *Return of the Master Killer*—1980), but this sequel, which was not quite a sequel, didn't have the inspiration of the original. This time, bald brother Liu Chia Hui played a street conman who impersonates San Te (the character he played in the original) to punish the Manchu owners of a dye mill.

When they call his bluff, he travels to Shaolin to actually learn kungfu. The switch here is that once the conman tricks his way into the Temple, he is put to work repairing the thirty-sixth chamber. Unbeknownst to the frustrated man, he is gaining the strength and learning kungfu techniques while building the bamboo scaffold around the chamber. He returns to his town, despondent and unknowing until he hurls a friend (Hsaio Ho) through the air with the greatest of ease. Then he returns to the mill and takes care of business.

Ku Feng, winner of several Asian Best Supporting Actor Awards, does "shocked surprise" during Ten Tigers of Kwangtung.

Return to the Thirty-Sixth Chamber was just fine, but the audience wanted more. Liang gave it to them with *My Young Auntie* (1981), a tradition-breaking kungfu film about breaking tradition. Liu Chia Liang plays the father of a Westernized son (Hsaio Ho again) who takes a strictly brought up young Chinese woman, who married his brother, into the house upon the brother's death. At its heart, this is a movie about the conflict between ancient Chinese traditions and Western influences personified by the son and aunt—who are roughly the same age.

But Liang is a martial arts movie director, and, through the cunning manipulations of the family's black sheep (Wang Lung Wei), he adds the commonplace conflict. Lung Wei wants the family's real estate titles and others don't want him to have them. He gets them anyway and secures them in his high security home (shades of *House of Traps*), where the son and auntie have to fight in and out to retrieve them.

Into this seemingly simple plot the director has mounted more wonderful scenes of "secret" martial arts—as in a ballroom sequence where everyone fights in costume—and added exquisite touches, such as the Westernized boy who constantly uses American slang and profanity incorrectly. The shining star of this movie, however, is Liang's protege, Hui Ying Hung. Although she was featured in his three previous films (as well as *Clan of the White Lotus*—U.S.: *Fists of the White Lotus*, directed by Lo Lieh as a sequel to *Executioners of Shaolin* in 1980), this was her first starring role.

The story goes that the actress had been working the streets and dancing in clubs before a talent scout spotted her and Chang Cheh cast her in *The Brave Archer/Kung Fu Warlords.* But it was Liu Chia Liang who took her under his wing and taught her everything she knows, as the saying goes. She did well by his training. Liang did a *"My Fair Lady"* on her here, transforming her from the prim girl in the film's first half to a stunner in slit gown and high heels in the second. He also managed to surprise jaded viewers with this transformation; nothing like it had ever been seen in a kungfu movie.

Liu Chia Liang was really on a roll now. His next movie was *Martial Club* (U.S.: *Instructors of Death*—1981), another young Huang Fei-Hong picture. Liu Chia Hui again played the youthful Huang, but not before Liang himself pops up during the credit sequence, lecturing the audience on the traditions and styles of the lion dance. The film then opens with a lion dance performed by Hui and his partner (Mai Te Lo, a young actor who has become the favorite of several directors).

The film unfolds as a classic kungfu school versus kungfu school story, complete with impressive battles and challenges, but basically the film is a setup for its final fight. The evil school has hired a Northern Chinese stylist (Wang Lung Wei once again) to defeat Huang Fei Hong. Instead, the pair test each other's skills in an extended fight in a long alleyway that gets narrower and twists.

This is an amazing fight scene, displaying a range of styles, techniques, and subtle as well as grandstand plays. It is a testament to Liang's, Hui's, and Wei's talents—which are prodigious. The Wei character winds up winning, but he never intended to kill the young man. He merely wanted to see what he could do, and was duly impressed. At the close he strongly suggests that the bad guys clean up their act. This was a special movie for Wang Lung Wei. He finally got to play a good guy.

THE GREATEST KUNGFU FILM EVER MADE

Legendary Weapons of China (U.S.: *Legendary Weapons of Kung Fu*—1982) is the quintessential martial arts movie. It is Liu Chia Liang's best movie and possibly the best genre film ever. We

Ten Tigers of Kwangtung *showcased the Shaw Brothers Studio's impressive sets and offered chances for young martial arists to be seen—not to mention torture each other.*

feel this way for several reasons. First it is about kungfu. It is not a western with kungfu; it is not a love story with kungfu thrown in; it is not a comedy with kungfu. It is a movie about the martial arts. If kungfu did not exist, this movie could not have been made. The martial arts here cannot be replaced with any other kind of fighting—which is not true of any other kungfu movie.

Second, it is about kungfu films. If the martial arts movie genre didn't exist, neither would this picture. It is about the strengths and the shortcomings of kungfu motion pictures. That is what the movie is about beneath the surface. On the surface it is about the end of the martial arts era in China. Outsiders, foreigners, have invaded. The various schools of kungfu band together to find a defense against their most dreaded, most powerful enemy: the gun.

The opening sequence prepares audiences for the wonder to come. Four barechested students stand before four aimed rifles. Chinese mystics and a Shaolin monk dance and mouth incantations to protect these supreme fighters from the weapons. As the action and voices rise to a frenzy, the quartet is shot point blank in their chests. They remain standing. The monk prays even harder and slaps written incantations on their chests. The ritual climaxes. The men still stand.

The collected school heads nod and smile at their success. Then the four men drop dead.

The glorious years of self-improvement have ended, perhaps even were for naught. Weaklings with guns can defeat the mightiest fighter. Only one sifu is willing to admit that. Lei Kung (Liu Chia Liang) refuses to force his students to commit suicide trying to find a nonexistant solution. He disbands his school and disappears. All the other schools want to kill him, to prevent the foreigners from discovering his doubts. They send Tieh Hou (Hsaio Ho) and Ti Tan the Shaolin monk (Liu Chia Hui) after him.

The duo find their own trail dogged by the monk's niece (Hui Ying Hung), who wants to warn Lei Kung of the danger. Complicating things further is Lei Kung's brother Lei Yung (played by Liang's brother, Lui Chia Yung), who also wants

Believe it or not, a belt has just turned into a sword and the young hero uses an umbrella and bowl to fight back. It's all in a day's work for the Ten Tigers of Kwangtung.

On the left, Wang Lung Wei, China's greatest screen villain. On the right, Ti Lung, playing the Ten Tigers of Kwangtung's *leader.*

to find the renegade fighter, but for reasons of his own. To do so, he hires a con man (Fu Sheng) to impersonate Lei Kung. To convince the townspeople he is Kung, Sheng fakes all manner of amazing kungfu feats, cleverly japing the feats of past serious genre movies (as did *The Spiritual Boxer* before this).

Liang doesn't leave it there. He adds to this movie's mix a new ingredient: magic. The Chinese "magician/spies" are the original operatives who were to become Ninjas in Japan years later. Here Liang takes the supernatural abilities of these fighters rather seriously, although using their talents mostly for humor. As in the memorable scene when Yung takes over Sheng's body with a voodoo doll. Whatever the doll does, Sheng does.

So when Sheng's accomplices try to wrest the doll back from Yung beneath a house built over a narrow river, it is Fu Sheng's time to shine. This sequence was especially poignant to audiences in that Fu Sheng had just recuperated from an accident on another film which broke both his legs. There was some question that he might ever work again.

Thankfully his "official" comeback film, *The Treasure Hunters* (U.S.: *Master of Disaster*—1982), directed by Liu Chia Yung (Liang's brother), laid that fear to rest. This was a film that was to establish Fu Sheng's screen persona for the rest of his career as a Chinese Bob Hope. *Master of Disaster* was essentially a kungfu "Road" picture with Sheng as Hope and his younger brother, Chang Chan Peng, as Bing Crosby. Sheng's performance in *Legendary Weapons* only reinforces this image.

The Hui Ying Hung character finally finds Lei Kung, who is disguised as an old woodcutter, and convinces him to start honing his rusting skills to confront the killers stalking him. In a few whirlwind confrontations, Lei Kung defeats both his pursuers, gaining their respect in the process. The monk returns to Shaolin Temple and the young fighter sides with Kung.

David Chiang returned to the Shaw Brothers Studio to shave his head, become a monk, and fight on the Shaolin Poles for A Slice of Death.

Only then does the truth emerge. Kung's own brother had arranged the hunt simply to ingratiate himself with the government, the kungfu schools, and the brothers' own clan. At the end, the two screen brothers, played by the two real-life brothers, face each other outside a temple at sundown to do battle with all eighteen legendary weapons of China.

It is no contest. Lei Kung's skill combined with his honorable nature defeats his evil brother every time. Although Lei Yung begs his brother to kill him rather than expose his plot or leave him with this dishonor, Lei Kung turns his back on his brother, letting him live with his guilt and shame.

Liu Chia Liang shot the works with this one. He threw in every kind of weapon except the Chinese kitchen sink. After this, there wasn't much more the man could say on screen, and, indeed, his subsequent films have been well done reiterations of his previous works. *Cat vs. Rat* (1982) was a strange comedy, very Cantonese in presentation and form, taking place during the Sung Dynasty.

In this one, taken from a tale of Judge Pao, Fu Sheng was once again a Bob Hope type, terribly envious of a fellow martial artist—who served as the elegant Bing Crosby type. *Cat vs. Rat*'s only distinction, really, is that it introduced Adam Cheng (Chinese name: Cheng Shao Chiu) to the masses. Cheng is the Chinese Cary Grant; athletic, sophisticated, fun-loving, rakish, and, as was said before, elegant.

He became an extremely popular movie star after this, thanks to an impressive performance as both the good and bad guy in Golden Harvest's production of *Zu, Warriors From the Magic Mountain* (1982). This was one of the "new wave"

The first great superhero kungfu movie. Here's The Five Deadly Venoms *wearing the masks that made them infamous.*

Chinese productions by young directors—in this case Tsui Hark, who made quite a splash with an impressionistic mystery thriller *The Butterfly Murders* (1979). *Zu* is a Sung Dynasty fantasy with demi-gods of good and evil fighting within the magic mountain for the fate of the earth. Although it completely loses control near the end, the first hour is a breathtaking stream of images and concepts that makes such American fantasies as *Conan the Barbarian* look ridiculous.

Cat vs. Rat looked just as ridiculous to Western eyes, and Liang compensated with *The Lady Is the Boss* (1983). This new film was a switch on *My Young Auntie*. This time Liang plays the traditionalist and Hui Ying Hung is the Westernized young lady who takes over his modern-day martial arts school. Leaving nothing to chance, Liang utilizes his whole crew of kungfu actors—Yung Wang Yu, Liu Chia Hui, Hsaio Ho, Chang Chan Peng, and Mai Te Lo—as co-starring school students.

They take to the streets on bicycles, battle in discos while dancing, and have a spectacular final bout in the gym with the bad real estate guys (once more led by Wang Lung Wei), before the girl decides to head back to San Francisco and leave the school to Liang. As a neat turnaround, it is the girl who wears traditional dress and Liang who is wearing modern clothes in the final scene. The message is clear. If people meet halfway, things can always be worked out.

Tragedy struck the martial arts industry after this. Fu Sheng died in a car accident July 7, 1983, at the age of twenty-nine. He had been in the midst of doing Liang's next movie *The Eight Diagram Pole Fighter*. The actor had also just made the transition from straight kungfu star to full-fledged comedy star in the box office success *Hong Kong Playboys*.

Muscular Lo Mang (left) fights to keep out of the pointed torture device in The Five Deadly Venoms.

The finished version of *The Eight Diagram Pole Fighter*, Liang's Sung Dynasty tragedy, was his angriest and bleakest film. Instead of his usual instructional prologue, Liang portrayed the death of most of the loyalist Yang family, betrayed on the Tartar battlefield by a treacherous general. As the credits roll, Chang Chan Peng, Hsaio Ho, Liu Chia Yung, Yung Wang Tu, and Mai Te Lo's characters all die graphically beneath the invader's swords and spears on an artificial indoor set that gives the scene even more of a nightmarish quality.

Only Liu Chia Hui and Fu Sheng's character survive, but the latter is driven insane by his brothers' deaths and his father's suicide. He returns home to his mother and two sisters, screaming and contorting almost uncontrollably. His brother, Hui, is almost killed by the invaders, but a hermit (Liu Chia Liang) gives up his own life to help him escape. He takes refuge in the Shaolin Temple where his practical, killing ways conflict with the monk's peaceful leanings.

They practice pole fighting on wood and steel mockups of wolves—the actual counterparts of which often harass the Temple. "Kill them," says the ex-soldier. "Defang them," suggests the sifu abbot. With the Fu Sheng character crazy, the mother (Lily Li) sends her eldest daughter (Hui Ying Hung) out for vengeance. At this point the Fu Sheng character completely disappears from the picture. Ying Hung runs afoul of the general (Ku Ming) and Tartar leader (Wang Lung Wei) at an inn where they hold her hostage.

To rescue his sister, Hui pole fights his sifu to a standstill using the Eight Diagram style (a technique which leaves an impression of an "8" on the floor), then marches to the inn to take on all the villains simultaneously. The scene awaiting him is impressive. Coffins have been piled high. Inside one of them is his bound and gagged sister.

Lo Mang lost the fight to keep out of an insidious torture device that left his skin perforated, in The Five Deadly Venoms.

All around them are the villains—with Wang Lung Wei at the very apex.

Hui is hopelessly outnumbered and is about to be killed when the Shaolin monks show up. Hui wonders in amazement if their attack doesn't go against their creed not to kill. "We will not kill," says the sifu. "Merely defang the wolves." Following is a weird, disconcerting, uncomfortable sequence in which the monks actually rip out all the Tartars' teeth. Hui personally hurls the two main villains head first into the coffins. At the close he does not return to the Temple—he marches to the sea.

At this writing, Liu Chia Liang's 1984 film is about to premiere in the Orient. It stars Lui Chia Hui as San Te, the "Master Killer," and Hsaio Ho as Fang Shih Yu, San Te's most famous student. It is called *Disciples of the Thirty-Sixth Chamber.* It is his third in this series and another example of how he is holding steady amid the continually changing Hong Kong film market. Whether he will be able to push the genre forward again with new concepts is yet to be seen. But we are certainly looking forward to it.

THE SECOND BIG STAR

"One thing you must learn. Fighting and practicing are two different things."—*Dragon Lord* (1982)

If Bruce Lee is the Chinese Clint Eastwood, then Jackie Chan is the Chinese Burt Reynolds. Lee was somber and serious. Chan is mischievous and clever. Lee was direct and vicious in his fighting. Chan is flamboyant and mutates the forms unmercifully. Lee made dramatic adventure movies. Chan makes comedy kungfu. It was through Chan's personality and talents that the sub-genre of comedy kungfu was concentrated and, perhaps, perfected.

It started in 1954 when he was born in Hong Kong under the Chinese name Chen Gangsheng (Jackie Chan was always his American name). His parents placed him in a Peking Opera school called the China Drama Academy where he studied gymnastics, acrobatics, and martial arts for ten years with sifu Yu Chan Yuan. He toiled in the academy from the age of seven to seventeen. His master remembers that he certainly wasn't the best in class, but when on stage he certainly gave it his all.

Like Bruce Lee and David Chiang before him,

The Five Deadly Venoms *fight! Kuo Chui learned "Centipede style" so he can stand on the wall.*

he appeared in movies as a child actor. The earlier comparison to Burt Reynolds is also apt here because both started adult careers as stuntmen and both had to toil in unexceptional, serious action films for years before someone gave their innate glib humor a chance to come out. The Oriental actor, now calling himself Chan Yuan Lung, was featured in 1971's *The Little Tiger of Canton* which wasn't even released until he became a star. Then it showed up in the East as *Stranger in Hong Kong* and in the West as *Snake Fist Fighter* or *Master With Cracked Fingers.*

By any name it was a cheap abomination, worked up by exploitive distributors eager to make money off the new star's fame by cheating the audience. The only interesting thing about this mess is seeing a seventeen-year-old Jackie Chan trying to do versions of Bruce Lee—before Chan had the cosmetic surgery to enlarge his eyelid openings.

Be that as it may, the young man's next major work was in 1975's *Hand of Death*, retitled *Countdown in Kung Fu* and released in the Orient in 1976. It was a Golden Harvest film starring Tan Tao Liang, one of the genre's great leg fighters (a fighter who can kick like the dickens), and was choreographed by Jackie's classmate Hung Chin Pao—known by his nickname of Samo Hung.

That seemed to be enough to bring Chan to the attention of Lo Wei, the director who was eager to find another Wang Yu or Bruce Lee. He cast Jackie as the star of *New Fist of Fury* (1976) and shortened his name to Cheng Lung. This film takes up where Bruce Lee's film (U.S.: *The Chinese Connection*) left off, with the survivors of the kungfu school escaping Japanese soldiers to come across the Chan character.

Nora Miao, who was the female lead in the Lee picture, returns to her role and teaches Jackie what is essentially Jeet Kune Do—here called Ching Wu. Then he goes back and takes vengeance on Lee's murderer. It's interesting to note that Jackie Chan really started his film career in a Bruce Lee exploitation picture. And, fittingly, he does mostly Lee moves, as he had in *Little Tiger from Canton.*

His performance fitted Lo Wei's bill, so he cast Chan in eight more movies over the next two years. But this was the American bicentennial year, 1976, the year Liu Chia Liang made his second film, the year Chang Cheh made three Shaolin movies with Fu Sheng and Ti Lung, and the year the redoubtable John Liu (perhaps the ultimate

Sun Chien is the incredible kicker in Mortal Combat *and many other Chang Cheh-directed movies.*

screen leg fighter) was introduced to a mass audience in director Ng Sze Yuen's *The Secret Rivals*. Jackie Chan/Cheng Lung's skills alone were not enough to make him an important star.

Nor was *Shoalin Wooden Man*, his second 1976 film for Wei's company, directed by Chen Chi Hwa. It was another straightforward kungfu film with Jackie taking revenge for his father's death thanks to the coaching of a handy Shaolin monk. But this was the first film in which Chan was given a little freedom in the fight scenes. Slowly, he started to find his way.

There was little chance to improve in *Killer Meteor* (1977), since Chan was playing the villain and Jimmy Wang Yu was playing the hero. In this one, based on a novel by Ku Lung, Wang Yu and Chan spin swords at each other, mostly, and Jackie bides his time. That is, until *Snake-Crane Art of Shaolin*, a Lo Wei produced–Chen Chi Hwa directed attempt to cut in on the Shaw Brothers' Shaolin profits. Their best hope was Jackie, who proved himself in the fight scenes again. He was becoming more and more proficient, displaying more and more charisma.

To Kill With Intrigue was the last straw. Lo Wei's company didn't have the money or the materials to make great kungfu films. Instead they had to rely on Jackie Chan's skill as a fighter. But even a fighter of Chan's ability couldn't do much with terrible working conditions and mediocre scripts. When this film also failed at the box office, drastic methods were called for.

Instead of fighting against the inevitable restraints of bad martial arts filmmaking, Chan went with them. He "fooled around." He helped make what was, in effect, a kungfu version of *Rocky and Bullwinkle*. This seminal cartoon show openly admitted it was inexpensive and utilized the fact. The animated squirrel and moose constantly jibed

Lo Mang (left) fights the venerable Chen Kuan Tai at the climax of Mortal Combat.

at their genre's limitations and clichés, as did *Half a Loaf of Kung Fu*, Chan's next Lo Wei production.

Bad kungfu movies usually contain ridiculous overstatements, outrageous sound effects, music stolen from American successes, and various other indulgences. Chan and company pushed these weaknesses as far as they could for this film. Chan plays a hapless bumbler who wants to be a great martial artist and the movie chronicles his ultimate lack of success. He lampoons Chinese, Japanese, and American movies in this "Jackie Chan's Laugh-In" variation, which just barely manages to please.

After that, Chan made three final straight kungfu movies for Lo Wei. The first was *Magnificent Bodyguard* (1978), a last-ditch effort to get viewers, since it was a period piece filmed in 3-D. Seeing Chan in any of these previous movies now is a lot like seeing Burt Reynolds in *Skullduggery* (1969), Roy Scheider in *Curse of the Living Corpse* (1964), or any well known film star in a movie way below his or her talents.

On his last two Lo Wei films, *Spiritual Kung Fu* and *Dragon Fist* (both 1978), Chan is named martial arts instructor, therefore both films have a look closer to what most fans recognize as the actor's style. Curiously, both films feature concepts that were either borrowed from or inspired by Liu Chia Liang. The former film is similar in tone and title to Liang's *Spiritual Boxer*, while the latter has a climax similar to *Dirty Ho*, which the Shaws released the same year. In both, one fighter becomes the legs of another.

Finally, producer/director Ng Sze Yuen, maker of everything from *The Secret Rivals* to *Bruce Lee: The True Story*, became aware of both Jackie and martial arts instructor Yuen Woo Ping. Ng was assistant director on Wang Yu's *The Chinese Boxer* before going on to do a vital, but tacky, anti-Japanese movie of his own, *The Bloody Fists* (1972). In 1975, he gave both the Shaws and Raymond Chow's Golden Harvest a run for their money by creating Seasonal Film Corporation, best known as Seasonal Films. To everyone's surprise, he put out exceptional martial arts movies that made money.

Not only does he seek out new talent, but he seems unafraid to try new approaches and promote the "new wave" of Chinese films. Films that are

Kuo Chui (center) is not at all happy about facing "Iron Head" (second from right) in one of the many fights during The Kid with the Golden Arm.

inventive and don't depend on traditional techniques to tell their stories. So saying, he teamed Yuen Woo Ping as director and Jackie Chan as star with his own script entitled *Snake in the Eagle's Shadow* (U.S.: *Eagle's Shadow*—1978).

The results were positive. The structure for Chan's next few films was also established by it. More often than not, the credits roll over Chan doing a "kata"—an exercise incorporating the techniques of the form he is showcasing. Immediately following is a fight between the main villain (in this case the head of the Eagle Claw kungfu school) and an expendable character (in this case supposedly the last of the Snake Fist school). The villains of these pieces, as with almost all period kungfu movies, are easy to identify. They wear beautiful clothes and have long, flowing white moustaches, hair, and sometimes eyebrows. This is a theatrical tradition which displays their elder status. And in China, white is the color which signifies death.

Jackie is revealed as a well-meaning bumbler who is tortured by his friends, father, sifu, or all three. When things appear darkest, along comes a wizened old bum, sometimes with a handicap, who just so happens to be the greatest teacher on two legs. Even so, Jackie is always defeated in his first fight with the bad guy. He goes off and makes a telling addition to his sifu's teaching, one of his own creation. Then, just as the villain is about to kill either the father or the sifu, the new, improved Chan arrives to save the day.

The variations Ping, and then Chan, were to create through what was to become six hours of action is awe-inspiring. For the first film, however, Chan played what was supposed to be Huang Fei-Hong in his very early, formative years. In the actual case, Chan's character was named Chien Fu, a menial at a mediocre kungfu school. He is rescued from his classmates' taunts by the arrival of an old man, who is, unbeknownst to Fu, the last of the Snake Fist fighters (Yuan Hsaio Tien, the director's father, better known as Simon Yuen).

Another classic Chan touch of his "second era" is the business of the student accidentally fingering the fugitive master by using his learned technique at the wrong time. This happens here. The

Chiang Sheng, alias "cutie-pie," uses his double axes against Chinese thugs in The Kid with the Golden Arm.

Eagle Claw killer finds Yuen and the chase is on. Chan tries to prevent the trouble but is mopped about the floor by the villain. Another common occurrence is the evil fighter letting the student live—thinking he'll never be good enough to beat him.

In this movie, Chan merely looks into the corner where a cat is fighting a snake. Instantly he conceives "Cat Claw" kungfu to beat the Eagle Claw man. Yuen is about to bite the dust when Chan fights through the murderer's minions and takes on the big boss himself. In this, and the succeeding three films, the climax often lasts as long as a half-hour as Chan fights the bad guy's bodyguards and the bad guy one after another.

Snake in the Eagle's Shadow was a huge success and the same team slaved to make the follow-up superior. They succeeded admirably. *Drunk Monkey in the Tiger's Eyes* (U.S.: *Drunken Master*—1979) was essentially a remake of *Eagle's Shadow*, but the concepts were streamlined, and this new picture stands as one of the sleekest, flat-out, action-filled kungfu comedies. But quantity of action is not enough. Quality of action was the object here, and while Chan's character, "Naughty Panther," simply moved from one fight to another, the imagination that went into creating the complex situations is staggering.

Although essentially one long action sequence (the outlandish training scenes can be considered part of the action), the movie manages to build until the battle between a Tiger Claw hired killer and the Naughty Panther.

Panther is such an incorrigible brawler that his father sends him to his sifu, a drunken old wino in the woods, again played by Simon Yuen.

Half the time Panther is being trained/tortured. The other half he tries to escape but is always outwitted by the drunken master who teaches him the "Eight Drunken Fairies"—a style that requires ample portions of alcohol. Chan "graduates" from the training part and moves into the kata sequence, where he shows the audience what he's learned. This is always the lead-in to the climax. Here, he must save his father from a hired killer. He does it by inventing a new amalgamation of the Eight Fairies on the spot.

After this success, Chan seemed to feel he knew enough to go out on his own. Making a deal with

Why, it's The Kid with the Golden Arm *himself, Lo Mang (center), showing Chiang Sheng (right) how useless blades are against him.*

Lo Wei's wife's production company, he wrote and directed his next film himself. Meanwhile, Simon Yuen, at the tender age of sixty-six, achieved the stardom that had eluded him throughout his forty-five year career. Before this he had appeared in many Huang Fei Hong movies, usually as villain Shih Kien's partner. He graduated to the role of elder sifu in Liu Chia Liang's *Heroes of the East/ Challenge of the Ninja* and *The Thirty-Sixth Chamber/Master Killer*. He recently passed away, but his seven children continue to work in films, maintaining the level of excellence their father sustained.

JACKIE CHAN SUPERSTAR

Fearless Hyena followed the previous two Jackie Chan films in both form and effect. Here he plays Lung, the grandson of the last of the Hsin-yi fighters. Like the Snake master before him, the head Hsin-yi man is being hunted down, this time by Ch'ing Dynasty General Yen and his trio of killers—all who carry a form of "switch-spear," a spear that folds like a switchblade.

Crafty, opportunistic Lung sneaks away from his grandfather's forest shack to perform as a martial artist for money. He takes on all comers, disguising himself as a buffoon and a girl, until he inadvertantly leads Yen to his grandfather. The old man is killed, but Lung is prevented from interfering by a crippled old sifu. He takes Lung away to train him in "Emotional kungfu."

The effect of seeing Chan turn the Emotional kungfu on Yen during the final ten-minute fight is delightful. Chan, as director, has already shown how powerful Yen is—his method of killing is by gripping the fallen victim's neck and dragging him to his feet. With the new martial arts technique—based on laughing and crying and the body positions thereof—Lung defeats the general and saves his sifu.

Fearless Hyena was not as polished as *Drunken Master*, but its roughness was part of its charm. Audiences probably wanted to see what Chan could do when left to his own devices, and the result was ingratiating. Jackie Chan owes more to Stan Laurel, Buster Keaton, Charlie Chaplin, and the Three Stooges—not to mention Benny Hill—than to any renowned filmmaker.

It's Sun Chien (left) versus Kuo Chui in the climactic leg fight of The Kid with the Golden Arm.

This is the sort of thing that happens when you're a villain in a kungfu movie. Lo Mang as The Kid with the Golden Arm *becomes the kid with the hole in his stomach.*

Kuo Chui (left) fights trident to trident with the unmasked Masked Avengers.

His is physical slapstick, utilizing every part of the body, every part of every other actor's body, and every part of the set. Furniture was to somersault, leap, climb, or flip over; to carry, throw, twist, or drop. The permutations of limbs and props seemed endlessly inventive.

With *The Young Master* (1980), his next film made for Golden Harvest, he came to the end of this particular line. *Drunken Master* was really as far as the subgenre could go in this direction. Both *Hyena* and *Young Master* were variations on it. This was Chan's "kitchen-sink" film, in which he throws in characters and conflicts at will. The plot, as it stands, has him trying to rescue a friend from a life of crime. As he attempts to bring the chief thief down, he keeps bumping into the sheriff and his two children—male and female martial artists.

There's a swordfight that becomes a complex juggling act, a lion dance, fights with elegant white fans, fights with furniture; and once more Chan dresses as a girl, this time to take out the main villain's cronies. The big switch this time is that Chan's character is not a good enough martial artist to defeat his enemy.

Throughout his last three films, Chan had made it quite clear that he likes torture/training scenes. The things he does to himself on screen are scarcely believable. In the climactic fight of *The Young Master*, Chan is pummelled unmercifully, but keeps coming back for more. He just keeps getting kicked and punched and hurled—sometimes in slow motion—until he beats the bad guy simply by surviving. The last shot shows every part of Chan's body bandaged except for two fingers of one hand. With those two fingers he waves to the audience, saying "bye-bye."

From there Chan headed to Hollywood. Fred Weintraub, the co-producer of *Enter the Dragon*, was co-producing *The Big Brawl* (also known as *Battle Creek Brawl*—1980) for Jackie. It was part of the deal with Raymond Chow and his Golden Harvest company. Chow, once the Shaws' second-in-command, was making up the distance that lay between the two companies for years. It started when he secured Bruce Lee's participation. It continued through Jackie Chan's.

The *Brawl* movie was written and directed by Robert Clouse and starred Chan as a 1930s Chicago resident who runs afoul of a mobster who participates in bare-knuckled boxing competi-

Kuo Chui (center) in a particulary uncomfortable spot during The Spearman of Death.

Lo Mang leaps over an adversary during Two Champions of Death *(Chinese title:* Two Champions of Shaolin*), while the extras look incredibly bored and the man second from the right scratches his moustache. This is a good example of what is wrong with Chinese movies.*

The Super Ninjas *attack with the ultimate rope trick in Chang Cheh's best film.*

The four last hopes for kungfu fight the Sun Ninjas in Super Ninjas.

Water Ninjas leap from their watery lair as the kungfu masters prepare to fight the Super Ninjas.

tions. It all starts when his father is muscled by some henchmen for protection money. Chan beats them up merely by dodging their blows in such a way that they hurt themselves. Throughout the film Chan utilizes his acrobatics to get the better of the crooks; included are some energetic roller skating scenes.

Even though the picture was directed too pedantically, Jackie Chan had, for all intents and purposes, become "the new Bruce Lee" by becoming the second international kungfu star. If *The Big Brawl* didn't convince people, The *Cannonball Run* (1981) did. Chan, as a Suburu driver, was a highpoint in the otherwise dreary picture starring, of all people, Burt Reynolds. Both Reynold and his Asian counterpart were in the even worse 1984 sequel, but that had no ill-effect on Chan's career. Between the two American films, he had made two groundbreaking Chinese movies.

The first was produced under the title *Young Master In Love.* Chan now had his own production company, with Golden Harvest as his distributor.

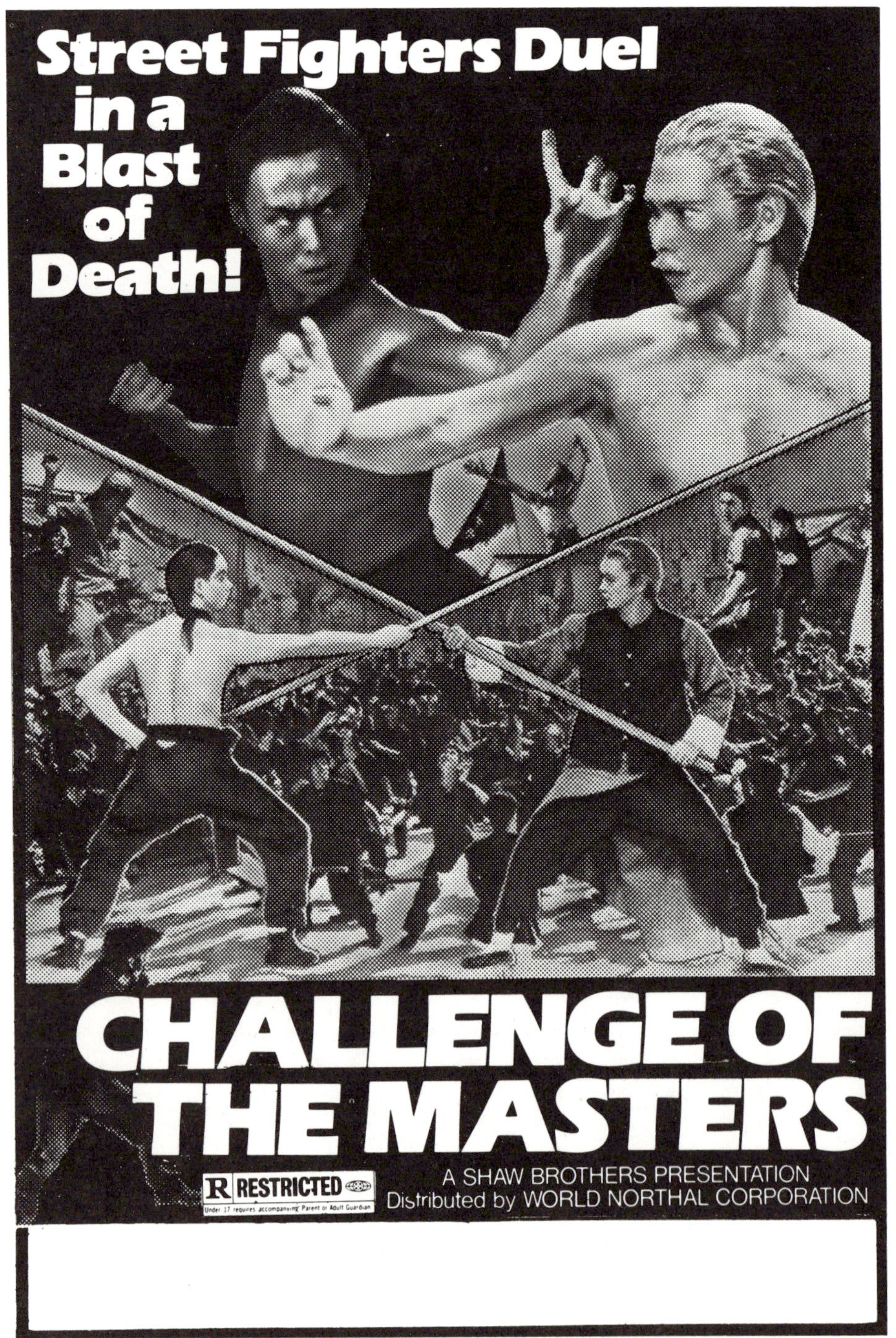
Street Fighters Duel
in a
Blast
of
Death!
CHALLENGE OF
THE MASTERS
R RESTRICTED
A SHAW BROTHERS PRESENTATION
Distributed by WORLD NORTHAL CORPORATION

He was given all the money and time he needed, and he took full advantage of both. The movie's drawback was that it was an unfocused affair. Too much freedom was the culprit. The film's success is that it brought home a telling fact about martial arts movies: Without growth they will stagnate and die. *Young Master in Love*, or, as its final title proclaims it, *Dragon Lord*, is a first sign of growth.

Chan purposefully downplays kungfu for other kinds of action. In the movie, set in the nineteenth century, Chan plays the happy-go-lucky son of a wealthy man. The lad's main interests are in sports and women. Actually, one particular woman, played by Hseuh Li. The film opens on a competition similar to vying for firecrackers, only the contestants have to climb up a bun-laden bamboo pyramid to grab the bun at the top. Reportedly ninety actors were hurt during this sequence.

The film meanders on, leading to another competition, this time a form of soccer using a feathered shuttlecock as the ball. Finally, the plot starts, with villains trying to steal art treasures. Chan gets wind of the plot when a kite with a message of love for Li goes awry and lands on the roof of the villains' headquarters. When Chan climbs to retrieve it, the guards try to perforate him with spears.

After he escapes, two henchmen try to rough him up at a temple, but Chan athletically foils them, even though he is not a consummate martial artist. He gets the inspiration he needs by the proximity of his love, Li. The film's strength is revealed when Chan's friend asks why the battle looked so haphazard. Chan tells him that learning kungfu and actually utilizing it are two different things.

That message is underlined in the twenty-minute climax, which is really the only fight in the film. Huang Ing Sik, the veteran villain who has worked with Bruce Lee and Angela Mao as well as Jackie Chan in the past, appears as a kungfu killer with one cataracted eye. He corners Chan and his friend in a barn and intends to tear them apart.

As always, Chan gets brutally beaten, but he shows that it takes more than martial artistry to win. Through luck and cleverness, Chan manages to defeat the expert fighter. This fight is the finest sustained realistic battle in the genre. Chan combines kungfu with street-fighting at a dizzying pace, making a fight look real for the first time. While there are acrobatics and kungfu, this is one of the few battles that doesn't look like ballet. It looks like a fight.

For this reason alone, Jackie Chan achieved something special in *Dragon Lord*. What he was to achieve in his next film, *Project A* (1984), was to drag the martial arts movie, kicking and screaming, into the twentieth century.

This next film, originally entitled Pirate Patrol, showed that Chan had a firmer grip on what he was trying to accomplish. The relatively poor box office response to *Dragon Lord* helped. Although it made a tidy profit, it was not as much as expected, and critical reaction made clear that fans were disappointed. *Project A* put the director/writer/star back on track again.

No faltering steps here. "Project A" was the name of the plan the 1903 Chinese Coast Guard had to clean the harbor of pirates who preyed on foreign ships. Chan plays one of the sailors, who are constantly at odds with the young Chinese police over who should get the bulk of the government's budget.

A "discussion" of this turns into a barroom

Liu Chia Hui learns "light" skills and balance at the first Shaolin Temple trial as he becomes a Master Killer.

Liu Chia Hui meets a nasty sword at the start of The Executioners of Death.

Chen Kuan Tai and Lily Li spar on their wedding night, testing their Tiger and Crane skills, in The Executioners of Death.

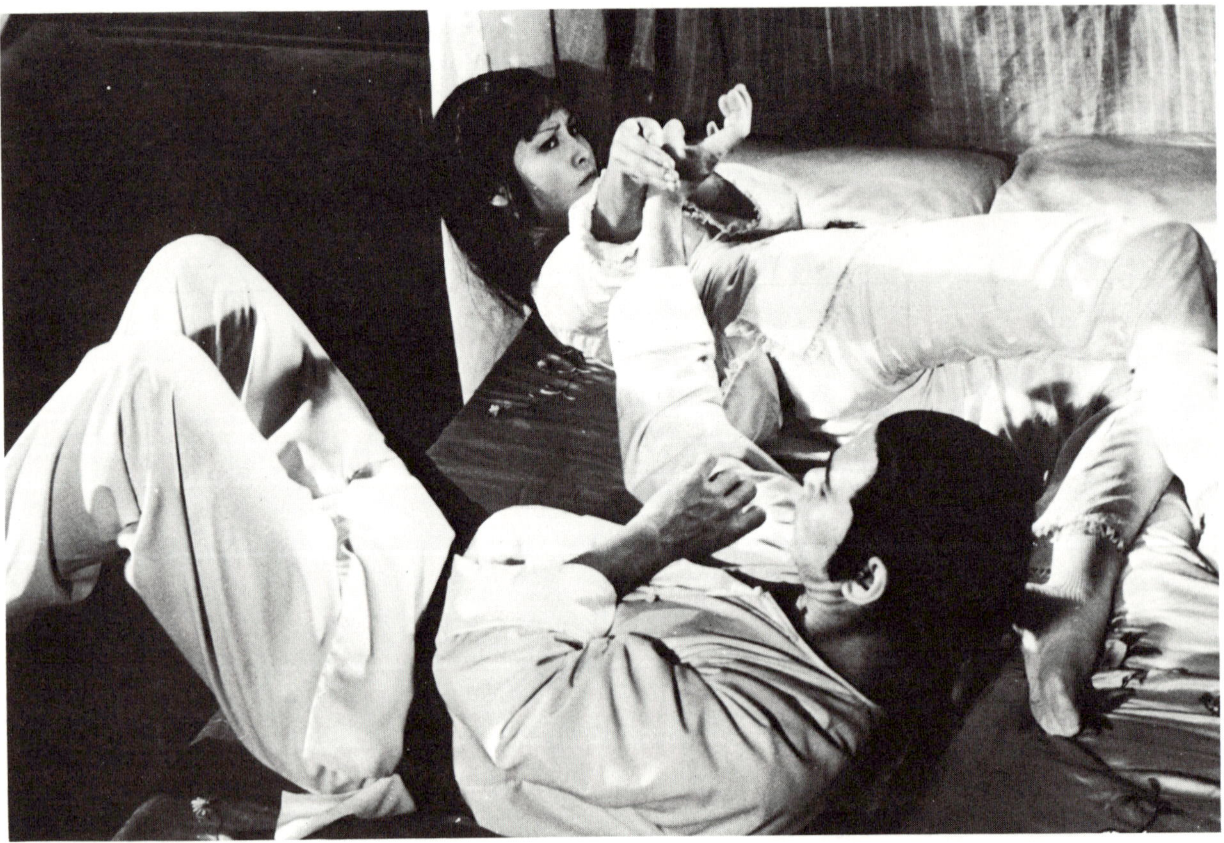

Long-time supporting actor Chen Kang Yeh (left) takes center stage after saving Chen Kuan Tai's life in The Executioners of Death.

Lo Lieh is under all that white hair, fighting good guy Yung Wang Yu at the climax of Executioners of Death.

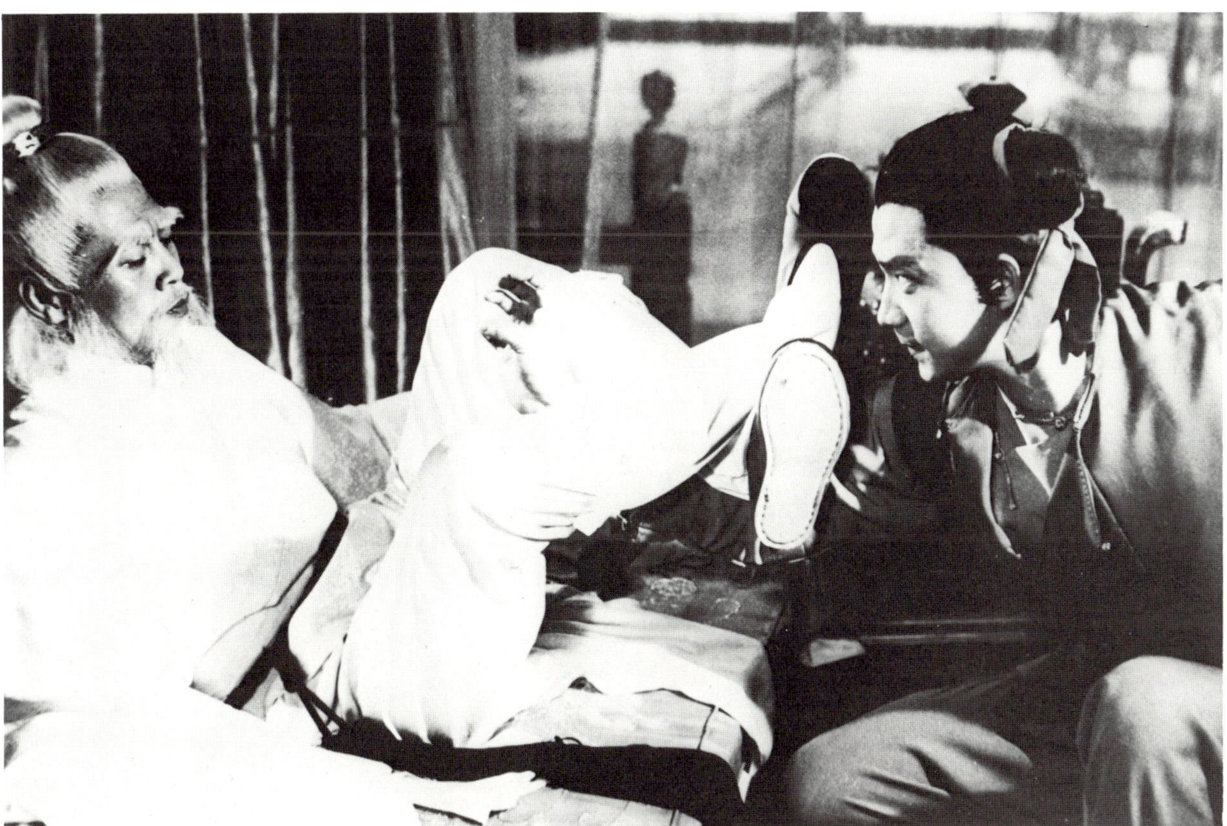

brawl where Chan shows off his sharpened physical skills both as actor and director. As a result of this fight, and the fact that their boats are sabotaged, the government assigns the sailors to the police force. After an initial conflict, Chan fits in with the cops, but finds his investigation into the sabotage and pirates stymied.

It seems the headquarters for illicit smuggling is in a swank nightclub, and the higher-ranked policemen don't want to make trouble there. Chan doesn't care and attacks the place straight on, again showcasing some literally breathtaking moments. Although he has uncovered the pirate's contacts, broken up the smuggling operation, and trashed the nightclub, he resigns his commission in disgust.

With the help of a conman friend (Samo Hung), he gets on the pirates' tail, and they get on his. A mid-film chase has Chan doing amazing things on a bicycle, climbing a flagpole while handcuffed, then twisting around in a clock tower's mechanism to escape villain Li Hai Sheng (the tall bald swordfighter of *Master Killer*), before dropping off the high tower, ripping through two awnings, and hitting the ground (all filmed in one continuous take—ouch!).

Finally he overhears a high-ranking official give in to the pirates' demands for a recently captured British admiral's ransom. Chan demands justice and the shamed official reinstates the Coast Guard. Chan disguises himself as the go-between for the ransom, Samo disguises himself as a pirate, and both infiltrate the pirates' cave hideout—meeting the ferocious leader (Ti Wei).

They are joined at the last minute by a young cop (Yuan Baio), and with kungfu and bombs they destroy the place. The sheer frenetic activity of the final scene makes for a thunderously satisfying conclusion.

Even the end credits are entertaining. As they roll, Chan shows outtakes from the film. But not outtakes of flubbed lines—rather, outtakes of flubbed *stunts*, including some painful shots of the barroom brawl and clock-tower fall that go horribly wrong. Watching Chan bounce off the awnings that refuse to break and then smash into the

This is the way the Shaolin Temple develops arm strength. Lower the arms and it's good-bye ribs. Liu Chia Hui gets closer to becoming the Master Killer.

The dangers of smoking? No, the Shaolin Temple way to develop eye coordination. Move the head and your cheeks are pierced. Liu Chia Hui gets even closer to being the Master Killer.

Liu Chia Hui develops wrist strength on the way to becoming a Master Killer.

That's Liu Chia Yung, director Liu Chia Liang's brother, fighting off proponents of The Deadly Mantis.

Liu Chia Hui has to use his head in this Shaolin Temple trial on the way to being Master Killer.

David Chiang (left) never looked better than in director Liu Chia Liang's The Deadly Mantis.

ground is a humbling sight.

Jackie Chan does an excellent synthesis of his past work in this film, combining the best of all three of his phases. There's action that is more satisfying to martial arts fans, kungfu that has the edge of reality, and some physical stunts that defy gravity (as well as sanity). These ingredients make *Project A* not only one of the best kungfu movies, but one of the great adventure movies, period.

KUNGFU FUTURES

For every good kungfu movie, there are at least ten which are unmitigated garbage. Of course, this is true of every nation's cinema, but it's especially obvious in kungfu films. Schlock artists in Hong Kong, the Philippines and Taiwan literally grind out junk with bad plots, bad acting, bad fighting, and music stolen from the soundtracks of *Star Wars* (1977), *Superman* (1978) and the James Bond movies. Some can be entertaining simply because they are so awful, like *Kung Fu Mama* (1973), *Any Which Way You Punch* (1978), *To Kill the Big Villain on Tai Mountain* (1981), and the greatly beloved *Kungfu Exorcist*.

Thankfully there are also honorable artists in all three locales who work toward excellence in the young genre. For all intents and purposes, kungfu films actually started in 1970 with *The Chinese Boxer*. But already it is beginning to show wrinkles. The influence of Chang Cheh, Wang Yu, Lo Wei, Bruce Lee, Liu Chia Liang, and Jackie Chan cannot be underestimated, but there are others who are also in there pitching.

Jackie Chan joined his classmate Samo Hung beneath the Golden Harvest banner. And it is Samo Hung's rare distinction to be able to combine kungfu comedy and tragedy in a unique way. That way is speed. Hung is not only a skilled martial artist and ambitious filmmaker, but he puts together laughs and gasps along the same razor's edge, sometimes within the same line of dialogue.

The expressive Yul Brynner lookalike, Liu Chia Hui, learns "Embroidery kungfu" to counter Fists of the White Lotus.

Lo Lieh is back under the white hair, doing an incredible leap during Fist of the White Lotus.

Liu Chia Hui does his own incredible leap over Lo Lieh, who also directed Fists of the White Lotus.

Challenge of the Ninja *is director Liu Chia Liang's* kungfu Kramer vs. Kramer, *as an interracial couple (she's Japanese, he's Chinese) decide whose martial arts is better.*

Liu Chia Hui (center) faces the disgruntled Japanese fighters who've given him a Challenge of the Ninja.

Shoji Kurata (right) gives Liu Chia Hui the final Challenge of the Ninja.

The mood can change faster in a Samo Hung-directed movie than any other.

Hung also has the distinction of being one of the few overweight masters of the screen. One critic called him the Chinese Pillsbury Doughboy. It is true that he is rotund and that he has several facial scars, but amazingly that doesn't prevent him from being an extremely ingratiating movie star. Two of his most effective works are *Warriors Two* (1979) and *The Prodigal Son* (1981), both concerning the life of the noted Wing Chun master Liang Tsan.

While the former film was a conflict during the character's later years, the latter is a powerful tale of his formative years, when he was the spoiled child of an overly protective father who had his servant pay his possible kungfu opponents to lose. When the cocky lad (Yuan Baio) is defeated by a Peking Opera star (Liu Cheng Ying, a veteran martial arts instructor who gives a powerful performance), he begs that person—who portrays a woman on stage—to be his sifu.

It has been a comedy this far. The tragedy arrives in the form of a second spoiled young man (Frankie Chan) whose wealthy father pays his servants to *kill* possible opponents. They go after the opera performer by murdering the rest of the troupe. Only through Baio's interference does the intended victim escape. He escapes to the home of his brother (Samo Hung), and together they teach Baio the Wing Chun. The opera star—fatally flawed with asthma—teaches him the basics, and Samo teaches him the tricks.

In rapid succession the opera star is killed by the rich man's servants, the rich man's son discovers the subterfuge and beheads the servants, then challenges Baio. Baio defeats the other prodigal son in a masterful display and walks off, no longer a prodigal son himself. The touches of warmth, humor, and emotion Samo Hung brings to this story are inspiring to watch. Recently the director has teamed with Jackie Chan for *Project A* and his own crime comedy *Winners and Sinners* (1983), but he is still a force to be reckoned with on the kungfu front.

Ng Sze Yuen worked with both Chan and Hung, constantly trying to broaden the kungfu category with new and inventive works. His collaboration with the Yuen family led twice to pay dirt. Once with Jackie Chan's movies, and a second time with *Ninja in the Dragon's Den* (U.S.: *Ninja Warriors*—

In Return of the Master Killer, *Liu Chia Hui gets beaten by some of the Orient's most dependable villains.*

1982), a showcase of innovative style combining excellent martial arts with seamless special effects.

Yuen Kuai directed the tale of a Japanese Ninja taking revenge on Chinese fighters for his father's death. Although the story was a hoary cliché, this was another movie that featured a Japanese as hero. It was also one of the first non-major studio works to concentrate on cinematography and lighting. This was a sumptuous-looking movie with action to match.

The first fight is probably the most memorable, even though it is incidental to the main plot. A fired member of a mediocre Peking Opera troupe attempts to ruin their performance during a festival. The young Chinese hero dresses up as the Monkey King and prevents him from doing so in a wondrously acrobatic fight. That, in itself, may not sound memorable, but the entire fight scene—kicks, flips, chases, somersaults and all—is performed on stilts.

Sadly, the film turns buffoonish in the very last minutes, as the young Chinese and Japanese team up to fight corny villains with stupid jokes. Hiroyuki "Henry" Sanada played the Ninja, with the awkwardly named Conan Lee as the hero. This film's director was the brother of Yuen Woo Ping, who went on from *Drunken Master* to do *The Magnificent Butcher* (1980), a ludicrously titled but wonderful vehicle for the oft-mentioned Samo Hung.

It was also the film that returned the original, Kwan Tak Hing, to the role of Huang Fei-Hong. He is only there for the opening and closing of the movie, but it is his first fight scene that remains the film's most impressive. The Yuen boys seem great at mounting special initial fights, and this one was no exception. Huang partakes in a "calligraphy duel" in which the villain tries to prevent the master from completing his lettering work of art.

In Return of the Master Killer, *Liu Chia Hui learns "construction kungfu" while repairing the Thirty-Sixth Chamber of Shaolin.*

Displaying dazzling skills unaffected by his seventy-four years, Kwan blocks, reblocks, twists, catapults, flips, and somersaults until he is calmly seated with the Chinese characters for "The Man of Virtue Is Invincible" calligraphed on the parchment. Kwan was so impressive in this film that Yuen starred him in the next, *Dreadnaught* (1981), a full-scale Huang Fei-Hong adventure with a modern twist.

In the early twentieth century, an insane murderer is guided by the jealous owner of a Peking Opera troupe (Kao Fei) to kill Huang. Coming between the adversaries is an unassuming young laundry boy (Yuan Baio once more) whose sister (Lily Li) has been teaching him Eagle Claw. There's a lion dance among the film's highlights before the unmasking of the killer (Yuen Shen Yi, the director's brother).

Soon after, Kao Fei, who played the villain of the preceding piece, took a page from Jackie Chan's book by directing and starring in *The Pier* (1984), another attempt at updating the martial arts movie. It is an underworld drama set in the fifties. The crime genre seems best suited for kungfu influences, and more and more Chinese underworld thrillers are becoming "new wave" martial arts films. The Shaw Studio added to the list with the crackling wild *Men from the Gutter* (1983), also starring Kao Fei.

On a more traditional note, Shaw directors are leading the way with well-structured and well-made period pieces. Tang Chia, the partner of Liu Chia Liang in their instructor days, became a director in his own right in 1983. He has done three films so far, the best of which is *Opium and the Kung Fu Master* (1984), reuniting Ti Lung and Chen Kuan Tai as hero and villain, respectively.

This is an extremely fine-tuned superheroic adventure in the Marvel Comics mold—that is, the tale of a superhero with flaws and problems. Ti

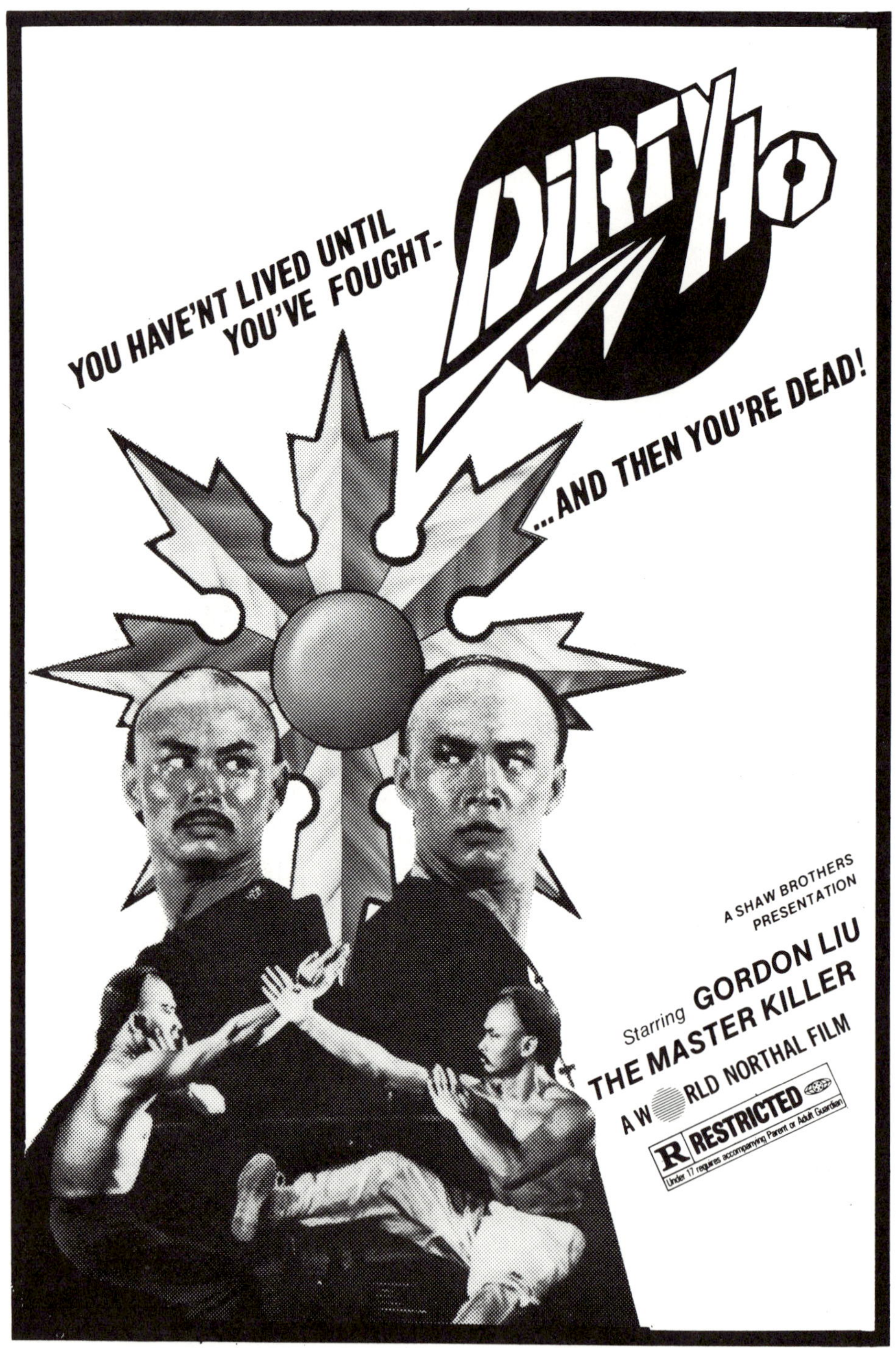
YOU HAVE'NT LIVED UNTIL
YOU'VE FOUGHT-
DIRTY HO
...AND THEN YOU'RE DEAD!
A SHAW BROTHERS PRESENTATION
Starring GORDON LIU
THE MASTER KILLER
A WORLD NORTHAL FILM
R RESTRICTED
Under 17 requires accompanying Parent or Adult Guardian

Lung returns to the role of the Ten Tigers of Kwantung's leader, whose problem is an addiction to opium. Because of it villains Chen Kuan Tai, Li Hai Sheng, and Kao Fei are able to take over the town, kill Lung's student (Mai Ti Lo), murder his student's girlfriend, and reduce the hero to a quivering, helpless mass. Tang Chia himself plays Lung's blind sifu who sees him through "cold turkey" and the final confrontation in which the dead student's teak grave marker becomes the instrument of the villains' destruction.

Another grand Shaw epic-maker is Sun Chung, whose output is nowhere near as prolific as his contemporaries'. But each of his kungfu movies

This is the climax of one of the greatest kungfu sequences in cinema history. It's Liu Chia Hui versus Wang Lung Wei in Dirty Ho.

Lo Lieh (left) would kill the wounded Liu Chia Hui (center) if it wasn't for Yung Wang Yu as Dirty Ho.

Instructors of Death pits Liu Chia Hui as the famous Huang Fei Hong against the queen of modern kungfu films, Hui Ying Hung.

is something special, characterized by his technique of dwarfing the fighters by their environment. He favors long shots in which the conflict is made small by the magnificence of China. He did it in 1978 with *The Avenging Eagle*, starring Ti Lung and Fu Sheng with martial arts instruction by Tang Chia, and he did it again in 1983 with *Wind, Forest, Fire, Mountain* (ludicrous U.S. title: *A Fistful of Talons*).

This is Billy Chong's best film to date. Actor Chong (Chinese name: Chuang Chuan Li) has been toiling in a series of uninspiring Jackie Chan exploitations such as *Crystal Fist* (U.S.: *The Jade Claw*—1979) and *Super Power* (1980), and kungfu horror movies like *Kung Fu Zombies*, a.k.a. *Kung Fu from Beyond the Grave*, for years now. Sun Chung's latest picture was his ticket out of the Hong Kong scrapheap. Chung encapsulated Chong's screen persona, that of an accomplished young martial artist who loves to fight.

In this fight-filled movie, set in 1918, Chong has many moments to shine. He is a supporter of the new Republic and goes around chopping off Ching supporters' long, braided pigtails (which are called queues). He corners a few in a barn and has a swirling, leaping time of it. Later, when he follows a Republic trouble-shooter, out of sheer hero worship, he captures four criminals as a good deed, literally bouncing off the walls to do it.

Finally, when he has incurred the wrath of a violent Ching revolutionary (Wang Ing Sik), he must learn a new form of kungfu from the hero he has followed. The training includes leaping across a gigantic, rèclining, candle-covered statue of Buddha. Chong must systematically put out the candles with the strength of his blows. With the help of his hawk-keeping girlfriend (therefore the stupid American title), he blinds and defeats the villain in the shadow of the statue.

Even with all these fine filmmakers, perhaps the most interesting recent influence on the genre is the entry of the People's Republic of China—Red China—into the fold. After Mao Tse Tung's death, the freedom of filmmakers opened up enor-

Mai Te Lo (second from right) and Liu Chia Hui (second from left) clean up the streets of this China town in Instructors of Death.

Pygmalion, Chinese style. Hui Ying Hung goes from plain Jane to knockout in the delightful My Young Auntie.

mously. After three years of production and supposedly ten million dollars in expenditure, the Chung Yuen Film Production Company presented *The Shaolin Temple* in 1981.

Filmed on location, using real martial artists in all the major roles, this film works on a traditional level. It is, in effect, a distillation of all the ingredients that made Hong Kong movies work for fifteen years. In fact, it used Shaw Brothers studio space and Liu Chia Liang's advice in certain scenes. The mainlanders also had the benefit of learning from Hong Kong's mistakes over the years. Entering the genre in the eighties allowed them to make use of the best equipment available.

The Shaolin Temple mirrors these facts. The attention to detail, sumptuous cinematography of awe-inspiring mainland Chinese locations, and truly exceptional kungfu scenes more than make up for the pat nature of the all-too-typical plot. It tells of the conflict which ended the Sui Dynasty and started the Tang, but from the viewpoint of a boy seeking revenge for the murder of his father. Sound familiar?

It's brother against brother at the climax of the greatest kungfu movie, Legendary Weapons of China. *Director Liu Chia Liang (left) fights Liu Chia Yung. They may not be great-looking, but they are great fighter/actors.*

導演 劉家良　　鄭少秋 傅聲 領銜主演

御猫三戲錦毛鼠
CAT VS RAT

龍天翔 唐偉成 王龍威 領銜主演　張展鵬 沈殿霞 特別客串　劉家輝 劉家榮 特別客串　小侯 惠英紅 領銜主演

Get a load of the usually bald Liu Chia Hui in Cat vs. Rat. *Also get a load of the Shaw Brothers Studio's ornate interior set—complete with a bird on the overhanging branch!*

Liu Chia Hui directed and co-starred in Shaolin and Wu Tang. *Here he practices the "Shaolin Hand-Out."*

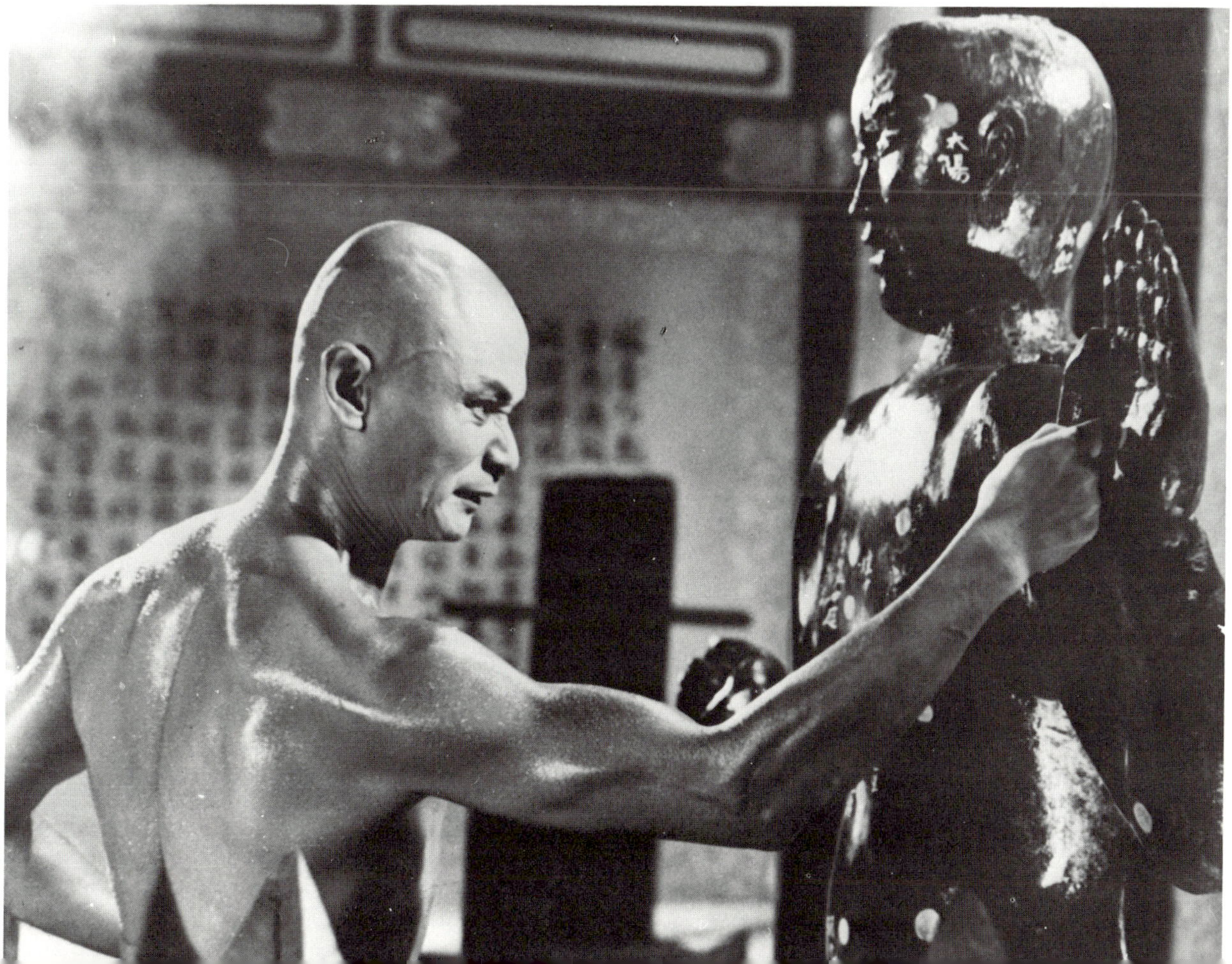

導演 劉家良

領銜主演 傅聲

御猫三戲錦

CAT VS RAT

特別客串 張展鵬 沈殿霞

特別客串 劉家輝 劉家榮

領銜主演 小侯 惠英紅

鼠

鄭少秋 領銜主演

龍天翔 唐偉成 王龍威 領銜主演

王清河 石崗 蕭玉 林輝煌 京柱 主演

It's Adam Cheng turning Fu Sheng every which way but loose in the strange kungfu comedy Cat vs. Rat.

Adam Cheng (left) loses most of his customary cool when fighting the powerfully precise Wang Lung Wei during Shaolin and Wu Tang.

The boy learns martial arts from an unusual bunch of Shaolin Temple monks—monks who aren't averse to drinking, eating meat, and killing when they have to. And, as far as they are concerned, when it comes to Sui soldiers, they have to. Li Lin Jei stars as the vengeance-seeking boy. At the time he was an eighteen-year-old who had already won five national wushu (martial arts) championships.

Yu Hsing Wei, the creator of what is called the "Shark Fin Broadswordplay," enacted the villain. The most important supporting actors were Ding Lan as the love interest, who loses her man to the Shaolin Temple; Mantis Fist champion Yu Hai as the Shaolin sifu; and 1981 National All Around Champion Hu Chien Chiang as the Monkey stylist.

Everybody has to start somewhere, and the personable Billy Chong started in Kungfu Zombies. *There was nowhere to go but up from there.*

莊泉利
羅 烈
大細眼
領銜主演

BLOODBROTHERS...

their hands are faster than guns ... and deadlier!

A HARD WAY TO DIE

FILMED ENTIRELY ON LOCATION IN PHOENIX, ARIZONA

STARRING:

BILLY CHONG ● CARL SCOTT ● LOUIS NEGLIA WORLD WELTERWEIGHT KARATE CHAMPION

Produced by PAL MING ● AN ETERNAL FILM (H.K.) CO. LTD. PRODUCTION

TD A TRANSMEDIA DISTRIBUTION CORP. RELEASE

R RESTRICTED
Under 17 requires accompanying Parent or Adult Guardian

THE BRUCE LEE OF THE 80'S
BILLY CHONG
STAR OF
"A HARD WAY TO DIE"

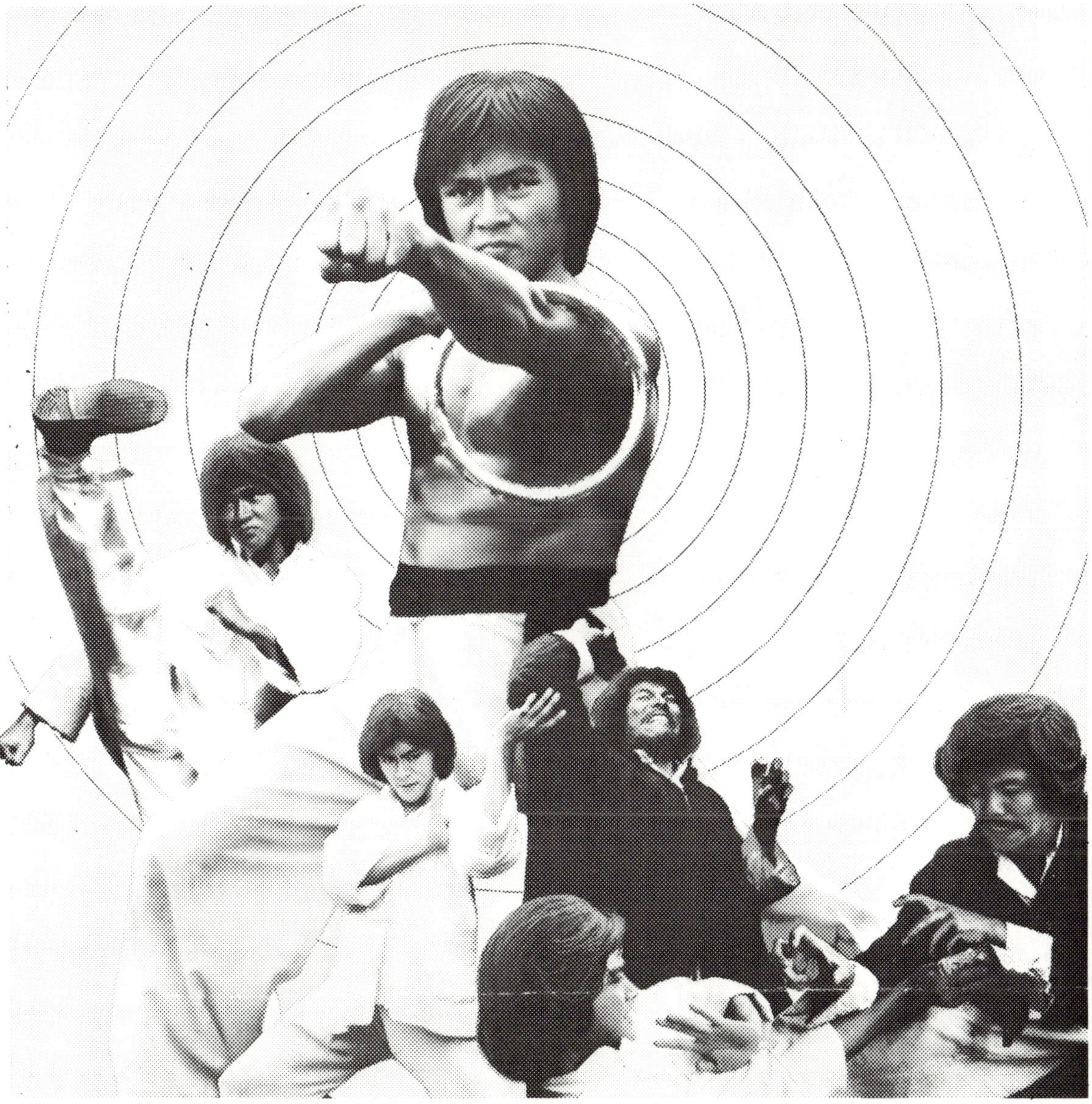

He takes them all on in...
SUPER POWER

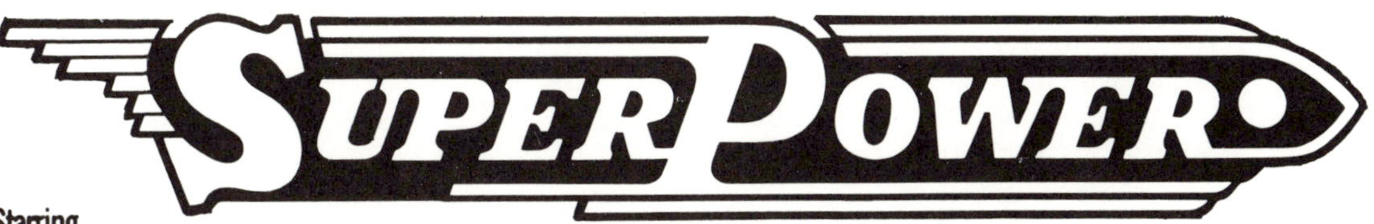

Starring
BILLY CHONG • **HAU CHIU SING** • Directed by **LIN CHAN WAI**
Produced by **PAL MING** • THE ETERNAL FILM (H.K.) CO. LTD.
Distributed by **TRANSMEDIA DISTRIBUTION CORPORATION**

R RESTRICTED
Under 17 requires accompanying Parent or Adult Guardian

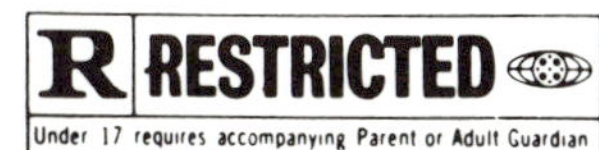

An example of director Sun Chong's favorite shot, dwarfing his kungfu fighters in their environment. In The Avenging Eagle *it makes their conflict small in comparison with the magnificence of China.*

The film was a far greater success than anyone had anticipated. The Chinese government was forced to issue a decree asking young students to stop leaving school to go in search of the Shaolin Temple. Li Lin Jei became an inter-Oriental star with the new name Jet Lee. In fact, one of the billboards that greeted President Reagan when he visited China (according to the photograph printed in *Time* Magazine) featured Jet Lee in an advertisement for "Shaolin Wine."

Such success called for a sequel. *Shaolin Temple Part II: Kids From Shaolin* (1983) was even better than the original. The cast and crew were the same, and everyone, from the actors to director Chang Hsin Yen, had improved. Comedy had been added to the plotline, which did not take up where the first movie ended. Instead it told of the Lung family long after the destruction of the Shaolin Temple.

On one side of the Likiang River lived the Lung family, consisting of an uncle and the six boys (dragons) he had saved from thieves years before. On the other side of the river lived the Pao family, of eight girls (phoenixes). The dragons knew Shaolin kungfu. The phoenixes knew Wu Tang swordsmanship. The girls' father had forbidden them to fraternize with the Lung dragons.

Unfortunately for him, his eldest daughter is secretly in love with the head of the Lung household and his second eldest daughter is in love with the eldest Lung son. Conflicts arise further when it's revealed that Pao's main adviser is a disguised thief preparing for his gang to attack the town—the same gang that had killed the dragons' parents.

Kids from Shaolin was a delight that featured truly spectacular martial arts as well as technical artistry. The locations were beautiful and their filming was crystal clear—rivaling the work of top Hollywood cinematographers. Although the plot falters once or twice, the film is so fascinating on

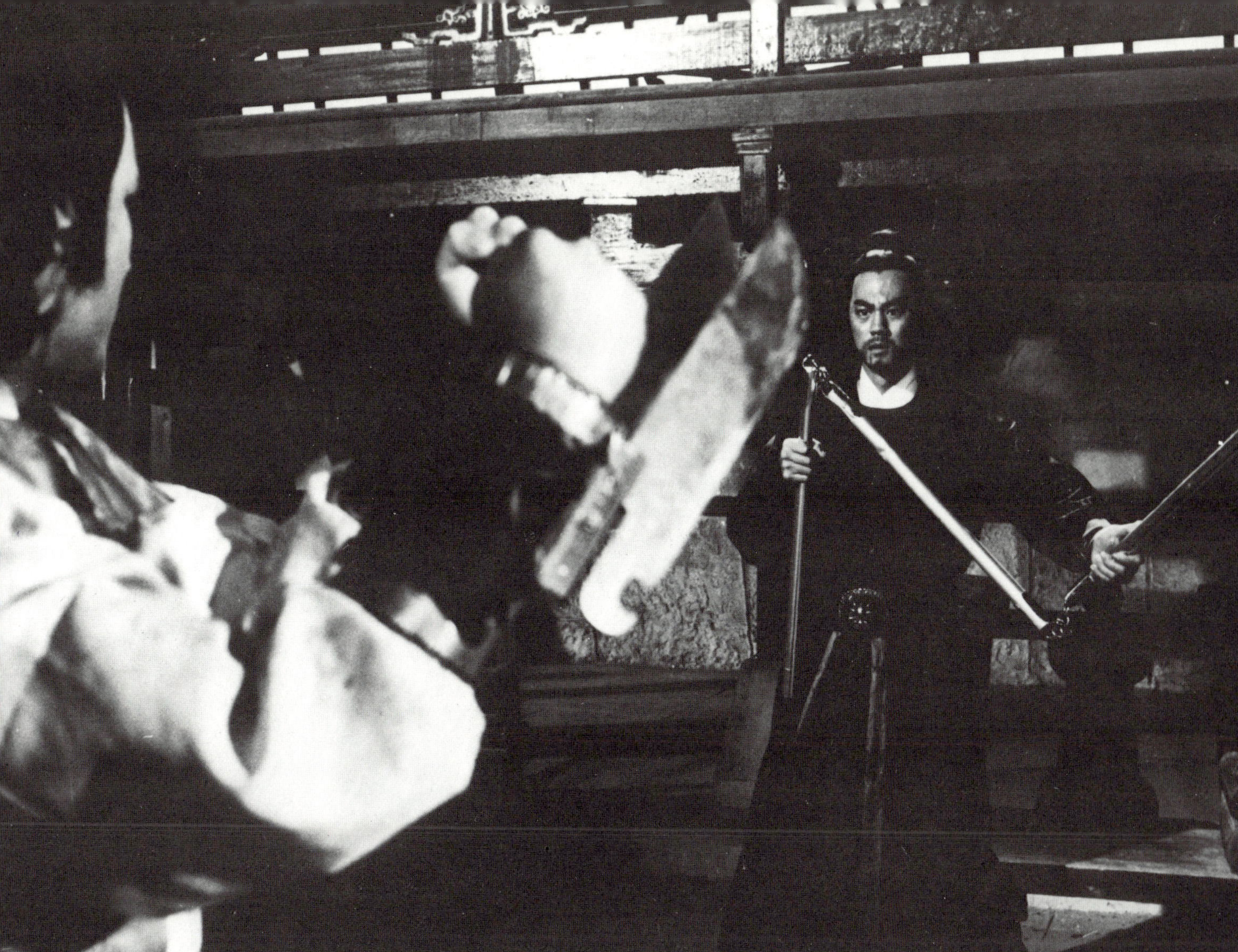

Ti Lung, with three-sectioned staff, faces Fu Sheng, with wrist blades, in the emotional final confrontation of The Avenging Eagle.

both a cultural and action level that it is hard not to be captured by its spell.

But people will be people. Following these two mainland Chinese productions were several more that didn't come close in terms of filmmaking technique and narrative structure. There was another Shaolin story about Fang Shih Yu (the first Red Chinese exploitation movie?) and a retelling of the "Outlaws of the Marshes" story, featuring the "108 Mountain Brothers" made famous by *Seven Blows of the Dragon*.

Even worse, Hong Kong filmmakers tried to muscle in on the mainland success, making one bad Shaolin movie after another. So far there's been *The Shaolin Temple Strikes Back, Shaolin vs. Lama, Shaolin Temple Against Lama, The 36 Shaolin Wonder Kids, Shaolin vs. Manchu, Shaolin Chastity Kung Fu, Thirteen Pugalist Monks from Shaolin, Offensive Shaolin Longfist,* and Lui Chia Hui's first directing assignment *Shaolin and Wu Tang*.

Still, everyone is doing their best, and it is just a matter of time now until kungfu movies receive their due. Recently audiences have discovered the vitality of German movies, New Zealand-based films, and Australian pictures. And in spite of the many crummy kungfu movies that make their way to the States, mass audiences will discover the great Hong Kong action films. They have already infiltrated exploitation movie houses and syndicated television stations, turning some of the most hardened viewers into happy children again. We've seen it. There's nothing quite like sitting in a New York 42nd Street or Chinatown theater with tough guys all around cheering as one.

There are kungfu filmmakers who slave, putting their very limbs on the line, to create the world's most exhilarating cinema. And with the campy, unimaginative works of superheroics made in English-speaking countries, it is nice to know that Hong Kong movies have someplace to go.

少林木人巷
JACKY
CHAN
in
SHAOLIN
WOODEN
MEN

JACKY CHAN
in
TO
KILL
WITH
INTRIGUE
劍花煙雨江南

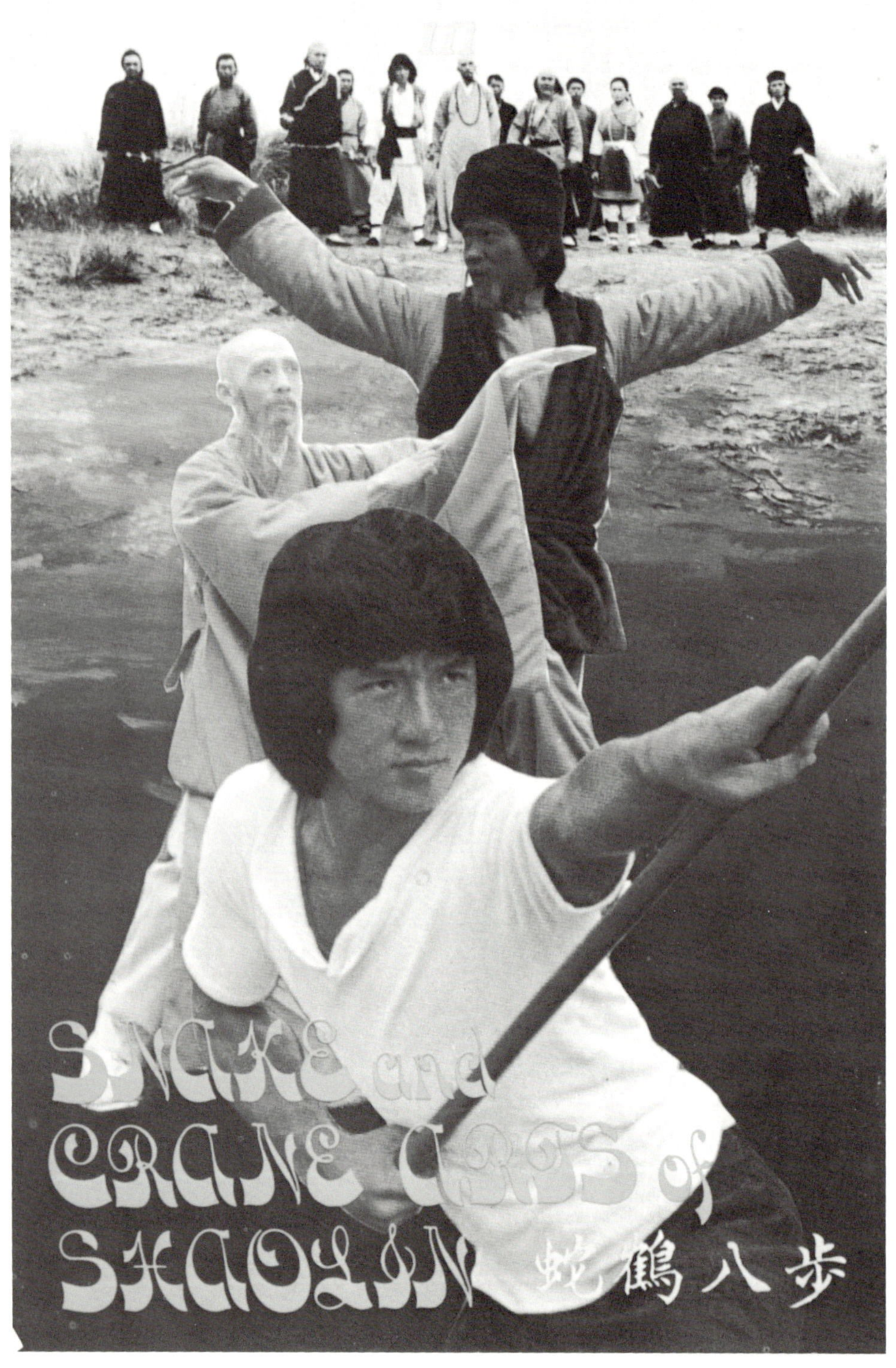
SNAKE and
CRANE ARTS of
SHAOLIN 蛇鶴八步

JACKY
CHAN
in
HALF A LOAF OF KUNG FU!
一招半式
闖江湖

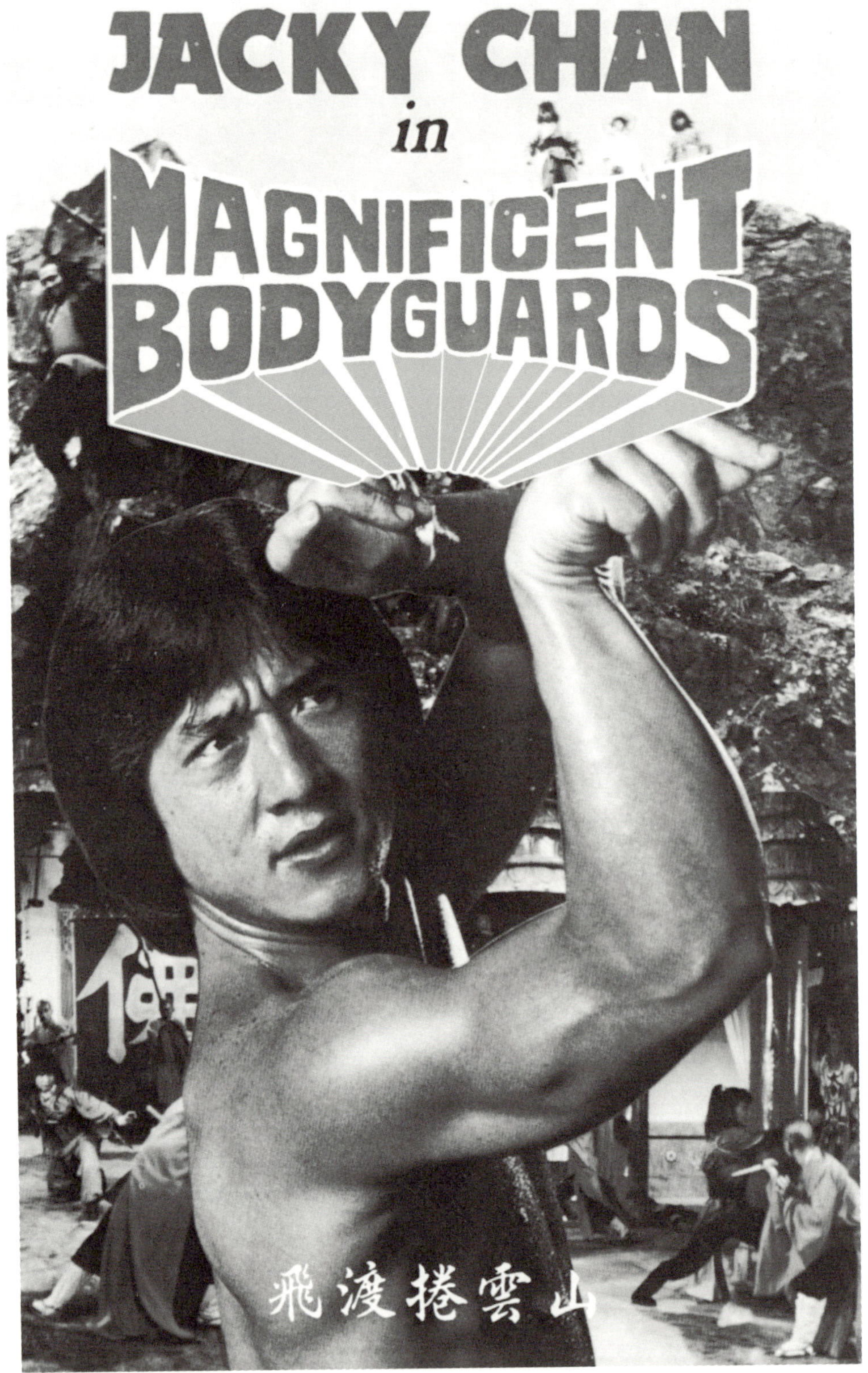
JACKY CHAN
in
MAGNIFICENT
BODYGUARDS
飛渡捲雲山

Jackie Chan in two highlights of Fearless Hyena: *an exercise on jugs, and the moment he shows off "Emotional kungfu."*

Athletic, gymnastic, buffoonish Jackie Chan shows what he's made of in Drunken Master.

This is just one of the tortures that passes for training in kungfu. Jackie Chan suffers under the feet of Simon Yuen, the Drunken Master.

Want a great way to show arm strength? How about crushing walnuts with two fingers? That's what Jackie Chan does to an adam's apple at the end of Drunken Master.

Jackie Chan, Chicago style. The international star is about to finish off The Big Brawl.

Jackie Chan, a symbol of elegance, in an unusually still moment from the otherwise action-packed Young Master.

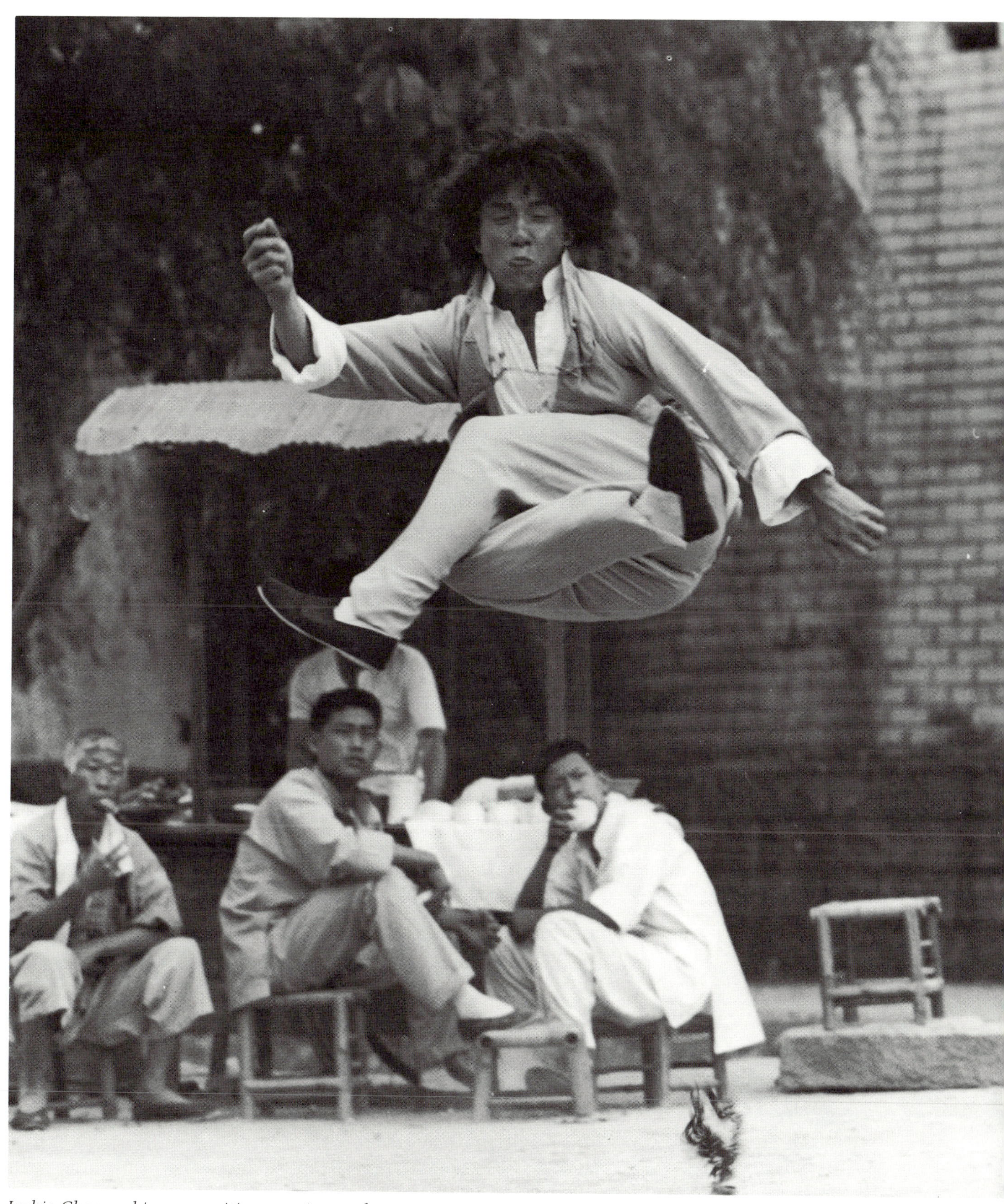

Jackie Chan on his own, writing, starring, and directing Dragon Lord.

Jackie Chan (right) supreme. The Chinese superstar gets his kicks in Project A *(U.S.:* Pirate Patrol*), his finest film yet.*

JACKY CHAN

EAGLE'S SHADOW

Serafim Karalexis presents "THE EAGLES SHADOW" an Ng SeeYuen film

starring JACKY CHAN · JUAN JAN LEE · SIMON YUEN · ROY HORAN

co-starring SHIH TIEN · CHEN HSIA · WANG CHANG · LOUIS FENG written by NG SEE YUEN

photography by CHANG HAI · action directors YUENWOO PING & SHU HSIA edited by PAN HSIUNG YOO

produced by NG SEE YUEN directed by YUEN WOO PING executive producer CHENG CHUAN

A SEASONAL FILM PRODUCTION

PG PARENTAL GUIDANCE SUGGESTED

SOME MATERIAL MAY NOT BE SUITABLE FOR PRE-TEENAGERS

IN CINEMASCOPE

IN COLOR

distributed by CINEMATIC RELEASING CORP.

© COPYRIGHT MCMLXXXII BY SEASONAL FILM CORP.

"EAGLE SHADOW"

Chan's star started to rise in the United States with the release of this effort.

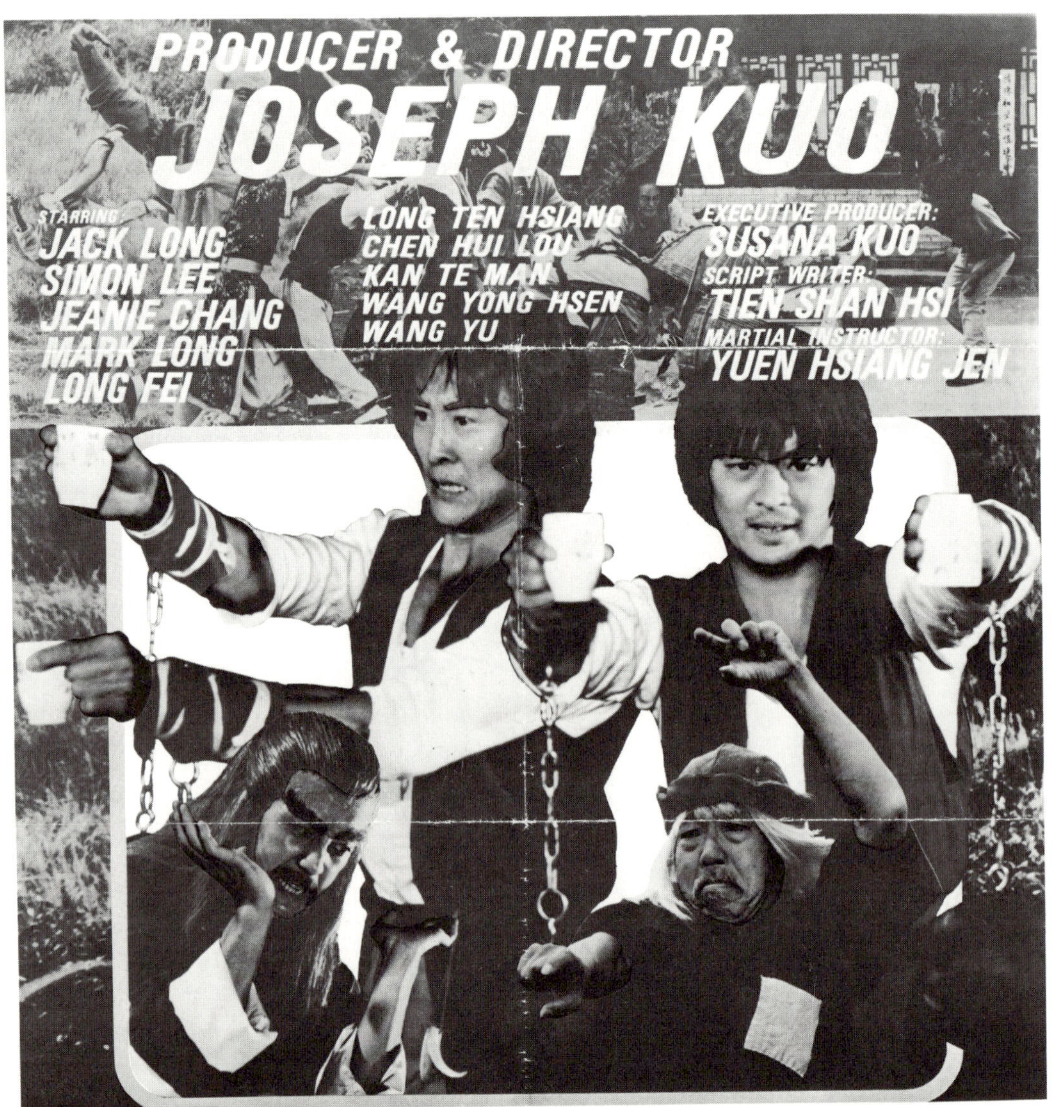

THE WORLD OF DRUNKEN MASTER

R RESTRICTED
UNDER 17 REQUIRES ACCOMPANYING PARENT OR ADULT GUARDIAN

In the wake of Drunken Master's *success came many inferior imitations.*

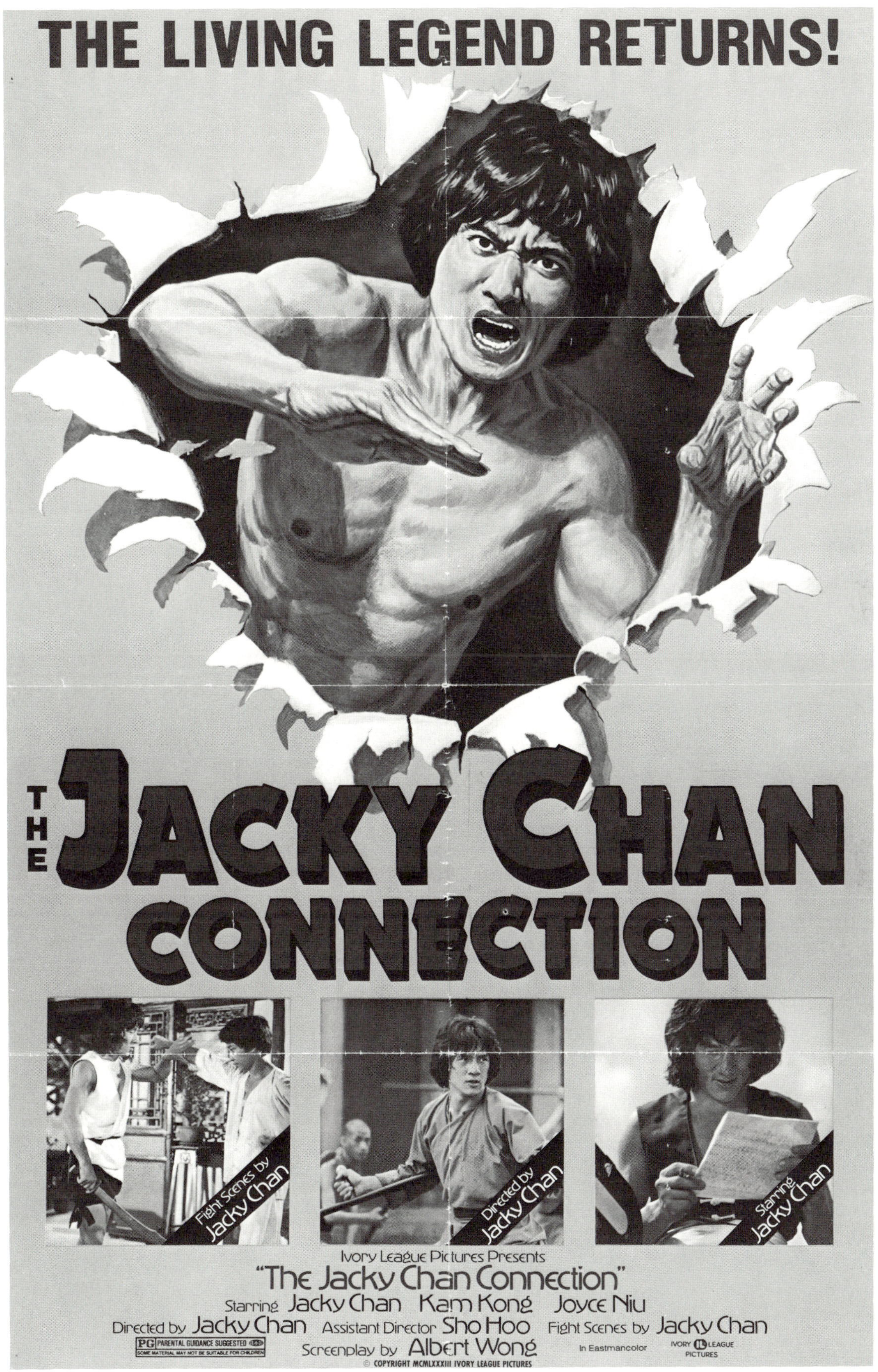

With the success of Jackie Chan came the same sort of exploitation that haunted Bruce Lee.

Yuen Baio, star of The Prodigal Son, Dreadnaught, Project A, *and many others.*

Samo Hung (left) plays The Magnificent Butcher, *one of Huang Fei Hong's famous students.*

Samo Hung (left) teaches Yuen Baio the shortcomings of Wing Chun and how to correct them, in The Prodigal Son.

Long, lean, handsome, and elegant, Adam Cheng was showcased in the Golden Harvest production of The Sword.

Adam Cheng (center, in white) became a star because of his looks, his Chinese television experience, and an excellent performance in this film, Zu, Warriors from the Magic Mountain.

The ultimate confrontation between Chinese and Japanese martial arts came in Golden Harvest's visually splendid Duel to the Death.

One of the first signs of Chinese/Japanese cooperation, as well as the sharpening of independent producing talents, came with Ninja in the Dragon's Den, *starring the impressive Conan Lee (left), here fighting on* stilts.

Kwan Tik Hing returns to the role of Huang Fei Hong in The Magnificent Butcher *during a dazzling "calligraphy" fight sequence.*

After the delight of The Magnificent Butcher, *director Yuen Woo Ping starred Kwan Tak Hing in* Dreadnaught, *in which Huang Fei Hong captures a Peking Opera killer.*

Jet Lee, the first martial arts star from the People's Republic of China.

Jet Lee in action, chopping down poles in a sequence filmed at the Shaw Brothers Studio in Hong Kong for The Shaolin Temple*—the People's Republic's first kungfu epic.*

Oceans of emotion could be read in Tatsuya Nakadai's expressive face, a visage that made him a memorable chambara actor.

CHAPTER FOUR

Japan: Samurai Swordsmen and Karate Killers

There's a distinct difference between Chinese and Japanese martial arts movies. While the martial arts originated in China, great Oriental filmmaking originated in Japan. China had the history; Japan had the cinematic ability. The world discovered it in 1951 when Akira Kurosawa's *Roshomon* (1950) was shown at the Venice Film Festival (where it won first prize). Even the strangest of Japan's action films look wonderful. The big difference between the best and the worst of these genre movies lies in the approach. The subject matter is usually the same. It is how artistically and poetically the director portrays the violent images that does the trick in this country.

Let's establish something at the very outset here. The martial arts movie is distinct from the samurai film—or, as it is known to afficianados, the chambara film. There are some samurai sagas that can be included on the basis of their violence. We'll create a simple distinction. If there's more argument than action, it's a mainstream chambara film. If there's more action than argument, it's a martial arts movie. Of course, some dialogue-laden movies will sneak in on the basis of their influence.

But first the foundation must be laid. To fully appreciate the films, it's best to appreciate the country they come from. The first hint of the Japanese came from Chinese history of 108 B.C. Then the series of islands and its people were called "Wo." At that time it consisted of more than a hundred states. By 250 A.D., it was thirty states. Early in the 400s, it was unified into a single nation with the "tenno" (emperor of heaven) as its leader. That's when the nation built on hypocrisy began to take shape.

Japan consists of four main islands: Hokkaido, Honshu, Shikoku, and Kyushu. To the south, there are the Ryukyu Islands between the East China and Philippine Seas. By 550 B.C., Korea split off on its own, but not before introducing Buddhism to the isles. In the early 600s the country created a constitution, and imposing Buddhist temples were built. They had an Emperor, they had a royal court, they had a Council of State (which took care of practical problems) and they had a Council of Deities (which was supposed to take care of heavenly ones).

The people were broken into two classes: freemen and slaves; while the land was broken into

Toshiro Mifune sits on the watchtower, cheering on the two warring gangs of Yojimbo.

It's ten against one at the climax of Yojimbo.

three classes: province, county, and village. Essentially, the government owned everything because it was charged with keeping the gods happy. In the late 700s, Buddhism was eliminated from affairs of state, but it had served its purpose. The government was a powerful entity which controlled the populace, and the infighting within the ruling ranks was rampant.

Throughout the tenth and eleventh centuries, the emperors and aristocracy lived rich lives, while the common folk—farmers, mostly—survived the best they could. At this time came the first stirrings of the social class which would become the samurai. Dissatisfied youth began to seek power in the towns, acquiring land and pressing locals into service. Combined with this class's innate instinct were special teachings, teachings that could make a person a better fighter.

An official Japanese language developed in the tenth century. No longer did they use complete Chinese lettering (characters); they used abbreviated Chinese lettering. The split between the leaders and the people became more and more pronounced. Even the religion was split. There were those monks who placed wealth over spiritual attainment, and so courted royalty's favors, and there were those "Pure Land" Buddhists who sought to purify themselves of negative desires.

Pure Japanese situations began to arise. Emperors would step down, supposedly to live a life of Buddhism, only to control the government from behind the scenes. Meanwhile the temples were being infiltrated by people who had less interest in wisdom and virtue and more in personal success and wealth. By the time the warrior class emerged, everything was factionalized.

The samurai had become a sort of military police with connections in the royal court. Each different samurai family jockeyed for position, hoping to establish themselves by knocking another family off, or hoping to curry the emperor's favor by putting down someone else's uprising. By this time, to become a samurai meant being born one.

Yojimbo *is no ordinary man. Toshiro Mifune cuts down his enemies.*

Tatsuya Nakadai (center) is an intense chambara actor, here showing his stuff in Harakiri.

Kinnosuke Nakamura has played nearly every great screen swordsman, including Tange Sazen and Itto Ogami.

The lines were already established. Heaven help the common man.

By the 1100s, the samurai had become so powerful that the emperor instituted a military government, called a shogunate. There was still an emperor and an emperor's family, but the real power now rested with the shogun and his samurai. There were military governors and military stewards and metropolitan guards—whose job it was to be policemen. Already the land was rife with thieves and gamblers, and other assorted scum. Again, pray for the common man.

In the 1200s, Kublai Khan tried to invade Japan from his base in China. A typhoon destroyed most of his ships and the samurai killed most of the survivors. Almost thirty thousand Mongols died, and the Japanese thanked the "kamikaze" (divine wind) for its protection. It filled the warrior class with the belief that they were blessed. At this point, the common man could forget about it.

The samurai were put in charge of entire districts and they ruled absolutely. Whenever they did a service for the shogun or fought bravely on the battlefield, they were often rewarded with more land. With time on their hands and the heavens on their side, the samurai developed the "Kyuba-no-michi" (The Way of Bow and Horse)—a creed which placed service to one's overlord more important than service to oneself, then placed service to one's family even higher than that.

The government continued on its merry way, cheating, lying, and killing to get ahead, while the samurai learned more about their swords. The samurai swords were magnificent works of art, created by master designers and metallurgists. In a long, secret process, soft and hard metal was folded hundreds of times, creating an incredibly thin, incredibly strong edge.

At first straight, and then slightly curved, the blades were tested, legend says, by cutting through a dead cow or a hanging corpse from shoulder through hip. If the blade slowed or stopped, it was discarded or sold to a lesser-ranked warrior. If it moved cleanly through the corpse, it was deemed suitable for a true samurai. Little wonder the

Raizo Ichikawa was a doomed but beloved actor, shown here in one of his earliest films, Hakai.

sword came to be considered the soul of the samurai.

During the Ashikaga (or "Muromachi") shogunate of two hundred years, from roughly 1300 to 1500, cities grew to be strong commercial and manufacturing centers. Corruption came along with it. When the Spanish and Portugese appeared and trade with China started, the corruption grew even worse. Corruption is a natural extension of hypocrisy, and the Japanese system was based on that. Combining pride with paranoia led the country to a ridiculous, but poetic, situation.

By the mid-1600s, the cycle was complete. Japan was locked into an amazing structure. The whole country belonged to the shogun, who was supposedly taking care of it for the emperor. The shogun divided the country up among his domain lords, in return for which, the domain lords had to provide any service to the shogun. *Any* service.

Beneath the domain lords were their retainers and feudal barons (called "daimyo"), who controlled the farmers. And everybody but the farmers had their samurai. And the samurai had their Bushido, their strict code of honor. There were certain things they could never do, primary of which was to go against their own clan (family) or the wishes of their overlord.

But all these people were human. Too human for the scheme of things. No one seemed happy with his lot, so there was constant insurrection and intrigue. Outside influences didn't help. With the Portugese came Catholic Christianity. With the Dutch and English came Protestant Christianity. The natural inclination of these religions is to make their influence felt. To maintain their treacherous lifestyle, the Japanese enforced "sakoku" (national seclusion). They cut themselves off from the outside world in the 1630s.

With outside influences cut off, the system became rigid. There were the warriors, farmers, artisans, and merchants. The warriors (seven percent of the thirty million population) levied taxes on the farmers (eighty percent of the population). Al-

Zatoichi the Blind Swordsman *cuts down his enemies.*

The usual climax of the twenty-four Zatoichi *movies. His enemies all lie dead. From* Zatoichi and the Scoundrels.

though the economic foundation of the empire, the farmers and common folk were treated as less than dirt. The samurai could do what they wished with them.

In the samurai households, the head of the family was absolute ruler; men were respected, women were chattel. Contrary to what male chauvinists might say, it was no way to live. Some managed to be content, essentially by ignoring these rules, but anyone who lived by Bushido was often forced to stare the hypocrisy of the system in its horrible face.

Therefore the Ninjas. The Ninjas fell through the cracks of Bushido. They were families of spies and assassins who hired themselves out to do the dirty deeds the samurai couldn't. Belief in the after-life was powerful in feudal Japan, and to go against Bushido meant giving up one's soul; ergo, no afterlife. The Ninjas had no place on earth and they had none in heaven. They only had their own pride and their own code. Their code: Get the job done and never reveal family secrets. Die if captured.

Incredibly, this system—what was essentially a police state—lasted three hundred years. While the outside world developed guns and industry, Japan fought with swords and poisons. The central government was in Edo (what was to become Tokyo) on the main, largest island. And all life seemed to eminate from there. The collapse of the system came in the late 1800s, heralded by, as usual, foreigners.

The Netherlands had exclusive trading rights with the Japanese at that time (they had what the Japanese needed), so they fought the British desire to open the country to other trade. The British empire's wealth was based on trade, so they always wanted other customers. The United States needed fueling outposts in the Pacific, so they had an interest as well. But when the shogun began to consider the offers, it factioned the country. Many saw trade as an invasion, a threat to the emperor. Many others saw it as a way to gain power for themselves.

The country was plunged into civil war by the 1860s. The sides were the shogun's and the emperor's. Samurai scrambled to be on what they hoped was the winning side. Bushido crumbled around them. There was no "right" side. There was no "wrong" side. It soon became clear that the correct side was the one that wanted the warrior class to continue. That was a toss-up.

The emperor won and established imperial rule. The samurai were slowly phased out. The wearing of swords was soon banned. Japan crawled out of the eighteenth century and painfully into the twentieth.

Zatoichi and the Fugitives *put actor Shintaro Katsu through his doubly difficult paces. Not only did he have to fight evil swordsmen, but the camera could never see his eyes.*

JAPANESE MARTIAL ARTS CHART

AIKIDO: All movements are circular rather than linear. The fighter uses his opponent's force to either throw him or apply a joint-lock. The fighter will usually move along the line of attack and grasp the opponent's wrist, gaining control. Aikido relies on momentum. There are no attacks in aikido. Only the opponent attacks.

ARNIS: Originally known as KALI. It is the most popular martial art of the Philippines. Although there are unarmed aspects to it, they are in the minority. It is usually practiced with a long wooden sword or short wooden dagger. Cinematically speaking, it is usually shown with one twenty-six-inch stick or two sticks of that same length.

HAPKIDO: A Korean martial art that resembles Japanese jujitsu. It is actually a forerunner of aikido. It is a synthesis of karate, judo, and aiki-jitsu.

IAI-DO—THE WAY OF THE SWORD:

1) Swordplay:	Parry ("uke") Exchange ("kawashi") Attack ("kogeki")
2) Sword Position:	Direct Overhead ("dai-jodan") Overhead Left ("hidari-jodan") Middle Position ("chudan") Pointed ("seigan") Vertical Right ("hasso") Vertical Left ("hidari-hasso") Point Lowered ("gedan")
3) Sword Cuts:	Thrust Horizontal Cut Vertical Cut Diagonal Up Diagonal Down

JUDO: Invented by Jigoro Kano and derived from jujitsu. Uses the fighter's opponent's weight against him. In sport judo, it uses throws, elbow locks, chokes, and hold-downs to score points. The striking aspects are practiced in the kata stage only.

JUJITSU: There are more than seven hundred styles of this self-defense art; most of them were practiced in the eighteenth and nineteenth centuries. Its basic concept is to do anything that is effective. Strikes, kicks, throws, chokes, joint-locks, and grappling techniques are all fair jujitsu game. Anything that works.

KARATE: Originated in Okinawa but brought to Japan in the 1920s. Brutal, direct, it is practiced as both a sport and a means of self-defense. Judo uses throws; karate uses punches, strikes, and kicks.

NINJUTSU: "The Art of Stealth." This is an ancient art that incorporates many ways of infiltrating an enemy's base and killing him. There are no opponents in ninjutsu. There are only enemies. Whatever is required to steal in, assassinate, and steal out again are part of ninjutsu. Related arts are how to escape after capture or to kill oneself if escape is impossible and interrogation is inevitable.

SAVATE: A French variation of karate that relies on lightning-quick kicks.

TAE KWON DO: A Korean art that concentrates on kicks, and flying kicks at that. But it also employs punches, blocks, and jumps.

EARLY SWORD SLASHERS

The Japanese film industry was formed in the twenties and thirties, then had to be reformed again after World War Two. Japan's martial arts movies grew out of its ritualized theater—in this case the highly stylized Kabuki dramas. There were stacks of samurai movies in the thirties, but most were staid glorifications of classical samurai heroes done in a very stiff, predictable style.

It wasn't until after the war that the particularly charged imaginations of the Japanese filmmakers conceived what was to become the most intense form of martial arts action. Keith Richards of the Rolling Stones rock group once said, "There's something about a naked blade that upsets people." Or words to that effect. In that he is correct. The chambara movie is the most personal of the martial arts films.

Kungfu films portray an intricate ballet of move and countermove, its purpose to introduce the loser to the wonderful world of internal bleeding. But the chambara cinema portrays people who

Three Ninja fall from the trees. They are dead before they hit the ground, killed by Tomisaburo Wakayama in Lightning Swords of Death.

slash and chop with an incredibly sharp extention of their *souls*. Here, the victims don't simply drop dead, the only clue to their destruction being blood-stained teeth (a mark of internal bleeding). Here, they lose arms, stomachs, heads.

But unlike the Chinese superhero cartoonists, the Japanese were artists, and were to do their killing on a grand canvas. In this country, after all, the martial arts movie genre was started, then revolutionized, then sustained by a certified cinematic genius—Akira Kurosawa.

Born in 1910, while the dissolution of the warrior class was still going on, Kurosawa was the youngest of seven children. As he grew he dreamed of being an artist, but when he graduated from school, he couldn't make a living in that field. In 1936 he answered an ad for assistant directors and was asked at the interview to write a paper on "what is wrong with Japanese movies and what would you do about it?"

His answer was his films, but first he was assigned to assist Kajiro Yamamoto, an eclectic filmmaker who concentrated on crime dramas in his later years. But in 1939 Yamamoto made his version of *The Loyal 47 Ronin*, a popular story of faithful retainers who first take vengeance for their lord's death, then kill themselves as per the code of Bushido. Kurosawa served as an assistant on this film. Two years later he had worked himself up to writing and directing entire portions of Yamamoto's movies. Two years after that, he was assigned to direct his own first film.

It was *Sanshiro Sugata (Judo Saga)*, which he wrote himself and in which he tells the story of that art through the eyes of a disillusioned martial

The astonishing ending of Lightning Swords of Death. *The Lone Wolf and Son leave the battlefield after killing an entire army.*

arts student. The screen was dense with multilayered images. Almost every visual Kurosawa created seemed to have easily graspable inner meanings. His characters also had depth and believability. Finally, the novice director seemed to have an inordinate grip on cinematic language—he knew how to say things with moving pictures and he knew how to say them in the clearest way possible.

Filmmaking involves getting across information. The art of great filmmaking is getting across this information in such a way that the audience is both amazed and delighted with the clarity of the information. In other words, the scene has the look, feel, sense, and even stink of truth. Like all the finest martial arts moviemakers, Kurosawa also had the morality. His *Judo Saga* promoted the humanitarian philosophy of the art.

Kurosawa completed the second part of the *Judo Saga* in 1945, after having made another film called *The Most Beautiful*. His *The Men Who Tread on the Tiger's Tail* and the *Judo Saga* were banned during the American occupation after the war and parts of the original prints were destroyed. Essentially, the entire film industry was put on hold until the early fifties.

But then a curious phenomenon took place. The Japanese had experienced the modern nightmare of a nuclear attack. In a very short time they went from being a humiliated people to a growing world power. They had a past that was colorful (to say the least), and, perhaps more importantly, very recent. The country had remained frozen for three centuries—and was just thawing out during most of the populace's youths.

Whatever the reason, the Japanese film industry started producing warped visions—visions that were totally opposite to the Japanese manner on the streets. In real life, the Japanese were polite, considerate, moralistic, and humane. But in their fantasy life, it was a completely different story.

The Baby Cart *series holds the distinction of being the bloodiest on record. In* Shogun Assassin, *Tomisaburo Wakayama shows why.*

Tomisaburo Wakayama holds the distinction of being one of the ugliest heroes on record. But in Shogun Assassin *he knew how to kill like nobody's business.*

Once they walked into a cinema for a chambara movie they were ready for some action.

And the Japanese film studios were ready to give it to them. The major studios controlled all three aspects of motion pictures: production, distribution, and exhibition. Hollywood studios did the same until the anti-trust laws of 1947. But the anti-trust situation passed the Orient by. Studios made movies for their own theater chains. The predominant chambara producer of the fifties was Toei.

The Japanese samurai have funny haircuts (called "top-knots") and wear funny clothes, but those are extensions of the Bushido malaise that both preserved and perverted the shogunate period. Like American cowboy movies, the chambara films rationalized what were essentially years of unfair slaughter—at first. Then came Saotome Mondonosuke, Tange Sazan, Kuro Genji, and Tengu Kurama.

Mondonosuke was the "Bored Samurai," a famous literary hero played by Utaemon Ichikawa. From the novel came the crescent shaped scar across his forehead that interrupts his hair bangs. But his cinematic swordstyle came from Ichikawa the actor. It is the "moroha ryu seigan kuzushi," two-sword eye-slashing cut. The Bored Samurai would leave his castle to go among the people and right wrongs in more than thirty movies made between 1931 and 1960.

Tange "Lefty" Sazan was one of the first samurai anti-heroes—a subgenre most often credited

Itto Ogami, played by Tomisaburo Wakayama (second from left), mows down the enemy during the Lone Wolf's best movie, Sword of Vengeance #5: Baby Cart in the Land of Demons.

to Akira Kurosawa. In a 1958 film, the character is shown losing his right arm and right eye to a jealous sword teacher. To most samurai, this would end their lives. The idea of using the left hand would mean putting the sword on the "wrong" side. Unthinkable! Because of the injustice done him, Sazan (who now has a scar across his closed right eyelid) rejects Bushido, becomes a "ronin" (masterless samurai) and slashes away at injustice with his one-armed style.

Kuro Genji was one of the first samurai superheroes. By day he was a gambler and general layabout, but by night he donned his white kimono and became a symbol of justice for all the downtrodden. He even had a catchy motto he tells the bad guys. "Whoever needs help, call my name. Then the white wings of the Fighting Genji Butterfly will rise. This is my parting gift. To send you to hell! My family is Genji. My name is Kuro." The wings are the sleeves of his kimono as he raises his swords, one in each hand. The influential, emperor-related Genji family crest is a butterfly.

Finally, there was Tengu Kurama, the Japanese Lone Ranger. It is quite possible that George Trendle, the creator of the Lone Ranger, was aware of this Oriental character, whose first film was produced in the 1920s. He is the masked do-gooder on the beautiful white horse named White Dragon. He is the man in black with the silver revolver fighting crime where e'er he roamed in the 1850s. He is Tengu Kurama!

It may already be apparent that the Japanese have as many varying sword styles as the Chinese have kungfu styles. In truth, each major chambara star had his own unique form of swordplay, as did these four characters. And while this quartet established chambara concepts which would lead to their being resurrected time and again by different directors and played by different actors, it wasn't until Akira Kurosawa turned his eye back to the samurai genre that it took its next major leap.

It was with *Yojimbo (The Bodyguard*—1961), starring Toshiro Mifune. In the intervening years, the eclectic director had done many dramas. He had also made *Seven Samurai* (1952), the influential epic which was to be remade into the inferior western *The Magnificent Seven* (1960) and the vastly inferior science-fiction film *Battle Beyond the Stars* (1980); *Throne of Blood* (1955), a Japanese period version of Shakespeare's *Macbeth*; and *The Hidden Fortress* (1957), a samurai movie whose characters helped inspire *Star Wars*.

All three prior films also starred Mifune, an actor who entered the industry in 1946 hoping for an assistant cameraman's job. Instead, he acci-

NOW!
THE INCREDIBLE
SONNY CHIBA
IS BACK TO BACK
AND TWICE AS MEAN!
THE STREET
FIGHTER
R
RETURN
OF THE
STREET
FIGHTER
R
IN ACTIONSCOPE AND EASTMANCOLOR FROM NEW LINE CINEMA
THEATRE

Don't mess with Shinichi "Sonny" Chiba, unless you want to lose some important piece of your anatomy. He's The Streetfighter.

This man messed with Sonny Chiba, The Streetfighter, *and got his teeth taken away.*

dentally stumbled into an audition and was hired by Toho Studios. In the years before *Yojimbo* was to turn the chambara cinema around, he starred in *Sword for Hire* (1952), a war movie set in 1573, *Miyamoto Musashi* (1954), the oft-told tale of Japan's greatest swordsman, and *Daredevil in the Castle* (1961), among many others. These films, however, were the work of chambara epic-maker Hiroshi Inagaki, who only directed samurai sagas, which ranged from small-scale mysteries *(Incident at Blood Pass*—1970) to "cast of thousands" costumers (*Samurai Banners*—1969).

But Inagaki's creations were traditional chambara. *Yojimbo* was something else again. The opening image of a stray wild dog sets the tone, as does the following image of Toshiro Mifune coming to a fork in the road and trying diffidently to decide which path to take. It is the end of the samurai era, and Mifune is playing a scruffy ronin out for a strange sort of fun. This was a Japanese western, and perfectly suited to the "stranger in town" cowboy films. In fact, *Yojimbo* was remade, plot twist for plot twist, into *A Fistful of Dollars* (1966)—the film that introduced Sergio Leone's "Man With No Name" and made a star of Clint Eastwood.

Mifune, playing an ex-samurai with a number for a name, comes to a bad town filled with two warring gangs which are too cowardly to kill each other off. Mifune, enacting a man named Sanjurò (which means "thirty"), plays both sides against each other, hiring himself out as a bodyguard to the highest bidder, until he forces the issue. The arrival of a man with a gun (Tatsuya Nakadai) almost foils his plan, but in the climactic showdown—ten men and a gun against one—Yojimbo lances the man's gun hand and cuts through everyone else.

The earlier superhero samurai had established a fascinating form of screen swordplay, but *Yojimbo* and its sequel, *Sanjuro*, (1962) added something more. Mifune had a vicious vitality to his blade in the first film. In the second, Kurosawa ends the more sedate story, of Sanjuro trying to save a clan, with a duel between the title character and a vaunted samurai (again, Tatsuya Nakadai). It consists of only one move each, the "iai" (fast sword draw), and ends with the two figures still as statues. Suddenly a spurt of blood erupts from the samurai's chest and he crumbles.

In all the years of chambara, in all the years of death by sword, no director had used blood so realistically. It would be almost ten years before directors would pour the scarlet stuff again. But when they did, they used buckets of it.

Sonny Chiba shows off the physique which made him a star in The Streetfighter.

He may be roped. He may have a gun at his head.
But don't bet against The Streetfighter.

BLIND MAN'S BLOOD

The year 1962 was a great one. In that year two chambara series premiered which featured heroes probably born of *Yojimbo/Sanjuro* influence. Yet these heroes went far beyond anything the Mifune character attempted. While director Kurosawa was subtle, these heroes were obvious. While other swordsmen fought against corrupt societies to create fine new ones, these heroes simply fought. Their aims were not to "save the society." The first of these new swordsmen fought to save individuals. The second fought to die.

The first was not blind the way most followers of Bushido were blind. The first was *literally blind.* He was Zatoichi, the justly famous blind swordsman. Rotund, scruffy, short-haired, he wandered the Japan of the 1800s, just barely surviving by gambling or hiring himself out as a masseur. Shintaro Katsu, the son of a musician, achieved stardom with this role, and little wonder. As the twenty-four films progressed between 1962 and 1972, his "playing blind" became more and more exact, filled with delightful nuances.

The audience never saw his eyes. Whenever his usually closed lids quivered, only the whites of his eyes could be seen. Still, the character seemed to have a radar-exact sense of hearing. He could "see" more than most people with his ears and his incisive mind. And his ears seemed directly connected to his sword-arm. He used a cane sword that guided him in times of peace. But for Zatoichi, there were few times of peace. His hearing-radar also seemed to be a signal to which trouble and death would surely be attracted.

But he was prepared for it. The character was a master swordsman, a nearly unbelievably fast and deadly fighter, and Katsu had the sword skill to pull this image off. The idea of a blind swordsman sounds ludicrous, but it has to be seen to be believed. And seeing this *is* believing it. Katsu would cut through three candles just by drawing his sword. In the same motion, he would return

The only man who can beat The Streetfighter *is tiny, rotund Masafumi Suzuki.*

The Streetfighter *may not be graceful, but he gets the job done.*

the sword to its cane-scabbard. There was no film edited; it was all done in one continuous take.

The character used the "gyakute-giri," the reversed grip sword cut, holding his blade in a downward, defensive position at all times. All the other swordsman held their blades up, the point above their gripping forefingers. But the unassuming Zatoichi, who never wanted to fight but always had to, held the blade pointed toward the ground, below his gripping pinkie. When he fought, he would slice back and forth with his fist.

Throughout the series, Katsu would do a startling dance of death, the sword appearing and disappearing as he slashed it across the bodies of his enemies—who almost always outnumbered him ten to one. Watching this innocuous, humble, shuffling lowlife turn into a whirling dervish of death was always exciting. And the filmmakers always put him in powerfully dramatic situations, which added volumes to the basic series structure.

He is already being hunted in the first film, *The Life and Opinion of Zatoichi*. Kan Shimosawa created the character and the story, while Minoru Inuzuka wrote the screenplay. Probably the greatest underrated Japanese action film director, Kenji Misumi, helmed this first picture—as he would most of the series' first films. Through it and the subsequent movies, the character unerringly points out the injustice of the feudal system.

The Zatoichi movies were comedy/tragedies in which Ichi would play the buffoon until he came across evil. Almost always, his attempts to right wrongs are confused or complicated by peoples' emotions and desires. Zatoichi wants what is best for the common man and always puts his life on the line for the often misunderstanding, ungrateful commoners. This leads to both scenes of effective heartbreak and final explosion of mass slaughter.

In the first film, the story of blind Ichi ("zato" means "masseur") is notably different than it is in the following films. (Ichi was not only famous to his fans, but his character was also infamous onscreen. Almost everyone knew of him in these early films' stories.) He is being tracked by vengeance-seeking members of a gang whose boss he had killed, when he stumbles across his brother—a man who reacted to Bushido as badly as Ichi but is not taking the path of righteousness. Instead he is leading a life of crime. And he has gotten in over his head.

The two reminisce about their youth as the brother lies dying in Zatoichi's arms—mortally wounded in a duel with his own brother. They remember the time when Ichi had his sight and they both loved the same girl. They remember how the brother stole her from Ichi and drove her to her death.

Ichi leaves his brother's body to confront the gang leader who hired his brother to kill him. In the very last second of the film, still surrounded by the gangster's henchman, Ichi swings his cane sword across the villain's neck in a freeze frame. It was an abrupt ending, but the following two sequels, produced in less than a year, added more to the character's history.

Both sequels seemed somewhat tenuous, as if the filmmakers weren't sure the series would last. At the end of 1962 came *The Return of Masseur Ichi*, and in early 1963 *Zatoichi Enters Again* premiered. The latter was directed by Tokuzo Tanaka, a regular on the series. This film establishes further Zatoichi traditions.

Most of the movies begin with the character minding his own business, but within seconds trouble finds him. Either a fight is going on nearby or enemies have finally tracked him down. For whatever reason, Zatoichi almost always finds himself fighting with someone for reasons he doesn't understand. He always finds himself killing the opponent in self-defense. Or he rescues a relative of someone he's killed in a previous picture, as is the case in *Zatoichi Enters Again*.

It is the brother of a gangster he had killed earlier, who, although Ichi had saved him, follows the masseur for revenge. He follows him to the man who taught Zatoichi swordplay, Zatoichi's "sensei." To the hero's horror, the man has been corrupted by lust for power. The sensei's sister loves the scruffy vagabond and wants to marry him. This is a seeming impossibility to Ichi, who thought an ugly low-ranked being such as himself would never find love. There's only one catch; she wants him never to fight again.

He agrees, leaving himself wide open to the vengeance of the gangster's brother. Although his instincts scream at him to fight back, he lays his cane sword at the brother's feet. He suggests that they gamble for his life. In a gut-wrenching scene, Ichi and his lady crouch at the man's feet in a side alley, throwing dice for the masseur's life. The vengeance-seeker wins, but he cannot bear to kill the honorable, humiliated man. He lies, saying the dice are in Ichi's favor.

But tragedy continues to stalk the hero. His own sensei forces him to duel, meaning to murder the man who constantly reminds him how low he has sunk. Zatoichi's skill gets the better of him, and he kills his own teacher. This means that he must leave his true love, for he has killed a member of her family, and, in Japan, family takes precedence over all, even love.

Tanaka directed the next few films, with Kan Shimozawa supplying all the stories. They developed the character to a delightful degree, creating

The Streetfighter *stares down his arch-enemy Jungo (Milton Ishibashi).*

Etsuko "Sue" Shiomi gets a knife all the way through her, trying to kill The Streetfighter.

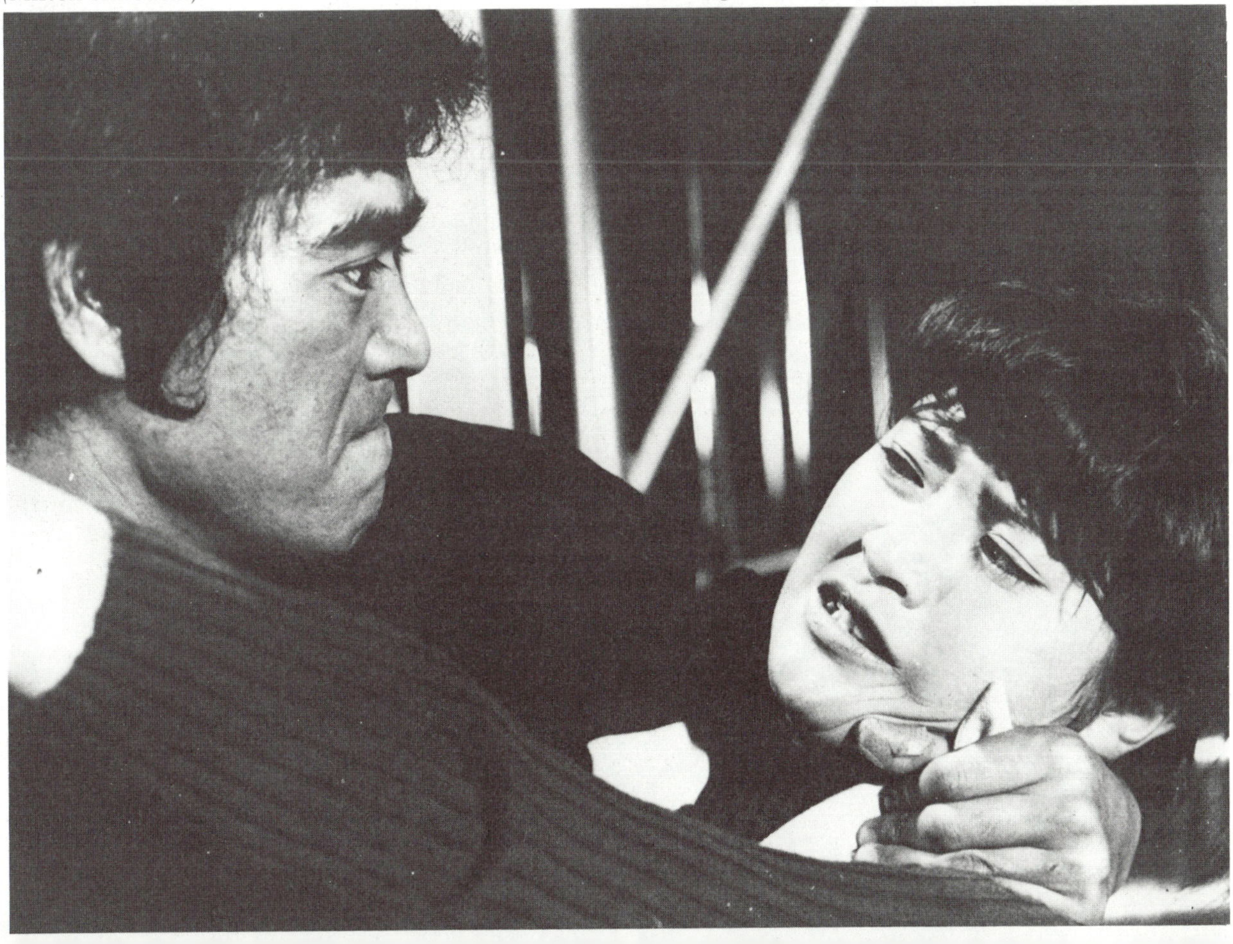

scenes that cleverly made use of both Ichi's blindness and his "seeing ears." Slowly but surely, Ichi was becoming a superman. Audiences flocked to the films, making them the greatest success of their time.

The fame grew to the point that *Zatoichi and the Scoundrels* (1964), the sixth in the series, the first to be filmed in color, and the first to be directed by Kimiyoshi Yasuda (who was soon to become the best director on the series) was dubbed into English and exported as *Zatoichi the Blind Swordsman*. But this translation didn't do as well as hoped, returning the character to Japanese cinemas and American "revival" theaters and "art" houses.

But even there, the movies often lost something in the subtitled translation. In one of the films, two kimonoed, top-knotted villians are discussing the masseur's arrival. "I hear Zatoichi is in town," the subtitles say for one. "Yeah," says the other. "He's one tough hombre."

The "tough hombre" fought through five more movies until coming to *Zatoichi's Pilgrimage* (1966), directed by Kasuo Ikehiro—another series regular. This was a milestone, in that Ichi promises to visit and pray at eighty-eight temples along the road—one for each of the men he has killed. Before the movie's eighty-two minutes are up, he has about a dozen more temples to visit.

Just one film later, something else unusual happens. In *The Blind Swordsman's Cane Sword* a master swordsmith warns Ichi that his blade is weak and will break if he kills just one more man. The masseur leaves it with the old smith for repair, not realizing that the master craftsman is making the Orient's strongest sword for a high ranking official—a sword many people want.

Ichi does some razzle-dazzle with sticks and an umbrella to fight off the villains until the climactic confrontation with the corrupt official. With the now dead smith's words of warning booming in Ichi's brain, the men fight . . . and the evil man's sword breaks. The old smith had

Guns? This is what Sonny Chiba thinks of guns, in Return of the Streetfighter.

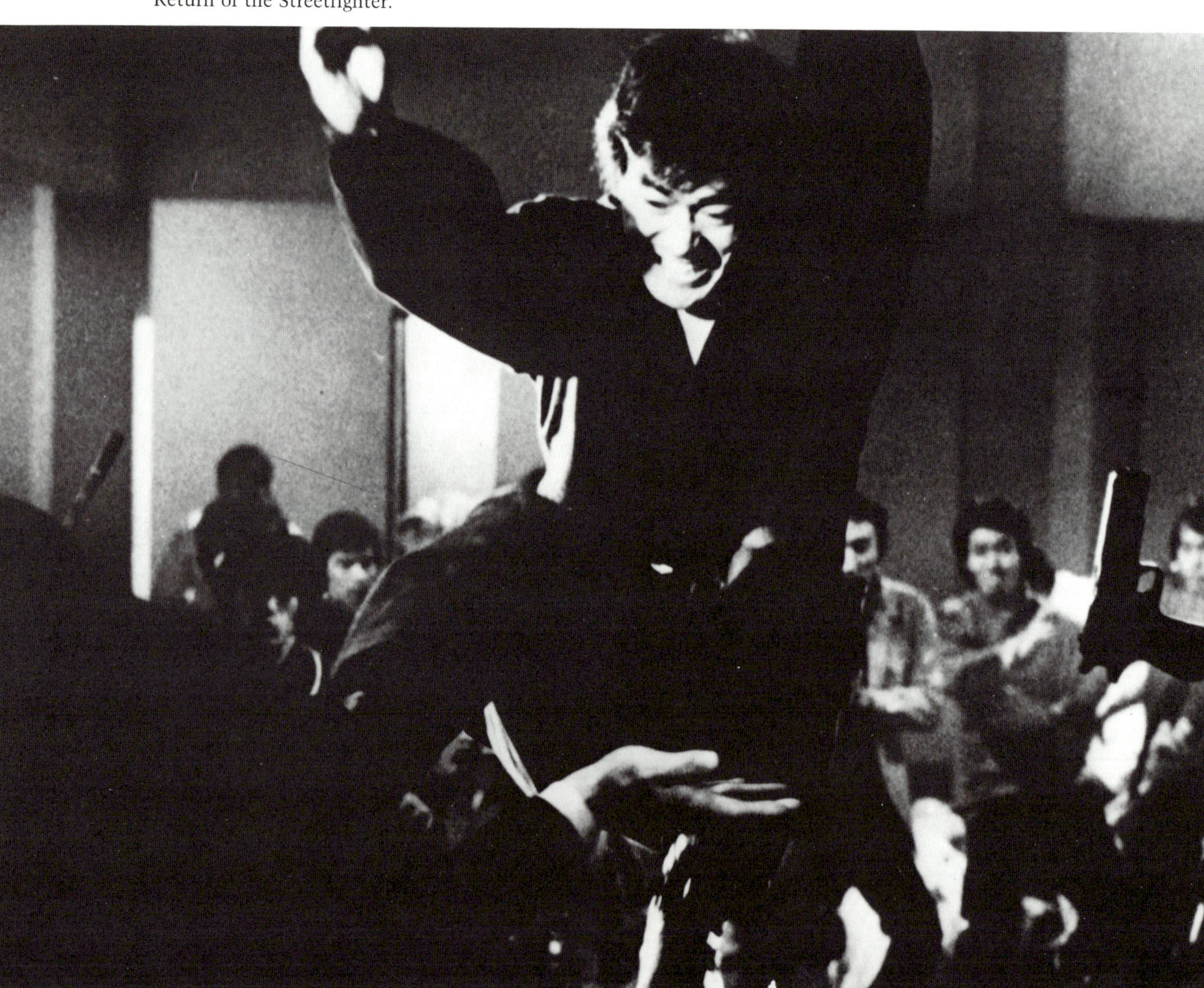

switched the blades. Now Zatoichi has the country's best sword. This was another excellent Kimiyoshi Yasuda film, one which many consider to be Zatoichi's best.

A personal favorite comes just two films later; after Zatoichi has continued to be both an amazing swordsman (in 1967's *Zatoichi Challenged* he cuts off the eyebrows of a corrupt official without breaking the skin) and an equally amazing humanitarian (in the same film he puts himself at the mercy of the shogun's agent to save the life of an innocent artist). It is *The Blind Swordsman and the Fugitives* (1968) wherein lie all of the series' traditions along with a brand new one.

It has been six years since the original film premiered, and already seventeen movies have been produced. By now Zatoichi is a masterful screen presence. After being hired as a masseur for the leader of a gang of cutthroats, the crooks purposefully place things in his way, including a sword edge. Ichi nonchalantly avoids and replaces all of them, finally stepping over the sword nimbly. The men torture him by surrounding his face with their blades, then later try to kill him.

Their leader silently picks up a bow and arrow while talking loudly to Ichi. He silently pulls the drawstring back and lets the arrow fly. Zatoichi merely pulls his sword out of his cane two inches. The arrow hits the blade edge and goes off on either side of the sitting masseur.

Three men try ambushing Ichi on the street. He swings his sword madly. The men freeze, certain thay have been killed. When they realize they haven't been touched, all three try to catch up with the shambling swordsmen. As they take their first steps, all their clothes fall off in tattered strips. Later, when a female assassin tries to cover Ichi with darts, he catches them on his sword hilt.

Director Yasuda and story writer Shimozawa have thus far reestablished the character's excellence. Then they bring in a new ingredient: a villain with a gun. When the hammer clicks back, Zatoichi's ears do not recognize the sound. He holds up his blade to deflect the weapon, only to have the bullet richochet into his shoulder. Escaping in the river, he digs out the lead and painfully cauterizes the wound by pouring sake into it.

Here was the rub. Since Zatoichi had gotten so good, the filmmakers were introducing additional handicaps. This led to an especially involving climactic battle in which a bleeding Ichi, one arm in a makeshift sling, faces the mob. He always seems ready to collapse. The enemy attacks and he viciously slashes, then immediately seems ready for collapse again.

No special effects blood shoots out of his victims, but his speed and the excellence of the swordfight choreography give the impression that Ichi's blade is so fast that men die three seconds before they become aware of it, their wounds cauterized.

Ichi slices right through a wall to reach the main villain. Thus ends another satisfying Zatoichi adventure. To keep the series going, the producers, Daiei Productions, started using guest stars, as in 1970's *Zatoichi Meets Yojimbo* (with Toshiro Mifune returning to the role) and 1971's *Zatoichi Meets His Equal* (featuring Wang Yu as the One-Armed Swordsman). Yasuda directed the latter, but Kihachi Okamoto, director of some of the most wondrously violent chambaras (*Sword of Doom*—1966, and *Kill!*—1968, being two) both wrote and directed the former.

Daiei went out of business in 1971, and the series went over to Toho Films for two last episodes. The final was 1973's *Zatoichi in Desperation*, produced and directed by the star, Shintaro Katsu. Once again, the ever-faithful masseur tries to help someone only to pay the piper. In this case, the villains drive spikes through his hands so that he will be unable to hold a sword.

In the climactic scene at a beach where Zatoichi is holed up in a shack, the smug villain sends in some men to kill the "helpless" blindman. To his amazement, the ruffians stumble back out, dying. Zatoichi follows like a hulking angel of doom. He had tied the sword to his wrist and forearm! He chases the screaming villains, cutting them down as he goes. The final film image of Zatoichi shows him stumbling along the shore, the waves getting ever louder until they drown out all sound.

Katsu was to take his famous character onto a successful television series, but the cinema had not seen the last of his particular skills. In 1972 Katsu Productions and Toho Films presented a series of *Sword of Justice* movies written by Yasuzo Masamura. These went way beyond Zatoichi. In them Katsu played "Razor" Hanzo, the most extreme policemen of the late 1800s.

Softcore pornography has become the prevalent genre of the modern Japanese cinema. Almost seventy-five percent of the films made are high quality sex-related stories. A major subgenre is that of "Roman porn," or as it is commonly known, "SM/BD" movies (Sado-Masochism, Bondage-Discipline). The *Sword of Justice* pictures were combinations of action and SM, but done in such a way that they seemed satirical.

The Snare, the second in the series, starts with Hanzo doing his morning exercizes. He goes into his rock garden, puts on brass knuckles, and starts punching stone statues, sending up sparks. He then goes inside his combination gym, sauna, and torture chamber to exercize his "prodigious member." In these movies, he uses his private parts as an interrogation device. The treatment of female characters in the films is embarrassing.

Whenever he comes across a woman in his work, he almost immediately rapes her. Whenever he comes across a reluctant female witness or suspect, he tortures, interrogates, and then has her lowered onto him. Then he spins her while she is (politely described) impaled upon him. In *every* case, the woman falls madly in love with him, desperately pines for him, and will do anything for him. All he wants, of course, are "Just the facts, ma'am."

In *The Snare,* Hanzo and his two bumbling assistants come upon a dead girl who recently had an abortion. They trace the abortion to a church where the nuns practice nasty rituals. They whip and molest captive women for the enjoyment of high-ranking officials. Because church land is sacred, Hanzo infiltrates the grounds by replacing the dead girl in her casket with himself and being buried alive in the church cemetery. The sight of him erupting from the ground is one of the great moments in martial arts cinema.

He attacks, breaks up the ritual and takes the head nun back to his torture chamber. He discovers that the rite's organizer is a high-ranking Treasury official he cannot legally touch. When reporting to his overlord, his jealous immediate superior demands he commit hara-kiri (or, "seppuku," as it is more accurately described in this case) for his failure to solve the girl's murder.

Hanzo immediately plunges his short sword into his stomach and pulls out some pulpy red stuff that he throws into his superior's face. Everyone, on screen and in the audience, is shocked, but it turns out to be watermelon pulp that Hanzo had secreted there for this very purpose. To save his life he must bring to justice Japan's most horrible pirate. He does so in an orgy of short-bladed violence.

Hanzo loves plunging his blade into enemies' joints (elbow or knee) and bending their limbs backwards. He also has a pagoda-home filled with hidden traps and secreted blades. When attacked in his bath, he pulls cords which send arrows and knives shooting into the ambushers. Finally, he manages to bring the Treasury man up on irrefutable charges.

Now, this series has to be seen *not* to be believed. It is the kinkiest and strangest of a strange lot. But it did not appear full-blown, without any antecedents. Its way into the hearts of martial arts lovers was heralded by the second chambara series to premiere in 1962. That of *Kyoshiro Nemuri: The Son of Black Mass.*

THE FULL MOON KILLER

Raizo Ichikawa could be called the Japanese James Dean. He was an intense young actor with glowing eyes, a weak chin, and a long nose. He was a commanding screen presence who also projected a great deal of vulnerability. His specialty was playing alienated characters. Audiences could clearly see great depths of sensitivity and suffering behind the tough exterior.

Arguably Ichikawa's greatest role was that of Kyoshiro Nemuri, the halfbreed samurai. Again, Kenji Misumi directed the first of the series, introducing a red-haired master swordsman born of the rape of his mother by a Portuguese missionary during a black mass. Quite understandably, the man hates most everything and especially Christianity. But again and again he voyages to towns where Christians are being persecuted by the Ienari Shogunate (1786–1838).

Nemuri is a seemingly amoral adventurer, intent on finding a situation or swordsman good enough to kill him. That is not easy considering that the "Son of Black Mass," as he calls himself, is the master of the "Engetsu Sappo"—the dreaded, mystical (fictional) Full Moon Cut.

In the later films of this eleven-film series, the full moon cut is pictured with a strobe effect so that Nemuri's sword seems to multiply. He moves it around in a circle in front of him, drawing the opponent toward him to deliver the killing slice. No opponent has been able to resist the hypnotizing effect of the Full Moon Cut.

But that was used for one-on-one duels only. Usually Nemuri would cut down tens of men in the outlandish situations he sought out. In the first few movies he is pictured less nilhilistically than he would later become. They were fairly straightforward adventures of Nemuri protecting children and the like.

But it was with the third film, *Kyoshiro Nemuri at Bay* (1964), the first directed by Kazuo Ikehiro, that things get out of hand. There he kills dozens of Christians as well as those shogun men planning to kill the Christians themselves. The most memorable moment, however, comes after he has been imprisoned in a dungeon with a babbling white man who turns out to be his father. Upon their escape, he beheads the crazy man.

From then on, the Nemuri series got down to the serious business of mass slaughter. The filmmakers slaughtered dozens on screen and slaughtered the concept of Bushido in the scripts. The highpoint of the series might very well be *The Human Tarantula* (1968, directed by Kimiyoshi Yasauda). The first image is of a beautiful woman in plush surroundings having an epileptic fit. Her

Sonny Chiba dresses up for his final appearance as Terry Surugy in The Streetfighter's Last Revenge.

maids bring a young girl to her. After she stabs the girl to death, splashing the walls with crimson streaks, the fit subsides. Toto, I don't think we're in Kansas anymore.

Here's the story: Two illegitimate children of the shogun have faked a suicide pact, then taken over a small town. The sister has these blood fits. The brother is in love with his sister and is a master of poisons. They have taken all the young people from the town and placed them in dungeon cages, the men on one side and the women on the other. They spend their days thinking of interesting ways to kill them.

Enter Kyoshiro Nemuri. Hearing about the village, he decides it deserves a look. When the villains get word of his coming, they arrange all sorts of traps along the road. One is a veiled woman who begs Nemuri to make love to her. His reputation is one of a degenerate rogue—a reputation he lives up to. Even though the woman reveals herself to be a leper, he takes her into a hut and has sex with her under a mosquito net.

Only then does he pull off the "leprosy," which was actually makeup. At that moment three men chop down the net and slash at it with their swords. Nemuri rises behind them. They look down. All they've succeeded in doing is killing their bait. The woman lies dead. Nemuri quickly kills all three. A fourth runs in, looking at the woman in shock.

"I can see by the way you look that she was your woman," Nemuri says. Then he smiles. "But she gave herself to me before she died." The enraged man charges. In one move Nemuri slices him, spins, cleans his blade with a hanky, puts it away and walks out of the hut. The fourth man stands, his sword raised, then falls dead.

By the time Nemuri reaches the town, the in-

Sonny Chiba's back...
and
Sue Shiomi's
got'm!
He's a one man army.
She's a one woman death squad.
Sister Street Fighter
Starring
Sonny Chiba · Sue Shiomi
FROM NEW LINE CINEMA
R RESTRICTED
UNDER 17 REQUIRES ACCOMPANYING PARENT OR ADULT GUARDIAN
THEATRE

sane sister will do anything to have him. She captures him, throwing open her kimono to reveal her naked form. Women were so well covered in those days that the sight of naked skin could drive a man crazy with lust. A normal man that is. Nemuri just glances at her chest. "I've seen that before," he says.

He escapes, only to come to a barn strewn with bloody corpses. Inside, tied to the ceiling beams, is a naked, dead girl—the ropes making her body a cross. The sister again approaches him and this time he takes her beneath the human cross. Then all the corpses jump up. They were live men playing dead bodies. Nemuri soon makes them real corpses.

He battles to the castle where the villains have chained another halfbreed in the courtyard. He arrives to find that the young man's eyes have been gouged out. Behind him a muscleman gloats that he did the deed and will do the same to Nemuri. Without turning, the Full Moon swordsman swirls his unsheathed sword and calmly returns it to his scabbard. He has cut through the muscleman's eyes.

He braves the castle, filled with traps such as spears coming through walls, to finish off the brother. Outside, the sister stands between him and the now-burning castle. Given a choice between facing Nemuri and the flames, she chooses the latter. She runs into the fire, and Kyoshiro Nemuri walks away.

And would you believe that these movies were done with high style and surprising taste? It's true. Although beyond the comprehension of many Western eyes, the Nemuri movies were done with demure sophistication. There was no complete nudity (even the girl in the barn was cleverly covered by the camera angles) and very little blood on screen.

The Son of Black Mass movies stand on their own, without these defenses. At their heart, they promoted belief in oneself. They also soundly condemned the society that allowed such a tortured halfbreed as Kyoshiro Nemuri to exist. *The Human Tarantula* was Raizo Ichikawa's second-to-last Nemuri movie. After completing 1969's *Castle Menagerie*, he died of colon cancer. Two more Nemuri movies were made with Hiroki Matsukata, but he paled in comparison to the beloved Ichikawa.

But Ichikawa lived on in his movies, which included one of the most popular Ninja series. Filmmakers on both sides of the world don't exactly know what to do with Ninjas. They exist mostly in legend and their legends dictate that they could disappear and sometimes fly. They were the most insidious creatures since the vampire.

Writers like Tomoyoshi Murayama and Hajime Takaiwa chose to portray the characters far more realistically. The concept of a person with no place on earth and none in the afterlife was fascinating. What kind of moral torture must their lives have been? Combining this intriguing character motivation with classic chambara ingredients led to the popular *Band of Assassins* series—seven films over three years tracing the lives of three Ninja, all played by Raizo Ichikawa.

The story is a true one: In the mid-1500s, a powerful warlord named Nobunaga tried to eradicate certain sects of Buddhism that stood in his way to the shogunate. The Iga family of Ninjas were descended from these sects and fought back for their lives. They sought to assassinate the warlord while working for Nobunaga's enemy.

All seven films were downbeat in keeping with the Ninja legend. Even when the black-garbed killers won they seemed to lose. Part One chronicled their unsuccessful assassination attempts. Part Two ended with the Ninja hero (Ichikawa) being led to a boiling pot of oil. In reality, the Ninja died in that pot, but on screen he escaped to fail again.

In the third episode, in which Ichikawa plays another Ninja, he is assigned to kill his own sensei, whose daughter is in love with him. In the last four episodes, the third Ninja Ichikawa plays decides to reject his heritage and try to take sides—rather than go with anyone who pays him. But first he must fight all manner of enemies.

After Ichikawa died, several more Ninja adventures were filmed, the one immediately following starring Hiroki Matsukata (who seemed to be making a living playing Ichikawa's parts for awhile there). It was called *Mission: Iron Castle* (1970) and told of the Ninja's attempt to escape the title location after having been captured. One of the most memorable Ninja gimmicks here was to eat ten days' worth of unboiled rice to stay alive while digging a tunnel out in nine days.

BABY CART TO HELL

With the success of Zatoichi and the Son of Black Mass, martial art sword movies became livelier and livelier. Also with the dawn of the 1970s came an increased Japanese public consumption of comic books. But these weren't the kind of comic books English-speaking countries were accustomed to. These comics were as thick as telephone books and came out weekly in mass quantities. As of 1984, comics make up forty percent of the entire Japanese publishing industry.

These comics range from love stories through

Sue Shiomi is a stranger in a strange land. Lucky she knows karate, in Sister Streetfighter.

sports stories to samurai adventures. One of the most popular of the latter was the *Kozure Ogami* (Lone Wolf and Cub) series written by Kazuo Koike and drawn by Goseki Kojimba. The most popular Japanese comics are later bound into volumes, and the Ogami series was to fill twenty-eight of them. It is generally regarded as the standard for samurai comic stories.

It told of a disgraced shogun executioner of the early 1600s who takes his revenge on an evil clan by becoming a hired assassin. That, in itself, was not enough to distinguish the series. But in addition, this killer brings along his three-year-old son for the ride in a wooden, weapon-laden baby carriage. In 1972, Katsu Productions bought the rights for the film version. Shintaro Katsu hired Koike to write the screenplay, Kenji Misumi to direct, and his own brother, Tomisaburo Wakayama, to star. The *Sword of Vengeance* series was off and rolling.

The first film told of the "Lone Wolf's" creation. Itto Ogami, a rising samurai in the ranks of the Iemitsu Shogunate, was dueling with Gunbei Yagyu—one of the six Yagyu family sons—to see who would become official decapitator. When someone committed seppuku (the more respectable form of hara-kiri) the decapitator was to cut the head from the suicide's body as per ancient traditions.

Gunbei wins the match but Ogami is declared winner because he has maneuvered the Yagyu son into pointing his blade toward the shogun—an inexcusable offense. To satisfy the shogun, the Yagyu father must bring him the head of Gunbei. The cunning, corrupt father merely sends for his son's double (all his sons have doubles for this very purpose) and beheads him. Then he starts seriously planning to frame Ogami.

But first he must kill a lord who has become aware of the Yagyu family's treachery. He arranges another bout between Ogami and himself. Ogami uses his "Suioryu Zambatto style" (Sea Gull-Horse Slashing cut) while Yagyu uses a wooden staff. This time the villain manipulates Ogami so that the cut tip of his pole lances the suspicious lord, killing him.

Only then does the plan go into effect. Ninjas attack Ogami's home in order to plant a memorial tablet with the shogun's name on it in the Ogami family shrine. Any hint of disloyalty—even this extremely questionable sort—is seen as betrayal and punishable by death. And since the Yagyus are essentially the shogun's secret police, it'll be easy.

Ogami's wife discovers the Ninjas and is killed. When the trap is sprung the next day, the shogun is fooled and Ogami is told to commit seppuku. He cannot decide whether to loyally die or take vengeance, go "on the road to Hades," as he calls it. He leaves it up to his baby son by putting a ball to one side, and his sword on the other. If the boy touches the ball, he and his father will die. If he touches the sword . . .

The child reaches for the ball but touches the sword. The next day, in the official seppuku ritual, Ogami goes wild, killing everyone around him and taking his son away. The Yagyu father is waiting for him outside. He suggests a duel with Gunbei and places the adversaries so that his son's back is to the sun. The plan is to blind Ogami, but the tables are turned. The samurai places his son on his back, the child outfitted with a metal headband which reflects the light back at the superior swordsman.

Itto Ogami kills the real Gunbei Yagyu and the adventure truly begins. He builds the baby cart and places a sign on it reading "My arm is your arm." For five hundred gold pieces he'll take on any assassination job, secure in the knowledge that any problem that requires that much expense would be created by the Yagyus. The succeeding films in the series tell of the Lone Wolf and Son's assignments as well as duels with the remaining Yagyu family members.

The films so impressed Americans David Weisman and Robert Houston that they bought the rights for the first two, re-edited them together, rescored them, dubbed them, and released them as one 1980 feature, *Shogun Assassin.* Here the head of the Yagyu family has become the shogun who kills his official decapitator's wife as a test of loyalty. Itto Ogami fails but accepts a duel with the Shogun's son to attain freedom—with the reflective results described previously.

Enraged, the shogun sends all manner of Ninja after Ogami, who has taken an assignment to kill the shogun's brother. Ogami defeats all the Ninja and faces the brother's bodyguards, the Three Masters of Death. One Master uses a studded club, another a studded glove, and the third, a razor-sharp claw. Ogami throws his sword into the first (an unthinkable act for a samurai). He uses another sword to chop the second's head down the middle, and then opens the third's neck.

Weisman and Houston do an exceptional job scripting and dubbing the American voices—one of the best jobs ever—and the new musical soundtrack by Mark Lindsay and W. Michael Lewis is terrific. Unfortunately without the interconnecting pure Japanese sequences, *Shogun Assassin* becomes one gory scene after another. The original language versions have a sense of epic poetry about them missing from this otherwise effective work.

The Japanese version of the second *Sword of Vengeance* film, *Baby Cart At the River Styx*, is considerably different in plot, but not in picture, from *Shogun Assassin.* Ogami still faces the Three Masters, but they are bodyguards of a man who has enough evidence to abolish a clan the Yagyus want out of the way. The female supreme Ninja of *Shogun Assassin* is actually a Yagyu daughter in the original version. In both versions, Ogami seduces her by his honorable nature and she cannot bring herself to kill him.

And the violence is the same in both versions: excessive. The screen blood pours, spurts, and drools in the Baby Cart movies—so much so, in fact, that the films become . . . cartoonish. In his review of *Shogun Assassin,* Chicago critic Roger Ebert said, "No one bleeds like this unless they have garden hoses for veins." And he's right.

An unadulterated version of the third in the series, *Baby Cart to Hades* (1973), was dubbed and exported years before *Shogun Assassin.* It played in America under the suitable title *Lightning Swords of Death* (1974). This episode had some notable highlights, including the opening.

Ogami walks in a bamboo forest, then suddenly, inexplicably, swings his sword madly. He then replaces the sword and waits. Three bamboo trees suddenly collapse and three Ninjas fall from them. Whipping out his sword a second time he kills all three before they hit the ground. In an ensuing duel with another Yagyu son, he defeats that superior swordsman by leaping upside down over the man and hurling his blade into the top of the Yagyu's skull.

Finally he turns the corner with the cart to face a literal army of opponents. In an exhausting but beautifully sustained fight scene, he kills every single one of them.

Number four, *Baby Cart in Peril* (1972), had an

The grace of Bruce Lee... The speed of Sonny Chiba... The force of Chuck Norris...
Duke Sanada is
ROARING
FIRE
He's total destruction.
Starring SONNY CHIBA and Introducing DUKE SANADA with ABDULLAH THE BUTCHER, SUE SHIOMI and MICKEY NARITA
Executive Producer N.J. OKADA Screenplay by NORRY SUZUKI Action Sequences Directed by SONNY CHIBA Directed by NORRY SUZUKI
R RESTRICTED
UNDER 17 REQUIRES ACCOMPANYING PARENT OR ADULT GUARDIAN
From New Line Cinema
(C) MCMLXXXII

interesting premise. Ogami has been hired by a father to kill his own daughter. The woman, once a promising martial artist, was tricked by her sensei and raped. To take revenge she had an ornate tattoo placed on her chest. When she is losing a duel, she throws open her shirt and kills her opponent while he's distracted. Unfortunately her burning desire for vengeance is threatening the safety of her clan. It is either her death or everyone's death.

Ogami waits until she has exacted revenge before killing her. Then he again confronts the head of the Yagyus. In this battle the villain wounds Ogami, so he is too weak to kill the old man when he pushes his sword into the Yagyu father's *eye.* Following that bloody picture, Kenji Misumi took the writer's fifth script, *Baby Cart in the Land of Demons* and made it the best in the series, if not one of the greatest martial arts movies.

The fifth Lone Wolf film is special, not only because of the ample action, but because it is such a trenchant statement on the feudal era. The opening is riveting. Five men attack Ogami in five atmospheric locations. As each is mortally wounded, each admits it was a test of Ogami's skill, and each tells him a different part of his assignment.

One dies beneath a water fall. One dies in a river, a circle of blood growing wider around him as he sinks lower and lower. One dies at a campsite, his leg in the campfire. As he speaks, the flames eat away at him. Finally, Ogami gets the full story. A warlord has gone insane and has fallen in love with a prostitiute. He has locked his own son and heir up, then disguised the prostitute's daughter as a boy so she can be the heir. To save the clan, Ogami must kill the man, the woman, and the female child.

The finale is nothing short of magnificent. Ogami has entered the insane lord's lair to try and talk the old man out of his insanity before all is lost. As he speaks, surrounded by enemy samurai, his son and the prostitute's daughter are making faces at each other, happily playing as children. When Ogami finishes, all eyes turn to the little girl for a decision. "Kill them," she says brightly.

The following fight scene is impressionistic, experimental, and inventive—one of Misumi's best. After the last man has been mortally wounded, the dying samurai basically suggests that now that the guards had fulfilled their duty to defend their lord, Ogami should go and kill the senile maniac. The guards *themselves* had hired Ogami, and all had died doing their best—knowing the truth all along. That is why they were so intent on testing Ogami at the opening. They wanted to be sure he was good enough to kill them all!

The following movies couldn't live up to that classic. They were excessively violent and clever, but number five had said it all. They started resorting to the supernatural, with Ogami versus Yagyu zombies and Ogami versus Ninjas on skis. Finally the series followed Zatoichi to television where Kinnosuke Nakamura—one of the great veterans of chambara cinema—played the leading role.

However, now it can be told. Recently the final volume of the comic series was published in America and the fate of Lone Wolf and son became known. As the final book opens, the shogun has become aware of the Yagyus' duplicity. He sends an army out to find and kill them. Knowing the end is near, the Yagyu father throws all he has left at Ogami. Ogami slaughters the rest of the Yagyu family but suffers mightily in the process. He faces the Yagyu father, one of the most hated villains in Japanese comic and cinematic history, in a weakened condition.

As they square off, the shogun's army surrounds them. They watch in tears as the antagonists battle. The sword fight is brutal, but no one can get the upper hand. The Lone Wolf feigns death, but even that doesn't work. Finally, Itto Ogami expires from his wounds. Daigoro, his tiny son, picks up a blade that has fallen from the cart and charges. The Yagyu father, seeing the army around him, opens his arms to accept his fate. The child plunges the knife into the man's chest. The Yagyu father dies embracing the child.

ENTER THE STREETFIGHTER

"I want karate fighters, not karate dancers!"—Shinichi "Sonny" Chiba, *Champion of Death* (1978)

The eighties were not good years for the big-screen chambara stars. Zatoichi, Kyoshiro Nemuri, and Itto Ogami went on television. The sword-slashing genre all but died out in movies. They were just too expensive to make, there were no new stories, and the Japanese public seemed far more interested in such softcore pornography as *Red Rope Rape* (1981).

The era might very well have died with Kenji Misumi in 1975. But before he died he made a fitting final movie. It was *The Last Samurai,* a two-hour-and-twenty-minute story of the end of the warrior class. Hideki Takahashi, a tall, muscular actor, starred as the title character, who must fight battles, lose loves, and take revenge (by chopping

Hiroyuki "Henry" Sanada in action, leaping over the Roaring Fire.

the villain completely in two down the middle) before becoming a barber in the brave new world.

No one could make movies move along like Misumi. His final work was an involving, exciting action picture with strong characters and affecting performances. No one can make them quite like Hideo Gosha, either. In 1978 and 1979, he made two samurai thrillers, *Bandits vs. Samurai Squad* and *Hunters in the Dark*, both starring Tatsuya Nakadai—an actor many feel is even superior to Toshiro Mifune.

Gosha's work is highly emotional, with violence to match. While he doesn't always keep the action coming, when it does come it is often teeth-grindingly intense. In *Hunters*, an amnesiatic hero charges through a half-dozen rice paper walls before coming upon a group he means to kill. When he attacks, the first move chops an opponent's arm off at the elbow. The opponent's sword had stuck into the ceiling so for the rest of the scene the arm hangs down like some sort of perverse chandelier.

Later in the same film the amnesiac is attacked in his bath by a female Ninja whom he kills by slowly, agonizingly pushing a bamboo tube into her side. Finally, the Nakadai character must challenge the man who had caused all the suffering—a corrupt member of the shogun's staff. The two kill each other in a farm yard. The villain of the movie was played by a brooding, strong figure with thick eyebrows and dark eyes. He was Shinichi Chiba, the man who had been known as "The Streetfighter" for years.

For many, the mention of that name is like pulling fingernails across the blackboard. Many remember the movie in disgust for its excessive violence. Many remember it with distaste for the editing job that came after its initial American release. Many remember it with disdain for Chiba's lack of martial arts grace. Many remember it with pain for the jumping, confusing camerawork that filmed it.

No matter how it is recalled, the original *Streetfighter* (1975) was an unforgettable theatrical experience. It was the first film ever to receive an "X" rating for violence instead of sexual content. Although some reports made this first release appear to be an amazing success, history bears it out as a dismal failure. Most theaters wouldn't show it—relegating it to cinemas that usually showed sexual pornography. Those audiences certainly didn't have the stomach for it.

The original, unedited *Streetfighter* is now pretty much a legend. Shinichi Chiba is not. He was born in 1939 and entered the film business in 1961 after having won a Toei Studios "New Faces" contest. He gained his higher learning at the Japanese University of Physical Education under the training of Mas Oyama Koncho—the World Karate Grandmaster. Chiba studied gymnastics and kyokushinkai karate, respectively.

Kyokushinkai karate is a formal competition version that requires knock-downs for points. It is one of the harsher forms of an already harsh art. "Harsh" is a word that doesn't quite do Chiba's film work justice. He came to the attention of the Japanese masses with 1970's *Karate Kiba* (also known as *Bodyguard Kiba* and *The Bodyguard*). It set the tone for his future films. In it he plays a master of an unusual form of "ken-karate" who foils a skyjacking singlehandedly. When interviewed by the television press, he takes the opportunity to offer himself out as a paid bodyguard.

From there he runs afoul of complex plots and the Oriental underworld. He succeeds by being the toughest guy around and not being afraid to get physical. From there it was onto 1971's *Gambler Cop* movie series—an extension of the Japanese crime genre generally known as the "yakuza" film. That led naturally into the *Lone Wolf Gambler* series, in which he plays a cigar chomping assassin of yakuza gangsters.

Then came a long stream of lookalike movies and television shows. By the time he became known in this country, he had reportedly done over seventy-five features. The feature he became known for was originally called *Sudden Attack: The Killing Fist*. Here it was named *The Streetfighter*. Chiba, now deemed "Sonny," played Terry Surugy (also spelled Tsurugi), a man who survives in modern-day Japan by his wits and fists. He is a professional "jobber." For a price, he'll do anything.

That is not to say he is always successful. While rescuing a murderer named Jungo (Milton Ishibashi), he accidentally kills the man's brother. Surugy goes on to other work, but Jungo promises revenge. The other work is protecting an oil sheik's daughter from the Five Dragon Society headed by an Englishman named King Stone. He's not too good at that, either. She gets kidnapped, he gets captured, and his good friend Ratnose gets killed trying to save him.

Escaping from torture, Terry tracks the villains down, only to find Jungo waiting for him. He leaves him in a pool of blood and rips the Five Dragon Society apart. Summarized this way, the movie seems like just another thriller. But during the proceedings, a man had pushed a knife through his own sister in an attempt to kill Surugy. Surugy himself had torn a man's genitals off, torn out another man's adam's apple, and, in the nauseating climax, smashed a man's head open—a scene which was both shown in slow motion and in X-ray! At the climactic moment, the screen became an X-ray machine showing internal effects.

Anyone who saw this picture either loved it or hated it. But New Line Cinema, its American distributor, hated the box office returns. In a hurried negotiation with the rating board, they promised to do anything to get an "R" rating. The result, which is available on videotape, is just short of incomprehensible. The mid-seventies rating board demands required the elimination of all screen blood, not just some of it.

The result was confusion. Fight scenes started and then almost immediately ended without the audience seeing what had happened. The same was true of *Return of the Streetfighter* (1976). This never had a chance of being seen in its complete form. What remains intact is the Streetfighter's youth. A flashback scene shows his father being killed by a firing squad. Surugy is a halfbreed and becomes a renegade. About the only man he respects is karate master Masaoka (Masafumi Suzuki), a tiny, fat expert who fights Surugy to a standstill.

A new employer hires Surugy to kill the karate master, then attempts to kill the Streetfighter when he refuses. It is all because the villain is embezzling money from a fund to build an All-Asian Military Art Center. Surugy kills all the attackers except one. Jungo has returned, seemingly from the grave, to battle his enemy on a rain-soaked roof. The anti-hero falls off the building but is nursed to health by the love interest (Yoko Ichiji).

Although not fully recovered, he goes after the villain, cornering both him and Jungo on a ship. The final fight also occurs in the rain. Surugy is shot in the back. He does something which is edited out and the film ends with him standing and the villains dead, the ship deck awash in blood. What director Shigehiro Ozawa and writers Koji Takada and Steve Autry originally intended is clear enough, but the result is frustrating.

What remains is a potent performance by Chiba. Martial arts lovers were captivated by his screen persona, which was several notches more severe than Bruce Lee's. As Chiba played him, Terry Surugy was an animal, and not a tame one. Surugy's face would contort, incomprehensible cries, grunts, and groans would burble out of his mouth, and then he would try to tear something off. Surugy wasn't a graceful fighter. He went for the juguler every time. And if he couldn't get that, he'd shoot for a less polite target.

Someone that practical and unforgiving was attractive to jaded filmgoers. A certain *Streetfighter* fever occurred, leading to some ludicrous publicity. Sonny Chiba's official American biography had him sired by an unknown father. His mother was a dancer, and he was the leader of a street gang called the Kamikaze Lords. He learned kungfu on the streets, according to this public relations release, but after a motorcycle accident, became a serious student of karate. The one-page bio went on to say that because of the public adoration following *The Streetfighter's* release, Chiba became a Shinto monk living in the foothills of Mount Fuji.

Henry Sanada had to do more than karate in Roaring Fire. *He jumps off buildings and crashes cars as well.*

Chiba left the mountain retreat long enough to make *The Streetfighter's Last Revenge* (Japanese title: *The Streetfighter Counterattacks*—1977), by far the worst of the lot. This time the violence wasn't that bad, it was the story. The basic idea of a company creating synthetic heroin is workable, but the remainder of the picture was incomprehensible junk. His subsequent films weren't much better.

Champion of Death should have been a great film. It purported to tell the life story of Mas Oyama. It started well: Shambling into a 1940s karate tournament is an unkempt bum who surprises everyone with his karate expertise. But when it comes time for the final "no injuries" bout (against "Jungo" actor Milton Ishibashi), his opponent cheats by hitting him in the stomach and he retaliates by smashing the cheater in the eye.

From there the film goes right down the drain. After World War II, Oyama sees a beautiful girl with an American general. He rapes her and is arrested. In jail he's forced to fight another prisoner handcuffed. When he is released, he apologizes to the woman he raped and she becomes his girlfriend. Then one day a bull goes wild in the street (!) and Oyama saves a small child from a trampling by beating the rampaging bull to death.

When a student is killed defending Oyama's reputation, Oyama gets drunk and kills someone else. After his second imprisonment, he goes to the murdered man's farm and helps his wife and

His uncle shoots him in the arm, and Henry Sanada bumps the guy off the cliff at the end of Roaring Fire.

Although a protégé of Sonny Chiba, Henry Sanada's best film was Ninja in the Dragon's Den, *where he got to spar with Conan Lee (right).*

child until she says it's all right. Finally, the jealous karate man Oyama defeated at that first bout sends hired killers to get revenge. Oyama defeats them all, kills the villain, and stumbles away. The End.

Oyama should sue and Chiba should be ashamed. Of far more importance to the genre, Chiba created the Japanese Action Club, a combination martial arts school and stunt association. The members are stuntmen and instructors on Japanese films, and several of the students have contributed more to the genre than Chiba himself.

The first of these is Etsuko "Sue" Shiomi, who initially played the girl stabbed through by her brother in *The Streetfighter.* She went on to star in *Sister Streetfighter* (1978), playing a karate student searching for the murderer of her brother. Since her sibling was a narcotics agent, she stumbles across a drug ring. In tried-and-true Streetfighter tradition, she is at first beaten and thrown off a cliff. Coming back she attacks the villains' headquarters with the help of Ninja Sonny Hibaki (Chiba), who knows the secret of invisibility.

Coming soon after that was *Sonny Chiba's Dragon Princess* (1980), which starts like a Streetfighter film but ends like *Champion of Death.* Chiba plays Shiomi's father, a bitter karate teacher who was crippled and handicapped years before in a rigged fight. The prologue shows the Tokyo fight, which took place in an atmospheric barn.

After defeating his opponent fair and square, villainous henchmen stab him in the eye, hand, and chest. He survives and escapes with his infant daughter to New York, where he raises her on karate. On his deathbed he tells her to seek revenge. She goes back to Tokyo and teams up with a handsome young fighter played by Shoji Kurata. Together they eliminate the bad guys.

Although a person may be an accomplished fighter and a good actor or actress, parts like these can impede a career. The modern Japanese action film industry tried to do that with Chiba's second major protégé, but it just wouldn't stick. Hiroyuki "Henry" Sanada first starred in *Roaring Fire* (1981), a movie so dreadful it is fun to watch. Norry Suzuki wrote and directed the film, which billed Hiroyuki as Duke Sanada.

"Duke" is called to his father's deathbed to hear that he was kidnapped from his rightful family by the dying man. The false father tells him that his real parents and brother have been murdered by the Tokyo syndicate and he should take revenge. Duke returns to the Orient to discover that his uncle is the head of a drug ring. Now the bad guy wants the family jewels to pay off his supplier, but only blind Chihiro (Sue Shiomi), Duke's sister, knows where they are.

Both brother and sister are taken hostage and tortured by Orientals dressed as Nazis. Duke escapes but Chihiro is given an overdose. Teaming up with "Mister Magic" (Sonny Chiba), a ventriloquist/magician/cop, Duke corners the villains on a cliff and knocks his evil uncle off. *Roaring Fire* could kill a normal man's career, but Sanada's talents were too great.

In 1982, Chiba was finally convinced to do a period piece of his own. This was *Shogun's Ninja*, and while it has some of the laughable ingredients that sank the earlier productions, mostly it showcased Sanada's martial arts skill. Chiba played the villain this time, and Shiomi played Sanada's heroic partner. Everyone but the hero and his love interest dies by the fadeout.

Following quickly was Sanada's call to China to make *Ninja in the Dragon's Den*. Upon his return to Japan, he found a growing audience for his films. Plans were quickly made for Chiba himself to direct Sanada in subsequent movies. It is hoped that these films will be about something other than a cheated fighter taking revenge for a relative's death.

Meanwhile the Japanese movie industry becomes less and less interested in quality of any kind. Akira Kurosawa had to look to Francis Ford Coppola and George Lucas to get enough money to make his monumental *Kagemusha: The Shadow Warrior* (1980). Other notable directors must slave to get their budgets. Actors must work on television or in pornography to survive.

The Chinese and Japanese cinema started at opposite poles and moved in opposite directions. The Chinese started with junk and worked toward excellence. The Japanese started at excellence and are moving toward junk.

Bong Soo Han was brought to the public's attention by Tom Laughlin, and then made audiences laugh in the "A Fistful of Yen" segment of the Kentucky Fried Movie.

America: Noble Norris and Nasty Ninjas

The history of American martial arts movies is very simple. There was almost no "Before Bruce Lee." The history of America and how it relates to martial arts movies is also very simple. It is the history of the gun. American history is not one containing kungfu or karate or sword slashing. The United States' action legacy isn't excellence of self. It is excellence of *aim.* As long as you've got the barrel pointed at the right thing and you know how to pull the trigger, you win.

To be fair, America's history is far shorter than Japan's or China's. There may have been a time when explorers didn't have guns, but in their time the European settlers certainly did. And they used them—on animals, on Indians, and on each other.

In fact, there's been only one period American martial arts film, made by the man who may have started it all—Tom Laughlin. Born in 1938, Laughlin became an actor in the fifties and was featured in several major Hollywood productions, such as *Tea and Sympathy* (1956), *South Pacific* (1958), and the original *Gidget* (1959).

By 1960, he had had enough. He retired to run a school in Santa Monica while rethinking the film industry's standard operating procedures. When he returned to show business, he came on his own terms. Now he wrote, directed, starred, produced, and edited his own films. The first was *The Young Sinner* (1965), which co-starred Stephanie Powers and established Laughlin's main screen theme of misunderstood youth.

Two years after that, he hit a mother lode. He produced, directed, wrote, and starred in *The Born Losers,* which introduced a halfbreed wanderer named Billy Jack. This film established the rest of Laughlin's approach. The Billy Jack character always attempts to do good but is fought against on all sides. When a motorcycle gang attacks a young man, Billy fights them off and is then arrested for assault. This scenario was all too plausible in the late sixties and fueled an audience's frustration.

The Born Losers made more than ten million dollars and gave Laughlin the inspiration for what was to be his most important work. *Billy Jack* took him four years to produce and distribute himself, outside the major studios' distribution stranglehold. Knowingly or not, he had timed it perfectly. The story of a halfbreed ex-Green Beret who fights redneck sheriffs persecuting a Freedom School for hippie runaways (located on an Indian reservation yet) attracted the polarized moviegoing youth.

The frosting on the cake was the fact that Billy Jack used karate to do it. The movie was an obvious, superficial, but heartfelt and well-meaning, work. Seen today it is almost funny, but at the time the sight of guffawing punk rednecks pouring flour and ice cream over redskins was the perfect excuse for Billy Jack to kick the rednecks' faces in. To top it off, Laughlin was a good actor. Not only could audiences be on the character's side, they could obviously see that the whole production was a labor of love.

Billy Jack cost eight hundred thousand dollars to make. It brought in over eighteen million. Laughlin now had the luxury of making almost any movie he wanted, as well as dropping the pseudonym T.C. Frank, which he had used for directing. *The Trial of Billy Jack* appeared in 1974, three years after the original. This was Laughlin's magnum opus, running almost three hours. The character had returned to the reservation after his prison term, but he didn't come alone.

Tom Laughlin kicks the stuffings out of rednecks in The Trial of Billy Jack.

He brought Bong Soo Han, a real-life hapkido expert, with him. Han supposedly doubled for Laughlin in the original *Billy Jack* and the auteur was paying him back with an on-screen role. While all the ingredients were doubled in this sequel, the reviews were universally awful. Even so, *The Trial of Billy Jack* made over twenty-eight million dollars. Tom Laughlin had it made, but was coming apart at the seams. He opened a new production building and announced plans for expansion into almost every area of the entertainment industry.

Then he fell into the danger-fraught trap of remakes. His next film was very well intended. It was an American western retelling of the 1969 Hideo Gosha Japanese chambara film *Goyokin,* which had starred Tatsuya Nakadai. *The Master Gunfighter* was two hours long, directed by the star's son, Frank Laughlin, and featured Tom as a California avenger complete with six-shooter and samurai sword. The material which had meshed so well for Billy Jack didn't transpose to the 1800s. The new movie was a box office failure.

Another Billy Jack movie was called for to recoup the losses. Unfortunately, Laughlin made *Billy Jack Goes to Washington,* an updated version

of director Frank Capra's classic *Mr. Smith Goes to Washington* (1939), which starred James Stewart. Remakes in and of themselves are questionable enough, but remakes of wonderful movies give the updated version no room to improve. And in the intervening years between 1971's *Billy Jack* and his 1977 sojourn to the nation's capital, attitudes had changed.

Finally the film business is a complicated one, filled with nooks and crannies into which money just seems to disappear. Laughlin ultimately fell victim to the creative bookkeeping that keeps a movie out of the profit column no matter what. With his company on the line, he was forced to make deals he hated; deals that seemed opposed to what his Billy Jack films promoted. Audiences went elsewhere for their action.

They went to the dozens of dubbed Chinese and Japanese movies which flooded the country after Bruce Lee's success. There were reams of movies with the words "Black Belt" or "Black" or "Chinese" or "Kung Fu" in their titles. It was the golden era of martial arts exploitation films, with the bad pictures outnumbering the good seven to one.

Fred Weintraub, the producer who brought Bruce Lee to this country, made several inferior works directed by Robert Clouse and starring Jim Kelly. They were all variations on the established Chinese formulas. In *Black Belt Jones*, Jim Kelly fights the mob for the freedom of a martial arts school in the heart of Watts, for heavens' sake. Then, in *Hot Potato* (1976), a Weintraub-produced Warner Brothers film directed by Oscar Williams, Kelly plays one of three mercenaries rescuing a senator's daughter from an Oriental general in Thailand.

Weintraub tried some more. *Golden Needles* (1974—directed by Robert Clouse) was a curious thriller, a combination of *Enter the Dragon* and *The Maltese Falcon.* Joe Don Baker, a brutish actor, starred as a hunter for a mythical Oriental statue which promised to give eternal youth . . . or painful death. Then there was the Clouse-directed *Ultimate Warrior* (1975), a science-fiction

Tom Laughlin uses a samurai sword in the California sands, circa 1850, in The Master Gunfighter.

post-World War Three adventure with Yul Brynner as a mysterious master killer.

Finally, the producer went on to other things. He made Steve McQueen's next to last movie, *Tom Horn* (1980), and a romantic tearjerker called *The Promise* (1979), before rediscovering the joys of kungfu from Jackie Chan. Warner Brothers, the studio that distributed Weintraub's work, has to be given credit, however. They certainly gave the martial arts their best shot.

In addition to *Enter the Dragon* and the others mentioned, Warners spent millions on *The Yakuza* (1975), paying first-time screenwriter Paul Schrader a then unheard of three hundred thousand dollars and letting Sydney Pollack (*They Shoot Horses Don't They*—1968; *Jerimiah Johnson*—1969; *The Way We Were*—1973; and *Three Days of the Condor*—1975) direct and produce.

Robert Mitchum and famed "yakuza genre" actor Ken Takakura co-starred in the violent modern-day drama of the Japanese underworld. Mitchum had the guns and Takakura had the swords as the duo fought to get an ultimately treacherous Brian Keith out of trouble. This was an exciting, well-made picture which could only attract a cult audience. But that cult saw some of the best American-made swordplay ever done.

About the only place American audiences can see better (outside revival cinemas, film festivals, art houses or videotapes) is in *The Empire Strikes Back* (1980), the best science-fiction samurai movie. In this, the second episode of the initial *Star Wars* trilogy, the "light-sabres" of the Jedi Knights are essentially futuristic samurai swords, and the climactic fight between Darth Vader, the Dark Lord of the Sith, and Luke Skywalker, his own son, is the most accurate translation of Chinese- and Japanese-influenced thrills around.

Many directors have been captivated by chambara movies and have done their best to transpose the excitement to these shores. Director John Frankenheimer and writers Richard Maxwell and

Jim Kelly smashes his way through Black Belt Jones.

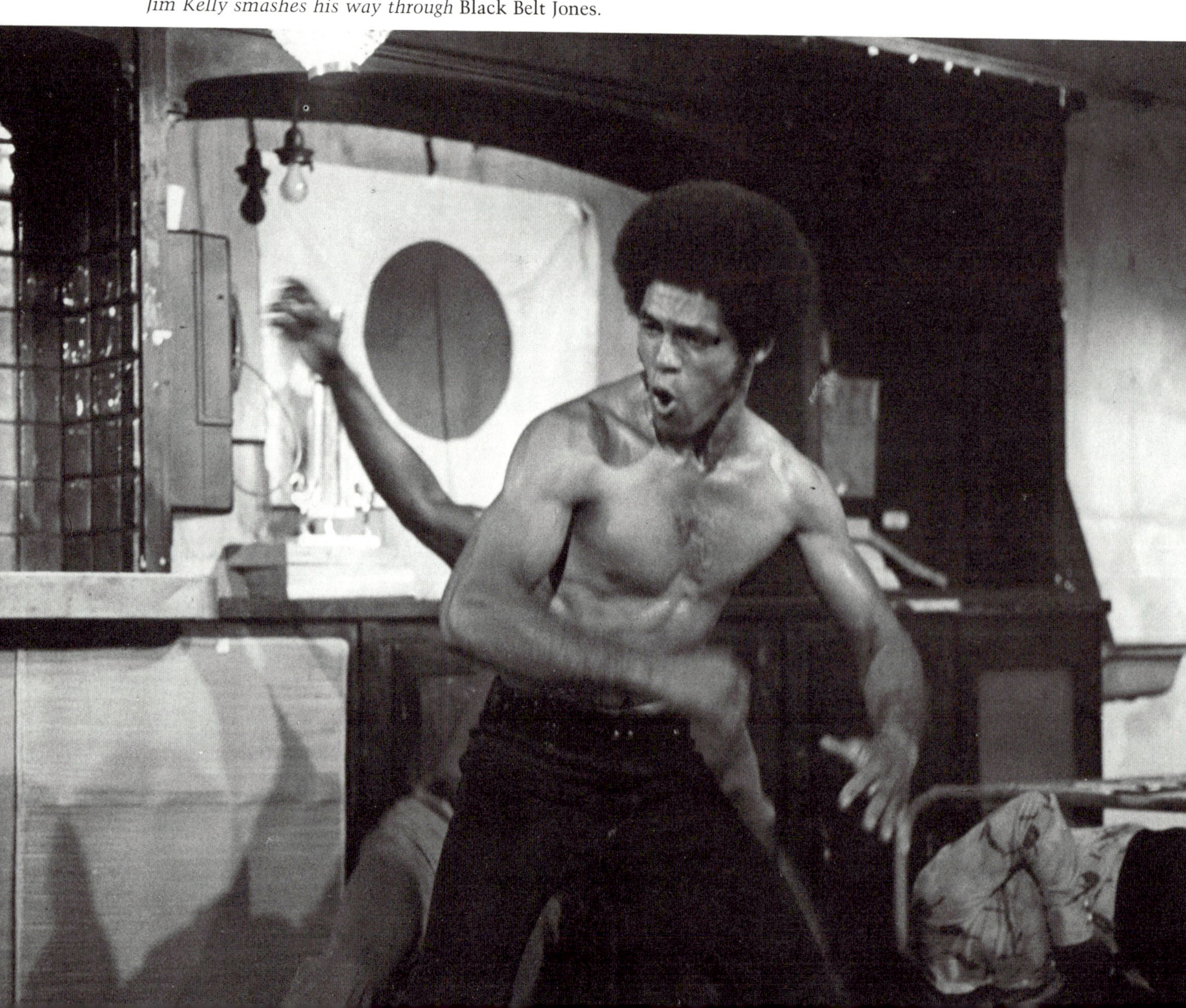

John Sayles tried with *The Challenge* (1982). But what they did was what has essentially been wrong with every American attempt. They clashed ancient Japanese traditions with modern Western weapons in a head-on confrontation.

Scott Glenn starred as a modern-day boxer who stumbles into a centuries-old conflict. So far, so good. He winds up helping an old man (Toshiro Mifune) try to reunite two ancient swords called "The Equals." Even better. But then it is revealed that the fight is between two brothers, one corrupt, one wonderful. The evil one stole one sword and killed his father to do it. Then he grows up to be a yakuza gangster. The good brother meanwhile has cloistered himself in a medieval monastery to train warriors to retrieve the sword.

This picture wouldn't even work as an inexpensive exploitation movie, let alone a big-budget, major studio release. The last nail in its coffin is that the martial arts are mediocre.

After *The Challenge,* the martial arts genre was left to the schlock artists. It seems that they were the best equipped to handle it. Two of the most prolific and influential American kungfu moviemakers are Serafim Karalexis and Harry Hope.

The former mostly distributes films like *Enter Three Dragons* and *The Real Bruce Lee.* His most important contribution was the distribution of Jackie Chan's *Eagle's Shadow.* The latter actually produces films like *Death Dimension,* starring "Myron Bruce Lee," and *Enter Another Dragon,* starring Bruce Le. Both men have been responsible for hundreds of variations on the action theme, and little things like coherent stories and character development don't sell tickets for them. They are in the interesting position of keeping the American kungfu film genre alive and killing it at the same time.

After the first wave of martial arts film mania subsided, everyone figured that the key to success was finding "the next Bruce Lee." They had tried all the fake Bruce Lees and the other stars of *Enter the Dragon,* and they hadn't worked. So the search began. In the case of *Firecracker* (1982), it led to a woman. Jillian Kesner was the girl who was thrust into a Philippine-filmed search for her missing sister. Who just so happened to be investigating martial arts bouts in Manila.

Jim Kelly went from America to China to battle Bolo in The Tattoo Connection.

While Kesner's karate style wasn't entirely convincing, her form was and the filmmakers took every opportunity to reveal it. Suddenly the villains' blades had an unerring ability to cut through women's underwear without breaking the skin. Kesner seemed to fight out of clothes more than in. The climax of the piece showed Kesner plunging arnis sticks through the villain's eyes.

The search went on to South Africa and a wiry young actor named James Ryan. In two laughable martial arts movies, *Kill or Be Killed* (1980) and *Kill and Kill Again* (1981), he joined up with a karate class to make what amounted to theatrical home movies. In the first, Ryan's character, Steve Chase, foils a modern-day Nazi's plan to unleash kungfu fighters on the world, and in the second, he foils a mad scientist's plan to unleash kungfu zombies on the world. Or was it the other way around?

It hardly makes any difference. Both Kesner and Ryan were personable performers, but neither had extensive martial arts experience, and it showed. Filmmakers continued looking for that perfect combination of actor and fighter. They tried Ed Parker, the famous karate instructor and tournament organizer, in *Kill the Golden Goose* (1981) and *The Revenge of the Pink Panther* (1978). Curiously he played a villain in both films. In the former his adversary was *Trial of Billy Jack* co-star Bong Soo Han.

Han was a good barometer of how the martial arts movie was doing in this country. After the Billy Jack debacle, he played "Mr. Han" in the "A Fistful of Yen" segment of *Kentucky Fried Movie* (1977). Made by the men responsible for *Animal House* (1978) and *Airplane* (1980), this was a rather vicious (and accurate) parody of *Enter the Dragon*, starring Evan Kim in the Bruce Lee part. Han then went on to replay the role seriously in *Force: Five* (1981), the last Fred Wientraub/Robert Clouse production to date.

After *The Big Brawl*, Weintraub thought the time might be right for yet another *Enter the Dragon* distillation. So saying, he sought out Joe Lewis, the first professional Heavyweight World Karate Champion, to star. Lewis had starred in one previous film, 1979's *Jaguar Lives*, which was supposed to be the first in a series featuring the karate hero. That one didn't work at all, so Lewis was hoping for the best on *Force: Five*.

Only Weintraub wasn't taking any chances this time. Not content to put the weight of the story

Tan Tao Liang shows off one of his trademark kicks in The Tattoo Connection.

Americans, for the most part, make pathetic martial arts movies, like this one.

on one man or even three, he rounded up four more martial artists and one love interest. The girl was Pam Huntington. The guys were Sonny Barnes, Benny Urguidez, Richard Norton, and Ron Hayden. The villain was Bong Soo Han, playing "Reverend Rhee," the sinister head of a worldwide "church." Naturally the bad guy lives on an island, and there are all sorts of guards to be chopped, slugged, and kicked out of the way before our hero corners the villain in his "Maze of Death."

Force: Five gave most audiences a severe case of *déjà vu.* It was an exercise in redundancy. But even this did not slow Fred Weintraub down. In the past few years he produced *High Road to China* (1982) and is intent on doing an American production of *Zatoichi.* He is certain that the blind swordsman will be the next "big thing."

Pam Huntington, the love interest, went on to become the love interest in *They Call Me Bruce,* which was at least meant to be a comedy. Korean comedian Johnny Yune starred in the slapdash satire, originally titled *A Fistful of Chopsticks.* Although supposedly lampooning kungfu movies, it actually was an extension of the *Get Smart* television show in that Yune played a bumbler who was so naïve that he appeared retarded.

The genre had started high only to sink very low. *They Call Me Bruce* was a pathetic indicator of just how low. It didn't work as a comedy or as a kungfu film. American martial arts movies needed something if they were going to survive. American martial arts movies needed an innovator. What they got instead was a focus. Its name was Chuck Norris.

The "blaxploitation" sub-genre of the seventies led to such mutations as the kungfu blaxploitation movie that this film represents.

The idea here seemed to be "the more the merrier." However "12 Hands . . . 12 Feet" aren't "Reasons to Die." They are "Ways to Die." So much for truth in advertising.

NICE GUYS KICK FAST

After Bruce Lee died, every kungfu film wanted a piece of him. Some used clones who had similar names. Others used Lee's co-stars. Chuck Norris had worked with Lee in *The Wrecking Crew* and, of course, the climatic duel in *Way/Return of the Dragon.* As a result, Lo Wei, the prolific Chinese filmmaker, cast him as the villain in *Yellow Faced Tiger* (U.S.: *Slaughter in San Francisco*—1973). Although the movie was terrible, it was one of Norris's better acting jobs. As a heinous mob boss in San Francisco, he gets to beat, rob, rape, and laugh.

The laughing was important. It is not easy to laugh for the camera, but Norris did it well. He also played the Chinese concept of a corrupt Caucasian well. Corrupt Caucasians always laugh when something bad happens. The bad guy constantly laughing is a cliché and the mark of a pedestrian movie. It is part of a deadening formula that Norris still has not shaken.

After that experience, Norris returned to teaching at his karate schools. He had started learning martial arts seventeen years before and had become a world champion in 1968 and held the title for six years. In 1975 he decided to become a movie star. That is the sort of person Chuck Norris is. Once he decides something, he puts all his considerable strength and will power to work toward that goal. It is a tribute to his strength that he has come this far.

In 1977, he got his next break. He played J.D. Dawes, an independant trucker fighting all comers in *Breaker Breaker.* After two villainous roles, he started establishing his good guy persona. His voice was high and thin, so he didn't talk much. His acting skills were far from honed, so he didn't react much. What he did was kick. His spinning back kick was one of the best in the game. In this movie, as in its successors, many stuntmen wait around on screen just to get his boot in their faces.

Breaker Breaker was a mediocre melodrama. It

Ken Takakura finishes off The Yakuza, *as Robert Mitchum slumps exhausted behind him.*

wasn't until *Good Guys Wear Black* (1978) that he came to major attention. Mar Vista Releasing got behind this picture, which was specifically tailored to Norris's talents by writers Joseph Fraley, Bruce Cohn and Mark Medoff. To put him through his paces, they got director Ted Post, who had garnered a good reputation from helming such Clint Eastwood movies as *Hang 'Em High* (1968) and *Magnum Force* (1973).

This introduces another continuing crack in Norris's armor. The goal he seemed to set for himself was *becoming* Clint Eastwood. Although he is often quoted that his desire is to become a star of Eastwood's magnitude, his parts seem like Eastwood hand-me-downs. In *Good Guys Wear Black,* he played John T. Booker, the leader of the Black Tiger unit in Vietnam. They are so good at their jobs that the Vietnamese require the extermination of the soldiers as part of the peace treaty negotiations.

Ed Parker tries to tear a guy's head off during Kill the Golden Goose. *And he's just the guy to do it, too.*

Although highly unlikely, the premise still had a grotesque workability. James Franciscus played an oily Undersecretary of State who agrees to the mass assassinations. In an exciting opening sequence, Booker leads his men to a supposed prisoner of war camp where the Cong are waiting. A half dozen Black Tigers die in the ambush but the hard-as-nails Booker leads the survivors out of the jungle.

Years later, after Booker has become an associate professor of political science—a role that fits Norris like a sleeping bag—the paranoid Franciscus tries to kill all the survivors so no one will ever uncover his treachery. At this point the movie unravels. Booker races from one survivor to the next, each one dying practically right under his nose. Why the assassin doesn't take the ample opportunity to kill Booker at the same time is never explained or understood.

There's a lot of gratuitous action in the film, but that's not the only thing that made it successful. Combining with a great title was a great advertising campaign based on two images. One

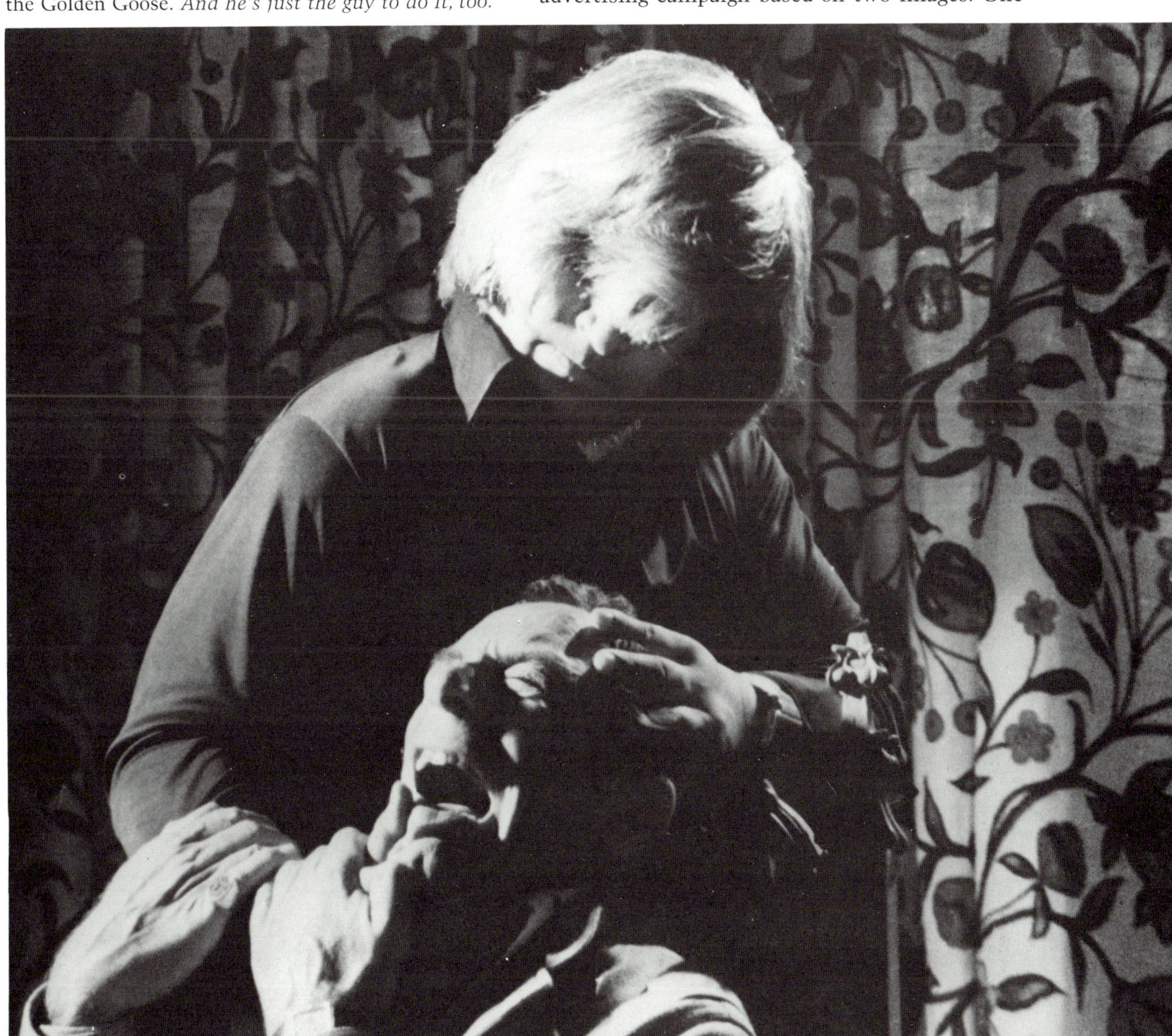

is of Norris dressed in a black pilot's jumpsuit standing before his Black Tigers beneath a helicopter. The other, more telling, is of Norris leaping through the windshield of a car.

To kill an Oriental assassin who is escaping by driving away, Norris delivers a flying kick through the car's windshield. In that moment, *Good Guys Wear Black* succeeded. No one forgot that stunt. Except, perhaps, the directors and writers of Norris's following films. The "one incredible stunt a film" concept should have been the core of the formula which *Good Guys* created. Instead, the next feature, *A Force of One* (1979), relied on the tried and true environment of a martial arts competition as its background.

The rest of the formula remained in place. The police are trying to eliminate a drug ring that a karate contestant is part of. Norris's young friend discovers the truth and is killed. A beautiful policewoman falls for Norris's character while he takes revenge. The thing director Paul Aaron apparently wanted to promote as the "big stunt" was Norris smashing of a box full of drugs in midair. It hardly replaced the windshield stunt.

Once again, good promotion made up for any deficiencies the pedestrian picture had. Although not as exciting as his previous film, *A Force of One* was superior to anything else that could be termed an American martial arts movie. Obviously, Chuck Norris cared about the kind of movie he made. Still, he wanted and needed a breakthrough film. A film that would bring him to the attention of the major studios.

That film was *The Octagon* (1981). Paul Aaron and Leigh Chapman conceived the story, while Eric Karson directed. It was Norris's quintessential role. Scott James, a nearly somnambulistic fighter, resists taking on a Ninja training camp although people are dropping like flies all around him. James had been raised by a great Japanese sensei who taught him and his adopted brother the art of Ninjutsu. When James proved superior to Seikura, the brother, it warped the brother's mind.

Seikura was played by Tadashi Yamashita,

James Ryan, the star of two feeble South African martial arts movies, Kill or Be Killed *and* Kill and Kill Again.

Jillian Kesner, who had a good face, a great body, and decent enough martial arts skills to star in the softcore kungfu movie Firecracker.

whose other main claim to fame was starring as *Bronson Lee, Champion* (1978), an unintentional comedy brought to you by the same folks who brought you *The Streetfighter.* Lee Van Cleef played a mercenary, also out to nail the Ninjas, while Carol Bagdasarian played a Ninja turncoat who helps Norris mop up the boys in black.

The story was far-fetched fun, as was the presentation. Almost everything was predictable here, but that was almost a relief. An audience could feel secure, since they always knew what was about to happen. And Norris managed to maintain a certain tension simply because his character continually refused to do anything. Although a hero, Scott James was responsible for several people's deaths because he had to be pushed beyond understanding before he'd fight back.

The final battle—an assault on the Ninja camp—is a good one, reminiscent of the opening attack in *Good Guys Wear Black,* but most of the stuntmen wait around to be kicked by Norris again. They just seem to stand there, like practice dummies. That didn't deter filmgoers, however, and *The Octagon* became Norris's best-looking and most successful film.

After that he reportedly wanted to do *The Destroyer.* The Destroyer is Remo Williams, hero of a long-running series of best-selling paperback books written by Richard Sapir and Warren Murphy. These novels are special for many reasons. First, they are satires; they poke accurate fun at everything from government to the martial arts. Second, the character chemistry is unique. Remo

It's Bill "Superfoot" Wallace as the villain versus Chuck Norris (left) in A Force of One.

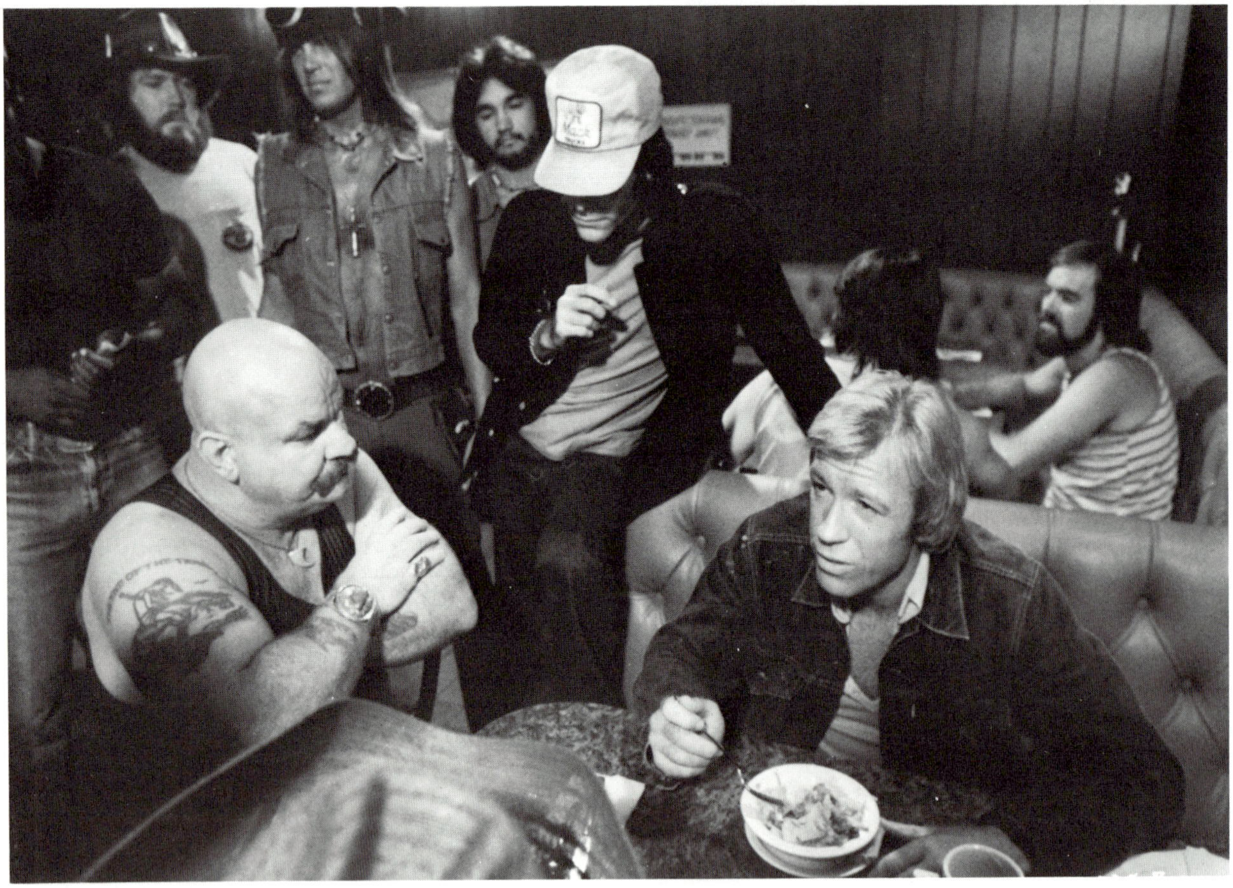

Chuck Norris (right) starts his solo star career in Breaker Breaker.

The great images of Good Guys Wear Black. *First there was this picture of Chuck Norris leading his "Black Tigers" into battle.*

The single best moment of Good Guys Wear Black. *Chuck Norris leaps through a car's windshield.*

Chuck Norris has the sword and Tadashi Yamashita has the "sais," in The Octagon.

is an ex-cop recruited by a secret organization (of one) to become the world's greatest assassin.

To help him accomplish that goal is a ninety-pound, one-hundred-year-old man named Chiun. Chiun is the master of "Sinanju," the sun source from which all the other martial arts eminate. Remo is an "everyman" and Chiun is, essentially, a Jewish mother who henpecks the now-amazing murderer. There are over sixty *Destroyer* novels at this writing, and over twenty million in print—with more to come.

However, Murphy and Sapir weren't selling to Norris. *An Eye for an Eye,* released by Avco Embassy, was made in 1981. Chuck Norris had accomplished that much, at least. He had stepped up to a more powerful distributor. The writers this time were William Gray and James Bruner, who seemed to take a page from *The Destroyer* and several pages from Norris's previous films to create another drug ring scenario.

Norris is "Sean," and Oriental actor Mako is "Chan." Together they take vengeance for the death of Sean's policewoman girlfriend at the hands of an Oriental giant. Norris's brother Aaron choreographed the fights which are in ample supply, but the *déjà vu* factor was back at work. How many times could an audience watch Norris do the same thing in essentially the same movie?

Clint Eastwood has a system. He makes whatever films he wants, usually acting and directing, until two in a row fail. Then he will make a film featuring a famous character, like Dirty Harry, or a western. The only reason *Sudden Impact* (1983) was made was because *Firefox* (1982) and *Honkytonk Man* (1938) didn't do as well as hoped. But when Eastwood does the films he wants, he always takes chances. Norris seemed to be making movies for his public, not himself.

Norris's following film was the worst. It was a perfect example of the kind of thinking that has hurt his upward climb. To make matters worse, it was his first major studio release. Columbia Pictures distributed *Silent Rage* (1982). The opening is very effective. A man named John Kirby goes slowly insane and starts hacking apart his rooming house neighbors with an ax. The sheriff, Dan Stevens (Norris), is called in and the film goes right down the tube.

Norris is his usual placid, stone-faced self while Kirby (Brian Libby) is a scenery chewing freak. In the ensuing fight and chase, the killer is gunned down. When he is brought to the morgue, some scientists decide for no other reason than to move the plot along that he is the perfect guinea pig for their regeneration serum. They bring him back to life with the elixer, and he goes hopping off to murder more innocents.

Here the film becomes two movies. One in which the sheriff goes around minding his own business, and another in which Kirby kills people in gruesome and gratuitous ways. Just to keep martial arts fans watching, Norris takes out a motorcyle gang in a barroom in a nicely edited scene.

Finally the two films come back together with the Kirby/sheriff fight. By then the filmmakers have made clear that the murderer can't be killed. Just to end the exploitive effort, Norris knocks Kirby down a well. The film ends in a freeze frame of the killer struggling in the water. Presumably the character will be unable to climb out and will starve to death.

It is this sort of uninvolved attitude in An Eye for an Eye *that has held Chuck Norris back from superstardom.*

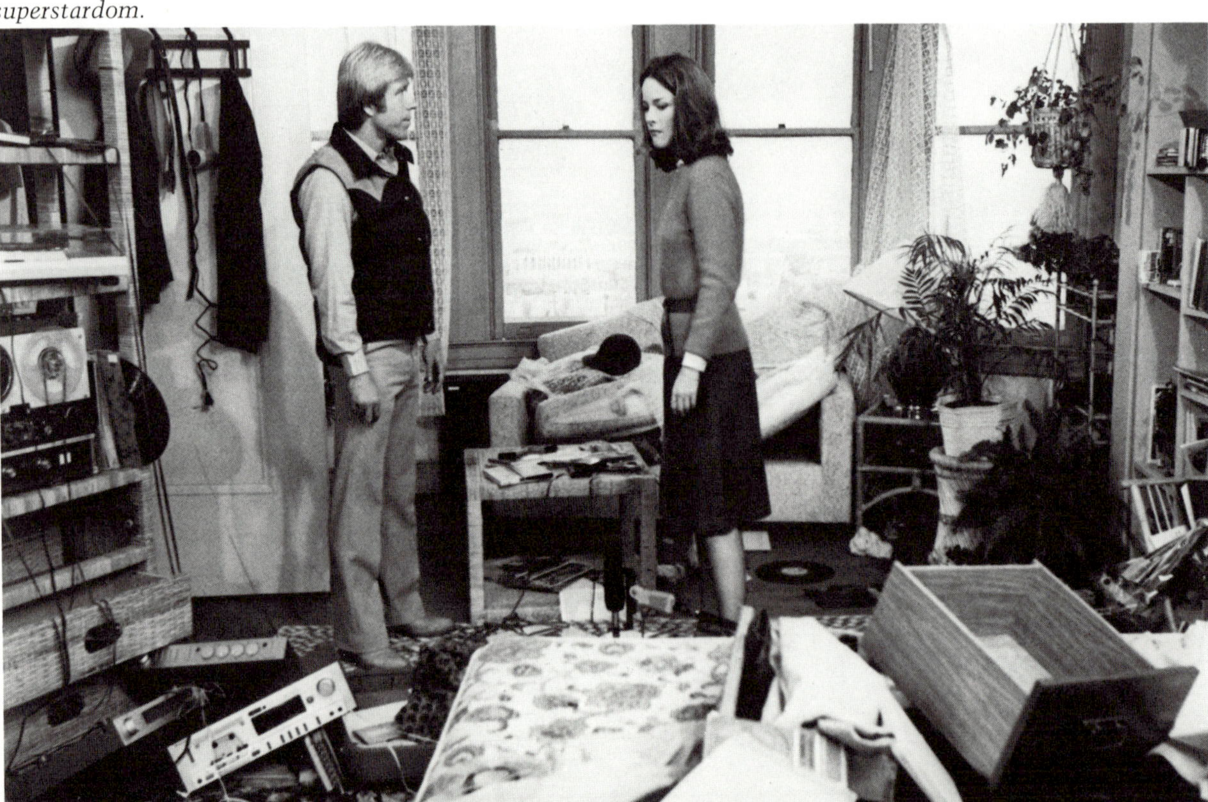

Words cannot suitably describe the pandering nature of this work. It is an insult to the audience, even to those who enjoy the "mad slasher" movies typified by *Halloween* (1978). It is as if some smug executives sat down to conceive the most derivative catch-all action film possible. It tries to cater to all and winds up catering to none. The only interesting aspect was that Norris was playing a live man like a zombie and Libby was playing a zombie like a live man.

There seemed to be little future for Norris at Columbia after that. His next film was released by MGM/UA Entertainment—still a major studio. Franklin Thompson wrote what was originally called *The Jade Jungle,* but when it was released in 1983 it was titled *Forced Vengeance.* James Fargo, a director who had worked up from the ranks on Clint Eastwood's crew, was at the helm here. Norris was wise enough to see the error of *Silent Rage.* It was back to human fights for him.

Forced Vengeance was essentially a recap of most of modern martial art movie themes. Norris plays a Vietnam vet who goes berserk in a Hong Kong casino. He's nursed back to mental health by the kindly casino owner. Enter the underworld, who want to take over the gambling den. They kill the owner and his son. Norris protects the daughter and his own beautiful girlfriend. To succeed, he must defeat a lot of henchman, a hulking bodyguard, and attack the villains' headquarters.

This picture also did badly at the box office. The question Norris had to ask himself was why fight scenes become boring. They get dull if the choreography isn't brilliant, or if the hero *has failed to create an engaging, believable character.* Throughout his career, Norris has seemed like an actor, not the character he is playing. The movies are constructed around him and he works his way through them—never giving an audience a chance to become involved.

Things are said about his character, but he never shows them in any action other than a kick or punch. His characters are given histories and motivations, but Chuck Norris never seems to be living them. He always seems to be trying to get through until the next fight.

When Gary Cooper, John Wayne, Clint Eastwood, or any of the strong, silent types Norris professes to admire, don't speak, an audience can see what they're thinking through their expressions or screen energy. Norris doesn't seem to have any screen energy. The only reason he isn't speaking, it appears, is that he is unsure how to deliver his lines.

It is painful to consider such things about the performer. He is an honorable man who is always trying to improve—characteristics to be admired. What is difficult to admire is his pedestrian, formula films. Only by breaking formulas and trying new ways of doing old things can a genre or an actor progress. To his credit, Norris tried again with his 1984 movie.

Lone Wolf McQuade should have been a great film. It could have been, if only clichés weren't standing in for realism. Norris plays J.J. McQuade, a legendary Texas Ranger who must fight a gunrunner who has injured his daughter and killed her boyfriend. There is abundant action and the leading role, based on real life Texas Ranger Lone Wolf Gonzales, required more from Norris than ever before.

It is just unfortunate that *Lone Wolf McQuade*

Mako (left) looks tired and Chuck Norris looks pained in An Eye for an Eye.

Chuck Norris has a problem. He seems to want to be Clint Eastwood. First there already is a Clint Eastwood—the public doesn't need another. Second, Chuck Norris's personality is not Eastwood's. Norris has to fake it—something he is not good at. Nowhere is this problem more apparent than in Lone Wolf McQuade.

"David Carradine is about as good a martial artist as I am an actor," Chuck Norris was quoted as saying. Sadly, they were evenly matched in Lone Wolf McQuade.

Tadashi Yamashita hits them where they live in Bronson Lee, Champion.

was an amalgamation of almost everything Clint Eastwood has ever done. The hero is a combination Dirty Harry and Man With No Name. The plot is a combination of the same two characters' stories. Even the soundtrack music is reminiscent of Sergio Leone's westerns' scores. The action film audience is limited, and they have seen all of Eastwood's movies. To presume that they wouldn't notice that the entire movie was a copy of an Eastwood film was a big mistake.

To make matters worse, it was not a good copy. It looked good, but the story was filled with big coincidences and all too obvious set-ups. Action happened just to move the plot along, not because it made any particular sense. And without common sense and characters the audience could believe in, no amount of action, no matter how competent, would suffice.

Lone Wolf McQuade's failure is unfortunate on another level. It featured David Carradine as the villain. Carradine played Bruce Lee's role in the *Kung Fu* television series, as well as in *The Silent Flute* (1974)—another project Bruce Lee was hoping to do before he died. Carradine wasn't convincing as the karate expert here because his skills aren't very good.

Norris has been quoted as saying that Carradine is about as good a martial artist as he (Norris) is an actor. While that is a very brave thing to say, and can be admired, it still doesn't say much for either man.

Joe Lewis (right) plays Jerry Martin, the head of Force: Five.

THE NINJA MASTERS

Bruce Lee was dead. Ed Parker, Joe Lewis, and Chuck Norris had all gone into the film business, but none had affected the industry the way Lee had. Mike Stone, the only undefeated karate champion, decided it was time to see what he could do. What he did was write a script entitled *Dance of Death.* He got it into the hands of Israel-born producer Menachem Golan. Golan promised to make the film with Stone as star. The entire crew was collected and sent to the Philippines to start work. Within three weeks everything changed.

"Not only was I fired," Stone recalls. "Everyone was fired. The producer, the director, the entire American crew with the exception of the sound man. Golan brought in a completely new crew from Israel. He brought in this other actor, Franco Nero, then rehired me for more money to stay as the stunt chorographer and double."

That was the birth of the movie *Enter the Ninja* (1982). Why it happened that way is still a mystery. "Apparently it's just the way they are with people," Stone now says of the producer, Yoram Globus, and the director, Menachem Golan. "That's just the way they deal with people. From what I hear that's just their standard operating procedure."

Benny Urguidez shows off his high-flying style in Force: Five.

Sonny Barnes plays Lockjaw, a silent giant, number three in Force: Five.

Richard Norton gets his kicks in Force: Five.

Franco Nero doesn't look at all happy replacing Mike Stone as the star of Enter the Ninja.

Mike Stone shows some fancy arm work, which made him the only undefeated karate champion in history. He went on to write, choreograph, and double the white Ninja in Enter the Ninja.

This Ninja movie, however, was not your standard kungfu film. The Ninja had been introduced to American audiences by James Bond. Sean Connery played 007 for what he promised would be the last time in 1967's *You Only Live Twice.* Bond stays at a Ninjutsu training camp for a time, and the memorable climax had an army of Ninjas attack a volcano stronghold with bombs, machine guns, and samurai swords.

Since that year, however, the Ninja concept has languished in the West. When Golan saw Stone's script, he obviously saw what could be "the next big thing." He and his company, Cannon Films, certainly promoted it as such. The opening of *Enter the Ninja* was promising. A Ninja clad all in white races through a jungle, killing red Ninjas as he goes. He invades a martial arts school and cleaves the sensei down the middle.

Surprise, surprise, it was all a hoax. It was a test for him to pass so he might graduate as a full-scale Ninja. Since he (Franco Nero) is the only Occidental ever to pass, his "brother" classmate (Sho Kosugi) is full of resentment. From here on, the Cannon "standard operating procedure" comes into effect. Nero travels to the Philippines to help out an old Vietnam war buddy with his plantation. The friend has become an impotent drunk, much to the displeasure of his beautiful English wife (Susan George).

A ruthless businessman (Christopher George) wants the friend's land and will do anything to get it, including kill everybody. Franco Nero is there to kick people. He does some nice bodyguard beating, thanks to his double, Mike Stone, until the bad guys hire a Ninja of their own. It turns out to be none other than the resentful classmate. Their war kills everyone but the wife.

The two Ninjas, one in white, the other in black (guess which is the good guy), face each other in the same Manila boxing ring that was used in the

Mike Stone kills red Ninjas in the jungle opening of Enter the Ninja.

Mike Stone prepares for battle at the climax of Enter the Ninja.

filming of *Firecracker*. "It turned out far better than I thought it would during filming," Stone admits. But what happened after the film's completion didn't turn out as Stone was led to believe.

"After they rehired me as choreographer, I took over a group of people which included Sho Kosugi, whom I hired to play the bad Ninja. All of them were extremely loyal. They all said that if I refused to work under those circumstances, they would as well. Except Sho Kosugi. But when we got back I was told that they, Menachem Golan and Yoram Globus, had made a mistake. They could have done this movie with me as the star and still made as much money. It was the subject that was the star, not the actor.

"They promised to do another film with me as the star. They also wanted Sho to co-star. During this negotiation period, Sho promised me orally that he would not sign before I signed. But then Cannon said they would use his son in the second picture. I didn't find out he had agreed until Cannon told me."

That was the birth of *Revenge of the Ninja* (1983). Sho Kosugi is an extremely ambitious man. He had dreams of being a movie star for years and trained every day since completing the first film in adapting actual martial arts to film choreography. It is his desire and expertise which permeate the otherwise exploitive ridiculousness of *Revenge of the Ninja*.

What can be said for both films is that they start

Mike Stone, with the moustache, faces his arch-enemy, Sho Kosugi, in Enter the Ninja.

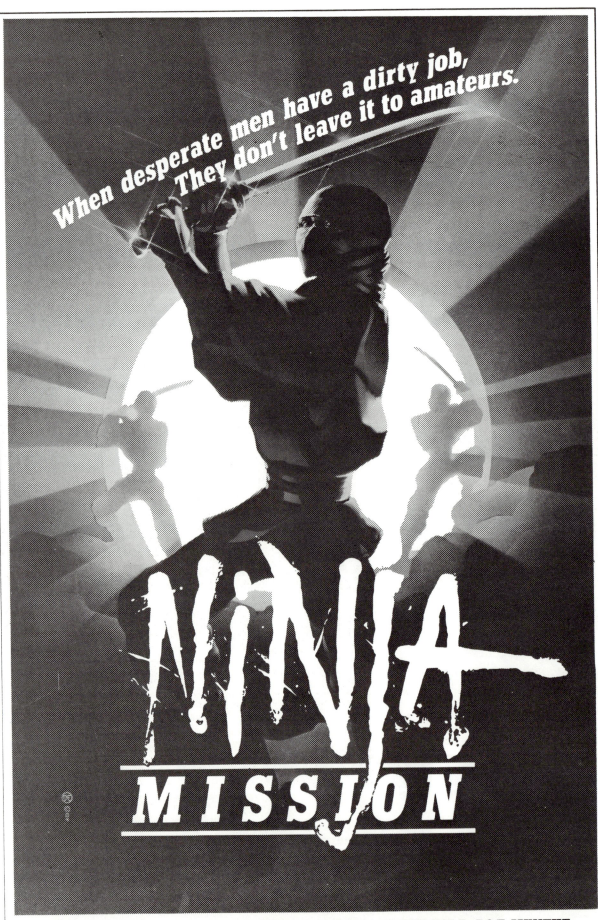

When desperate men have a dirty job,
They don't leave it to amateurs.

NINJA MISSION

"NINJA MISSION" Starring CHRISTOPHER KOHLBERG · HANNA POLA · BO F. MUNTHE
Music Composed and Performed by DANNY YOUNG Executive Producers CHARLES APERIA · GUY COLLINS
Produced by ROGER LUNDEY Directed by MATS HELGE A VTC Production

World Film Alliance From New Line Cinema

Swedish Ninjas? Why not? This film just shows how powerful the Ninja concept is.

well. In the sequel, Kosugi plays Cho Osaki, who returns to his Japanese house from a meeting with his American partner to find almost all of his family dead and Ninjas crawling all over the place. He takes them all out, then decides to pack up his infant son and honored mother and go to America. He opens a Japanese art gallery with his partner (Arthur Roberts) who is, in actuality, a heinous drug runner and a Ninja himself.

When the mob refuses to buy the cocaine Roberts has smuggled into the country inside Japanese dolls, he dons a silver mask, suits up in the all-black Ninja costume and kills the syndicate members one by one. The hero becomes involved when thugs try to steal the drug-filled dolls, then he investigates with a karate-trained policeman. His mother is murdered by the villain and his eight-year-old son is kidnapped by the girlfriend Roberts had set him up with.

The finale finds the black Ninja and silver masked Ninja battling through an office building, using almost every ancient weapon in the Ninjutsu arsenal. *Legendary Weapons of Japan* it's not.

Sho Kosugi's influence was obviously felt, but the Cannon approach kept undermining his integrity and historical accuracy. A much-vaunted truth of fiction is that the way it works in real life is always more interesting than what a writer can imagine. In this case it is true. If *Revenge of the Ninja* had been done as a serious film, the movie might have worked far better than the exploitive approach Cannon gave it.

It still makes for an impressive martial arts showcase. Deficiencies aside, Menachem Golan's instincts have borne fruit. At this writing a third—

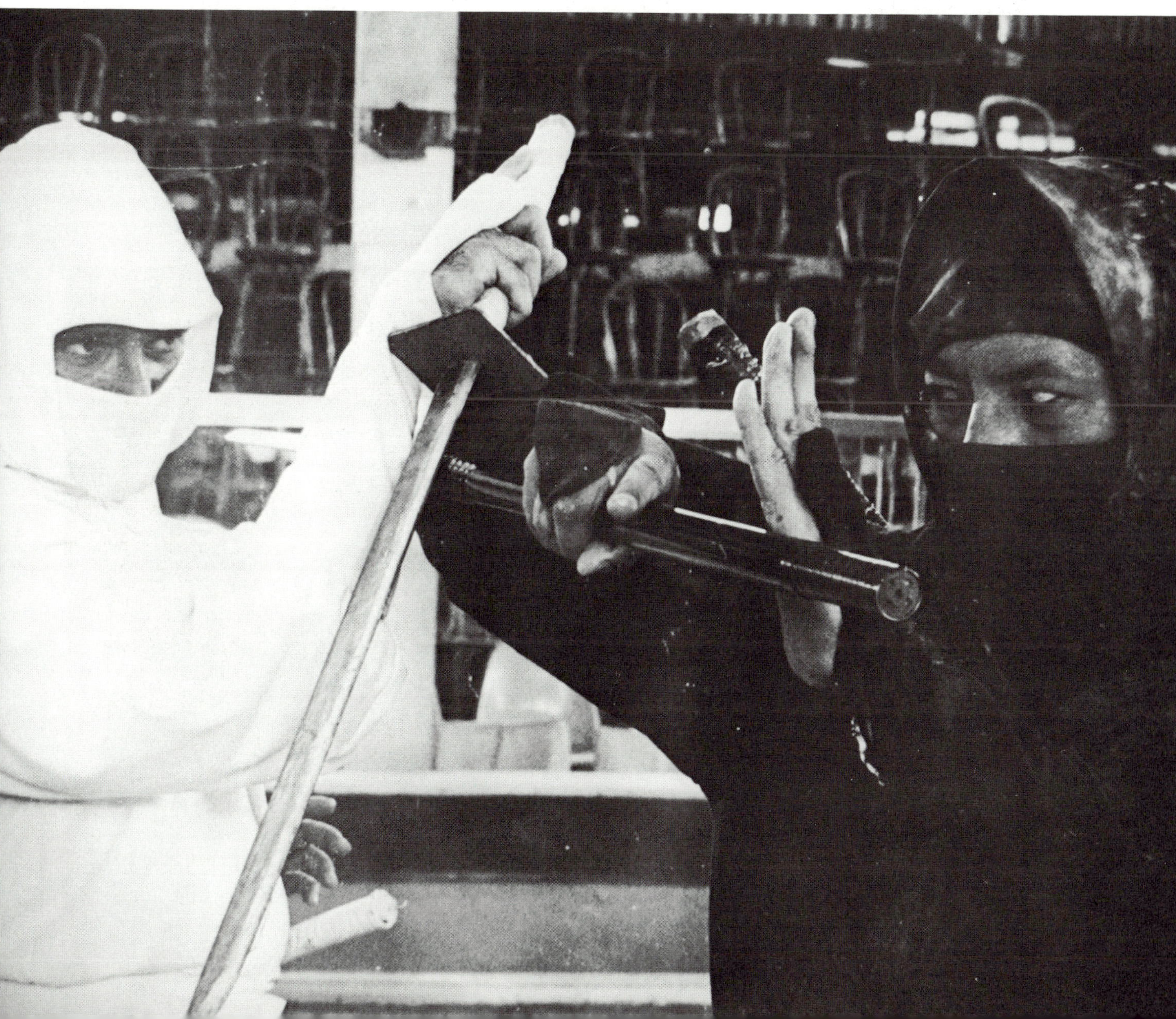

Close-up of enemy Ninjas—Mike Stone in white, Sho Kosugi in black—for Enter the Ninja.

Manachem Golan (far left) smiles with a friend as Franco Nero and Susan George discuss Enter the Ninja.

Mike Stone confers with actor Michael Beck and the stunt arranger on the television pilot movie that premiered before The Master *television series.*

THEY ARE DEADLY!

YOU CAN'T HEAR THEM...

YOU CAN'T SEE THEM...

DRAGON LEE in

the SECRET NINJA

AIMI PICTURES™ RELEASE

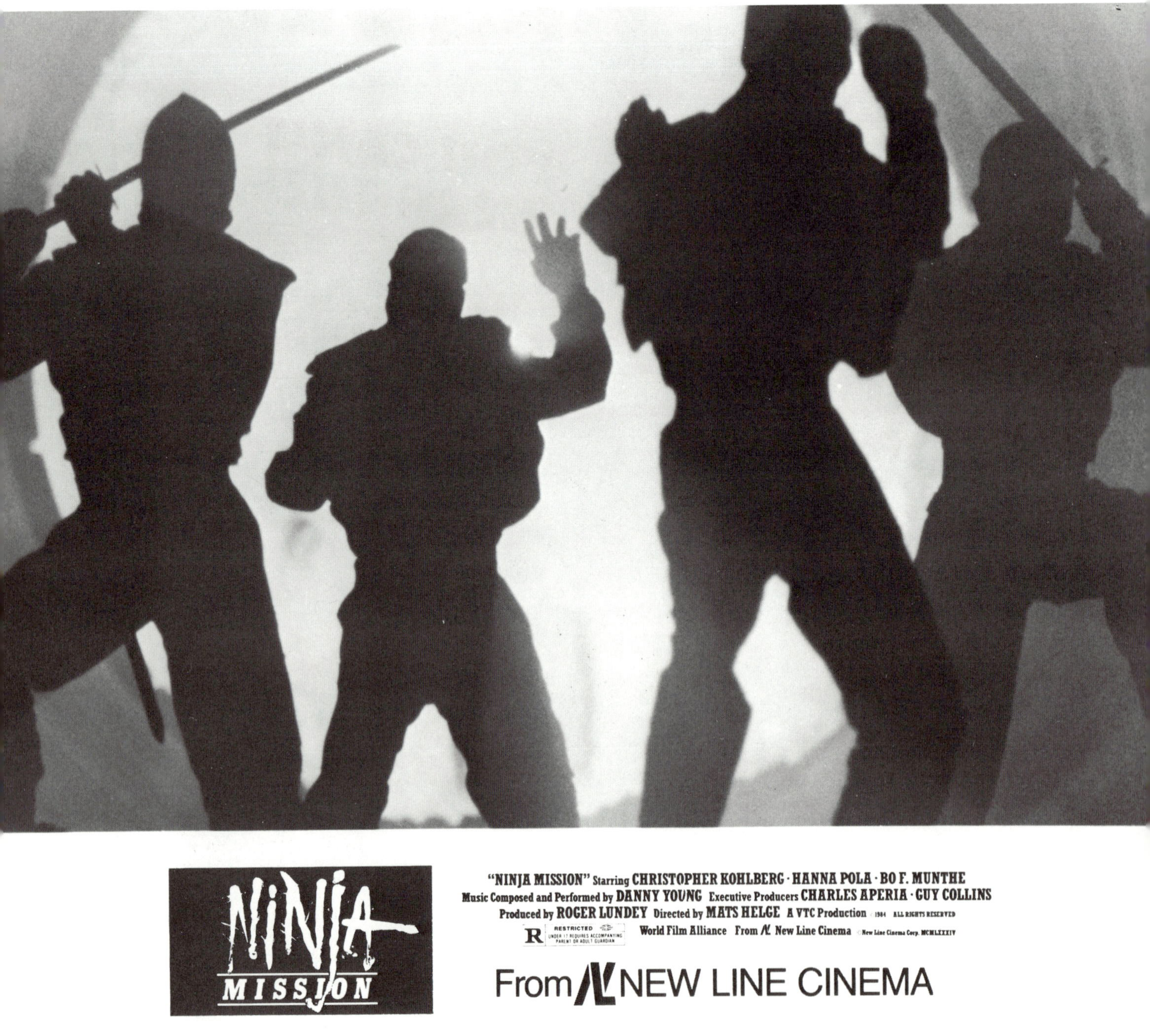

"NINJA MISSION" Starring CHRISTOPHER KOHLBERG · HANNA POLA · BO F. MUNTHE
Music Composed and Performed by DANNY YOUNG Executive Producers CHARLES APERIA · GUY COLLINS
Produced by ROGER LUNDEY Directed by MATS HELGE A VTC Production © 1984 ALL RIGHTS RESERVED
R RESTRICTED UNDER 17 REQUIRES ACCOMPANYING PARENT OR ADULT GUARDIAN World Film Alliance From NL New Line Cinema © New Line Cinema Corp. MCMLXXXIV

From NL NEW LINE CINEMA

Ninjas are everywhere!

and possibly most ludicrous—Cannon Ninja film is being finished. *Ninja III: The Domination,* in which an evil Ninja takes over the body of, as the press releases declare, "a beautiful blonde."

Ninjas are everywhere now. On movie screens, on television, on book racks, in comics, and even in toy stores. Kosugi has already signed for three more Ninja movies with other producers. Cannon has signed Chuck Norris for an "American Ninja" project of its own, and Mike Stone quietly works on his own new project—quite possibly the best martial arts movie of all.

The Master, another Kosugi-influenced work, came and went on NBC television. Warner Books has just released the ambitious and engrossing *Year of the Ninja Master* paperbacks, starting with *Dragon Rising.* Larry Hama, the creator of Marvel Comics' *G.I. Joe* series, has so successfully incorporated Ninjas that a white Ninja—complete with swords, bow, arrows, throwing stars, and nunchaka—is now part of the *G.I. Joe* toy soldier collection from Hasbro.

Elsewhere signs of a second American wave of martial arts movies grow. WW Entertainment has made an exclusive pact with Shaw Brothers to release their movies in America, including *Legendary Weapons of Kung Fu. The Karate Kid,* a movie about the philosophy of that violent art, was premiered in 1984 to good reviews and box office. Everywhere there is Japanese and Chinese lettering on clothes, on furniture, even on coffee mugs.

But if the second wave never materializes, America won't miss it. Americans may not be able to do another country's history better than the parent country, but kungfu, samurai, and karate pictures will never completely die out, as the western won't completely disappear from U.S. entertainment either. They are a part of our culture. A part of our past. No matter how violent or outlandish they get, they will always contain important messages about our lands and ourselves.

Why the martial arts movie? Because it can be beautiful, extreme, emotional, soaring, and freeing for an audience. That is what it is all about. Exhilaration.

THE TEN BEST MARTIAL ARTS MOVIES OF ALL TIME

In no particular order, they are:

1) THE CHINESE CONNECTION

(Directed by Wo Lei/starring Bruce Lee)
Bruce Lee's best overall film, directed by Lo Wei. Exceptional action and a strong, relevant plot were two ingredients the Chinese movie industry had never experienced together before this.

2) ENTER THE DRAGON

(Robert Clouse/Bruce Lee)
Not the greatest script ever written, or the greatest directing job ever done, nor did it contain the finest performances ever seen. Although a James Bond movie by way of Fu Manchu, Bruce Lee's presence and contribution created a sensation and instituted an American martial arts movie genre which became enfeebled after his death.

3) DRUNKEN MASTER

(Yuen Woo Ping/Jackie Chan)
Jackie Chan encapsulized and streamlined the Chinese kungfu comedy genre with this nonstop showcase of his acrobatic art.

4) PROJECT A

(Jackie Chan/Jackie Chan)
Jackie Chan takes the martial arts movie three giant steps further with this pirate adventure set in 1904 Hong Kong.

5) THE SHAOLIN TEMPLE

(Chang Hsin Yen/Jet Lee)
The People's Republic of China entered the kungfu film industry with an impressive distillation of traditional martial arts movie ingredients.

6) EIGHTEEN LEGENDARY WEAPONS OF CHINA

(Liu Chia Liang/Liu Chia Liang)
The quintessential kungfu movie.

7) BABY CART IN THE LAND OF DEMONS

(Kenji Misumi/Tomisaburo Wakayama)
A savage samurai thriller and a vicious indictment of feudal Japanese society seen through the eyes of an ugly decapitator and his young son.

8) THE HUMAN TARANTULA

(Kimiyoshi Yasuda/Raizo Ichikawa)
A nihilistic halfbreed samurai cuts down all in his path in an attempt to understand his love/hate relationship with Christianity.

9) ZATOICHI'S CANE SWORD

(Kimiyoshi Yasuda/Shintaro Katsu)
A wandering, humble, pathetic blind masseur gets the most powerful blade in all of Japan.

10) SEVEN SAMURAI

(Akira Kurosawa/Toshiro Mifune)
The engrossing epic that guided the Japanese film industry and influenced American action dramas.

Bruce Lee, the King of Kungfu.

Jackie Chan, the heir apparent to the throne of the martial arts movie world.

Tomisaburo Wakayama cuts through armies in the Baby Cart *movies.*

Toshiro Mifune, the "Japanese John Wayne."

THE 25 BEST AND WORST KUNGFU VIDEOTAPES

Now that you know everything you'll need to enjoy martial arts movies, the question is: Where do you get to see the movies mentioned? Well, most of them will come to you . . . on television. World Northal, or WW Entertainment, as it is also known, has an exclusive pact with Shaw Brothers' studio. This New York based distributor sells these movies, unedited, to theaters, as well as well edited versions (by the knowledgeable Larry Bensky) to TV stations. If you don't get them in your area, you can write your local stations to suggest they investigate World Northal's "Black Belt Theater" packages.

Meanwhile PBS stations irregularly run Japanese samurai classics. To see the wilder sword slashers—which will probably never be seen on TV—it is best to find the revival theaters or art houses in your communities and suggest they try to run some of the *Zatoichi, Sword of Vengeance, Sword of Justice,* or *Son of Black Mass* series. These Japanese chambara pictures have played all along the East and West coats.

However, perhaps the best place to seek out martial arts adventures is in videotape stores. Almost all the movies in the "Noble Norris and Nasty Ninjas" section are on videotape. Akira Kurosawa's great classics, *Yojimbo, Sanjuro, Seven Samurai,* and *Kagemusha,* are on tape. The viciously edited *Streetfighter* movies are on tape, as are *Roaring Fire* and *Shogun's Ninja.* Even *Shogun Assassin* is on tape.

In addition, there are dozens of kungfu movies on tape, from such companies as Video Gems, Vestron, Master Arts, Budget, QVC, VL-Vision Star, Orchids International, Omni, Wild West, and Value Video. Now you can have your local store order all of these tapes so you can see how they are for yourself, or you can listen to us. We've viewed over three hundred kungfu videotapes—some in English, some subtitled, some in Chinese—just so we could tell you what's what.

THE BEST

1) AVENGING BOXER (FEARLESS YOUNG BOXER)

(No director listed)
Peter Chen and Ca Sa Fa (Casanova) Wong beat each other and everybody else silly in order to possess a gold plate—a symbol of leadership for an insidious gang. But few can do better beating than Chen and Wong. The sets for this American Intercontinental film are far above those of the usual independently produced movie, and the plot rolls right along.

2) THE BLOODED TREASURY FIGHT (DRAGON DEVIL DIE)

(Pao Hsueh)
A titanic teamup of Tan Tao Liang, the great leg fighter, and David Chiang, the ex-Shaw Brothers superstar. The Chinese loved the plotline for *The Dirty Dozen* (1967) and this sub-titled videotape directed by Pao Hsueh is a prime example of its influence. Liang is the cop and Chiang the crook on the trail of ping-pong sized pearls hidden in "The Bloody Mill." There's an evil general, a map tattooed on a leg, traitors, and double and triple crosses galore in addition to some fine fighting.

3) THE BONE CRUSHING KID (KUNG FU CRUSHER)

(Hsieh Shing)
An independent production structured to feature the talents of goofy-looking Chin Lung. He has toiled as a supporting actor in dozens of features, so he takes advantage of this tale loosely based on Jackie Chan's *Eagle's Shadow.* He dresses as the Peking Opera Monkey King and as a woman to take vengeance on the villains. As they fight, the film also becomes a showcase for Monkey, Mantis, Tiger, and Crane styles.

4) CANTONEN IRON KUNG FU (IRON FIST OF KWANTUNG)

(Li Chao)
This particular effort is a nicely mixed bunch of clichés which serve to let Liang Chia Jen do his impressive stuff. He is a powerful martial artist who is very convincing doing his Iron Bridge kungfu style against the villains Eagle stylings.

5) CRACK SHADOW BOXERS

(Wan Yao Hua)
A charming and funny kungfu comedy featuring able supporting players Ku Feng and Chou Li Chung as stars. Through a series of mixups and mistaken identities, two conmen must face the evil Tiger Wu and his pair of henchmen, Leopard and Wolf. This film satirizes martial arts styles in addition to throwing in sight gags and sexual in-

Lo Lieh always seems buried under white hair, playing villains in innumerable action films.

nuendoes. A kungfu *Porky's?* Not quite, but well worth the viewing for the yuks as well as such esoteric styles as Shadow, Butterfly and Flying Fist—especially after seeing stacks of serious martial arts flicks.

6) DEADLY SHAOLIN KICKS (FLASH LEGS)

(Wuu Maa)

In the mid-1900s, eight thieves steal the "Eight Trigrams Map" and break it into eight pieces—vowing to meet again in three years after things cool down. What they don't count on is Tan Tao Liang, playing an undercover cop. Tan tracks one

Chi Kuan Chun (right) battles another veteran villain, Chaing Tao.

crook after another until he faces the eighth crook, played by Lo Lieh. The action is plentiful and Liang shows off his impressive taekwondo kicks to great advantage.

7) DRUNKEN ARTS AND CRIPPLED FIST

(Yuen Chien Yu)
Of all the movies that came in the wake of Jackie Chan's *Drunken Master,* this is one of the best. Simon Yuen returns in the company of his family to teach Li Yi Min how to get along in the world. The usual kungfu confusion ensues, what with jealous martial artists testing each other's skills, getting upset, and taking revenge; but there is no bloodshed—just impressive, exciting fight scenes.

8) THE EAGLE FIST

(Cheng Kay Ying)
The story of one man's training in Eagle Fist kungfu. Once he masters the technique, he is sent by his sifu in search of the infamous "18 Styles

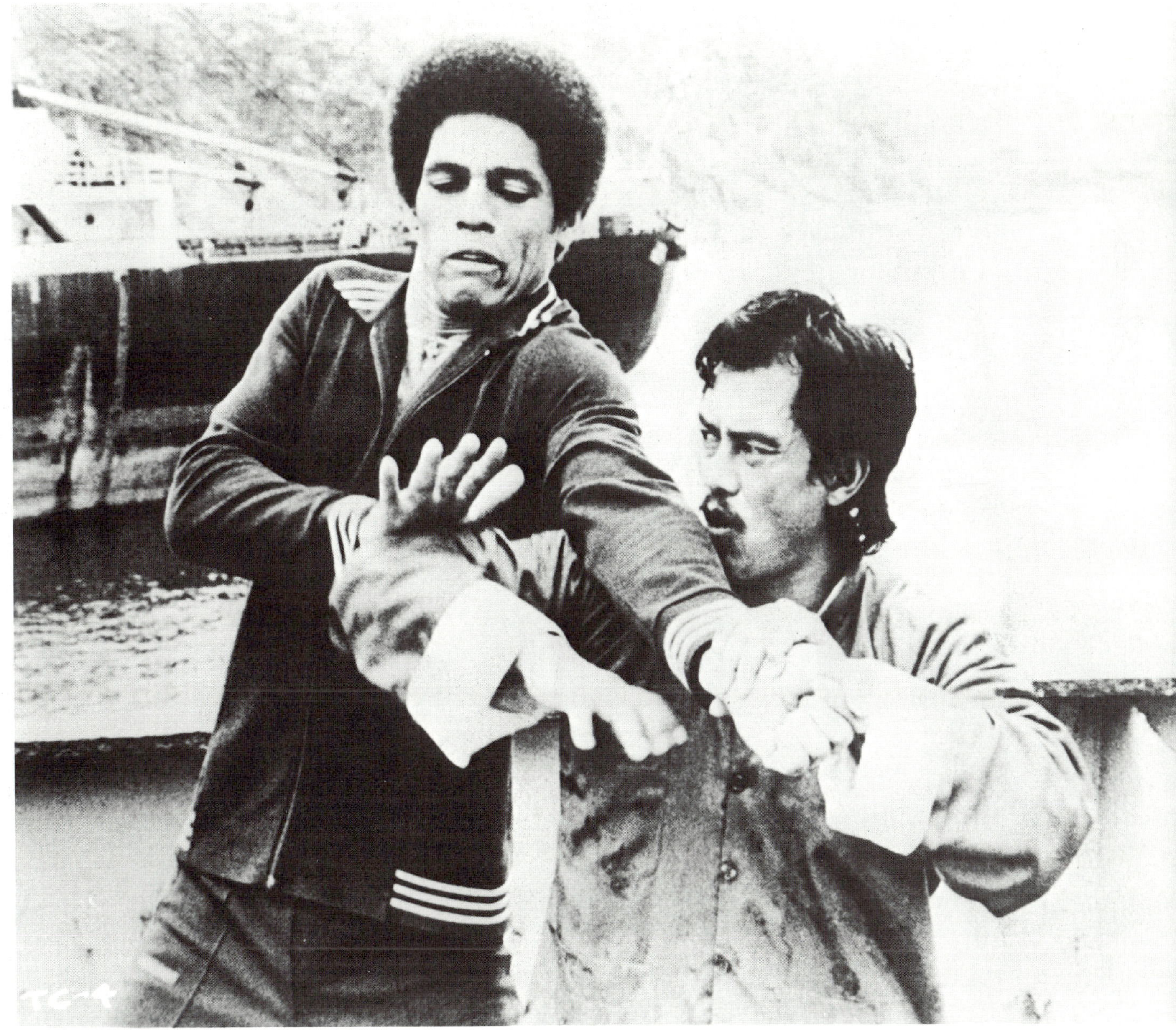

Chen Sing outclasses Jim Kelly, as he outclasses many other stars.

of the Monkey" and "Unlocking Vital Points Attack" books. Chi Kuan Chun is the student who toils for what turns out to be a villainous master. This twist ending elevates the otherwise common story line, but the fight scenes speak for themselves.

9) THE GOOSE BOXER

(Dai Shifu)

One of the best. Charles Heung plays a hapless bumpkin who just manages to survive all sorts of crazy goings-on as a maddened White Crane killer tries to flush out his enemies. It would be difficult to describe the charming combinations of training, fight, and comedy sequences which make this a top tape for any martial arts library, but how about this for a try: The hero mistakenly uses a sex manual to learn kungfu and flabbergasts the villain with such styles as "Pushing the Cart Uphill" and "Rowing Upstream."

China's greatest villain, Wang Lung Wei (right), spars with a new Chinese star, Mai Te Lo.

10) A HERO'S TEARS

(Li Tao)

The title should tip the viewer off. Instead of the usual *Bloody Fingernails* type title, this movie promises a more mature approach to the martial arts. And, for the most part, it delivers. A somber theme, well-drawn characters, beautiful sets, costumes, and lighting all make this videotape a fine change of pace. "Three Days Light," a famous hired killer, goes on a trek with a worshipful student to find expensive medicines to cure the assassin's sister's blindness. Their trip is fraught with danger.

11) HERO TATTOO WITH NINE DRAGONS

(Pao Hsueh Li)

Bandits kill a martial artist's family and he swears revenge. Sound familiar? Well, it is familiar, but this adventure is special because of its stars, Chen Kuan Tai and Chia Ling. Tai, of course, started his career at the Shaw Brothers, but Ling is a female star who has been featured in dozens of films. This movie is one of the best places to see the two—he for his Hung Gar techniques and she for her humorous martial arts antics.

The Dirty Half-Dozen, Chinese style. John Liu (far right) leads the Kung Fu Commandos.

12) INCREDIBLE MASTER BEGGERS (12 KUNG FU KICKS)

(Tu Lu Po)
The star of this movie is a personable, fast, acrobatic, chunky young fighter with strong screen presence. It is only too bad he's named Bruce Liang. But don't let the name put you off. He doesn't mimic the famous Lee and he has a style all his own. He uses Dragon, Snake, Wing Chun, Tiger, Crane, as well as the twelve kicks of the "Tan Toy" style in this tale of a begger who takes vengeance for his girlfriend's savage murder.

13) THE JADE CLAW (CRYSTAL FIST)

(Hwa I Hung)
Another Jackie Chan variant, but one starring Billy Chong, the best of the Chan imitations. Simon Yuen himself is in this one, playing a kungfu cook who teases Chong before getting down to the se-

rious business of teaching the young man Eagle Claw so he can avenge his father's death at the hands of Master Yen's (Double Phoenix Eye style—not to mention his henchmen, "Deaf" and "Blind." The plot, almost as always, is secondary to the fights, choreographed by the always special Yuen family. But between them and Chong, who can make the extremely difficult look almost effortless, they are amazing to watch.

14) KUNG FU COMMANDOS (INCREDIBLE KUNG FU MISSION)

(Chang Hsin Yi)

The most accessible of the *Dirty Dozen* variants. John Liu, the amazing leg fighter, is hired to rescue a rebel from the fortress of a deadly enemy. His only help are five unskilled mercenaries: an ex-undertaker (Chen Lung), a juggler, a brothel worker, a carpenter, and a streetfighter. At first they don't want to help, but Liu's amazing legs kick them into line. The Dirty Half-Dozen rescue the rebel, but only Liu survives to deliver the man to his treacherous employer. Lui is truly the star here and lives up to his billing. He uses such techniques as "Sticky Feet" and "Lui Foot," climaxing the showcase by delivering fourteen rapid fire consecutive kicks without putting his foot down!

15) THE INCREDIBLE KUNG FU LEGS (THE LEG FIGHTERS)

(Li Tso Nan)

Another one of our favorites. Not only does it have Chen Lung and Tan Tao Liang, it showcases Hsia Kuang Li, a tall, beautiful, female fighter who can kick with (and at) the best of them. And Tan Tao *is* one of the best. Watching this trio glide through the familiar story of a stubborn girl learning kungfu so she can defeat a heinous villain is a comfortable joy. Imagine the Rockettes trained in kungfu and you get only a small idea of the kind of athletics you're in for. People fight each other, pairs, trios, and more—with arms, legs, and weapons.

16) THE MASTER STRIKES

(No director listed)

Ca Sa Fa (Casanova) Wong is one of the great secrets of the martial arts film. You could haunt the best Chinatown theaters and see the best martial arts movies without getting a glimpse of him. The best place to find him is on videotape, and this is one of his best videotapes. He is not exactly handsome and he is not exactly ugly, but he is a good actor, a great acrobat, and a terrific fighter. There's only one problem with this videotape—a story of Casanova trying to retrieve a stolen jade lion. The two middle reels of the film were reversed! The plot is a jigsaw puzzle, but it is worth piecing the story together to see Wong in action.

17) THE PRODIGAL BOXER—PART ONE

(Chai Yang Min)

THE PRODIGAL BOXER II: THE SECRET OF THE SHAOLIN POLES

(Au Yang Chu)

These tales of the famous Shaolin student Fang Shih Yu feature Meng Fei, one of the *The Five Masters of Death.* Both films start as if they are going to be straight kungfu adventures, only to turn tragic in the middle. Meng Fei must suffer mightily—as must all those around him—before he takes vengeance on the bad guys. Both Fei and the movie become more accomplished, personable, and watchable in the second film, from the opening "warfan" fight to the impressive final battle on the booby-trapped poles.

18) RENEGADE MONK

(Chang Shin I)

John Liu is back and kicking. This time he's after a murdering monk. With the help of an adoring student, he tracks the killer. The only problem with this workable video is the all-too-obvious special effects used to "enhance" the fight scenes. Instead, they reduce the reality in a genre whose verisimilitude is already frightfully low. Even so, great kicks, jumps, splits, and weapons abound in abundant kungfu confrontations.

19) SEVEN GRANDMASTERS

(Joseph Kuo)

Want a great story? Great acting? Great sets? Great costumes? Well, forget about it. This video features great fighting and that's about it. Still, the battles with butterfly knives, swords, spears staffs, hands, feet, heads and bodies are well worth the price of admission. Director/producer Joseph Kuo didn't have much money but he has great martial arts expertise. That much is obvious from the very first chop in this fight-filled film.

Ca Sa Fa, otherwise known as Casanova Wong (center), kicks while Samo Hung charges. Both are terrific actor/fighters.

Tan Tao Liang (left) as he's known and loved best—the baddest leg fighter in the Orient—taking on the villain in The Incredible Kung Fu Legs.

20) SHAOLIN INVINCIBLE STICKS

(Lee Tso Nam)
It's easy to tell the good guys from the bad guys in this period piece. The former all wear their hair cut short while the latter have "queues." That means it's the Republic versus the Imperialists near the start of the twentieth century. The title also means that this is the ultimate "stick fighting" movie on videotape. Hsia Kuang Li, the Incredible Kung Fu Legs, is back, only this time in the company of Don Wong Tao, and they both use staffs—short sticks, tri-sectional sticks, the heavy Chen Kang stick, and the Tzu Wu stick—to a fare-thee-well.

21) SUPERPOWER

(Lin Chan Wei)
Billy Chong is back in action—this time without Simon Yuen. An old Manchu group, the Eight Banners Clan, decide to take vengeance on the descendants of five kungfu masters who had humiliated them years before. The son of one of the five is sent to an aged sifu who teaches him enough to beat the avengers. Although the tape has music stolen from American movies and features the usual ludicrous sound effects of arms swishing through the air and bone meeting bone, Billy Chong's exuberance and spectacular skills save the day.

22) THREE SHAOLIN MUSKETEERS (THREE SWORDSMEN)

(Ou Yang Chun)
What can be said about a kungfu film which starts with a food fight instead of a fist fight? Namely this: it is a good combination of comedy and fighting featuring a few personable martial arts stars. Lo Lieh, Meng Fei, Liang Chia Jen, and veteran actress Lung Chung Erh all let their hair down in this funny film in which the battles take a back seat to the humor. Even the most rabid fight fanatic should be disarmed by the wit as well as the kicks.

23) THUNDERING MANTIS (MANTIS FIST FIGHTER)

(Yeh Yung Tsu)
Liang Chia Jen puts his hair back up for this one, which is considered to contain his finest ninety minutes. When the rough, strong Jen enacts a hero, he almost always plays an honorable character who fights for the downtrodden. Here the injustice is so immense that his character literally goes insane. And since that character knows Mantis Fist, it sets the stage for a savage, virtuoso climactic performance that has not been surpassed for sheer raw energy. Everybody dies in this picture, except the hero, who becomes a gibbering animal. An amazing viewing experience.

24) TWINS OF KUNG FU

(No director listed)
This is a mob kungfu film. There are lots of heroes, lots of villains, and lots of kungfu styles, like Dragon, Phoenix, and the "Plum Flower Fist." The twins are a son and daughter team of a martial arts master who must defeat a mountain killer who is filling a village river with poison and the countryside with corpses.

25) THE YOUNG AVENGER

(Wilson Tong)
An unusual effort starring Yung Wang Yu as an undertaker's assistant who doubles as a grave robber. In payment for his evil deeds, a ghost chases him around town, only to reveal itself as a wronged sifu. The ghost/sifu trains the lad and sends him out after four thieves. The variants that make this one a winner are the consistently unusual approaches on traditional concepts and themes. Instead of foiling the villain with a classic kungfu weapon, Yu uses what could be described as a "Swiss Army spade."

HONORABLE MENTION

Look for these too:

26) ADVENTURE FOR IMPERIAL TREASURE (starring Don Wang Dao)
27) BANDITS, PROSTITUTES, AND SILVER (Don Wang Dao)
28) THE BIG RASCAL (Chi Kuan Chun)
29) CUTE FOSTER SISTER (Yan Hsaio)
30) DREAMING FAST WITH SLENDER HAND (Tsing Yuan Pao)
31) DRUNKEN SWORDSMAN (Yo Hua)
32) MYSTERIOUS FOOTWORKS OF KUNG FU (Chaing Tao)
33) THE NEW SOUTH HAND BLOWS AND NORTH KICK BLOWS (John Liu)
34) THE ROVING HEROES (Chi Kuan Chun)
35) SIX DIRECTION BOXING (David Chiang)

The Chinese could have an astonishing team of high kicking Rockettes, if Hsia Kuang Li (right) is any evidence. She's the other pair of The Incredible Kung Fu Legs.

THE WORST

It wasn't easy picking the twenty-five worst kungfu movies on videotape. There were so many. We didn't want simply to choose the most mediocre—there were legions of them, too. We wanted the absolute worst. The garbage. The dreck. The ones with the incomprehensible plots, the laughable stories, the horrible acting, the stupid sound effects, the absurd special effects, and the absolutely worst fighting. Interestingly enough, almost all of them take place in modern times.

1) THE AMSTERDAM CONNECTION

(Directed by Lo Ke and Fang Mui San)
This film is strung together like a police report. Big Louie (Yang Sze—also known as Bolo) and Ah Bun decide to put their casino competition out of business by telling the police about their enemy's drug dealing. The enemy, in addition to pushing drugs, makes porno movies and sells the actresses to white slavery rings. One of these girls, Fanny, proves to be everybody's undoing.

2) BLOOD ON THE SUN

(No director found)
Not to be confused with the 1945 thriller starring James Cagney. This pathetic number stars a variety of bozos in a 1936 Japanese-occupied Chinese village. As a change of pace from raping and killing, the Japanese hold a martial arts tournament to demoralize the citizens. After much swearing and bloodshed, the tournament demoralizes the viewer.

3) THE BLOODY FIGHT

(Ng Tien Tsu)
There's the "who's the fastest gun" sub-genre of the western. This here's the "who's the fastest fist" sub-genre of the eastern. A Japanese wanders around killing all the Chinese he can with his "knife-fingers"—ramming his digets into chests, and the like. He's stopped by an intrepid band of kungfu fighters. The camera work here is so poor one can usually see the blows falling short by about two feet. The fight scenes are so poorly done that there is one where the hero jumps into the air and beats his opponent to death while floating.

4) THE BLOODY FISTS

(Ng See Yuen)
Believe it or not, this was the director's first film, a grimy little number with reputable Chen Sing fighting Chen Kuan-Tai to the death. Tai plays a long-haired Japanese fighter who wears a loud kimono (they *all* wear loud kimonos), while Sing is an escaped fugitive patriot. The two antagonists beat each other to death on the beach. The sound effects for the punches and kicks are "ricocheting bullets."

5) DUEL OF THE IRON FIST

(Chang Cheh)
Tang Chia choreographed and Ti Lung and David Chiang starred in this early (1971) Shaw Brothers work. Still, their efforts were not enough to elevate this dated blood bath. Chiang plays "Rover," an assassin with some sort of throat disease, and Lung plays a handsome young swain whose dad is killed, whose family is slaughtered, and whose girlfriend is forced to become a prostitute before committing suicide. With knives in each hand, the heroes plough through a battalion before finally expiring themselves.

6) DUMB BOXER

(Liu Yang)
The title says it all.

7) EIGHTEEN BRONZEGIRLS OF SHAOLIN

(Chian Lai Ya)
They paint these eighteen women bronze, you see, and every time somebody on screen hits one, they go "bong!"

8) FIGHT FOR SURVIVAL

(No director remembered)
The pits, especially since this movie was released by CBS/FOX Video, a major American distributor known for packaging the Bruce Lee videotapes. Although advertised as an "R" rated thriller, this is actually the stupidest of children's movies with a confusing plot and bad martial arts.

9) THE FISTS OF VENGEANCE (TWO FISTS VS. SEVEN SAMURAI)

(Chen Hung Man)
Kung Bun is a Jimmy Wang Yu lookalike. Here he fights Shoji Karada for a trainload of sand. The final fight on the moving train could probably set records for overwrought ridiculousness. By the looks of it, this film was inspired by Buster Keaton.

10) FURY OF THE SHAOLIN MASTER (THE SHAOLIN MASTER AND THE KID)

(Lin Fu di)
A man returns home to find his family slaughtered, save for his four-year-old nephew. The man travels the road of vengeance with the child. *Lone Wolf and Son* this is not, as viewers vainly try to follow the knotted storyline. There's a man with a sword inside his arm, another guy with ball-shaped bombs, and a white-haired villain who gets hanged in a flying finale.

11) THE GHOSTLY FACE

(S.K. Yang)
The only kungfu movie with "scenes of Bali tribal ceremonies!" In addition, people leap tall trees in a single bound while trying to capture a mysterious killer who has stolen a magic sword.

12) THE INVINCIBLE

(Lo Jun)
Jimmy Wang Yu out to save the Sung Dynasty, to the soundtrack strains of music from the movie *Shaft* (1971).

13) THE INVINCIBLE (SWIFT SHAOLIN BOXER)

(Chen Hung Min)
This is the "Match Game" of martial arts movies. The viewers can fill in their own plot since the film doesn't have one. "Do you know what this means?" says one character. "Yes," says the other. "Good," says the first. "Then we don't have to discuss it." Only the audience is left in the dark. Lo Lieh is in this, as is Angela Mao Ying, and some ghosts. Aside from that, you're on your own.

14) JAPANESE CONNECTION (A TOOTH FOR A TOOTH)

(Kong Hung)
A film made in the Philippines, with Japanese smuggling opium into modern-day China. This seemed natural for a sequel entitled *An Upper Lip for an Upper Lip.*

15) THE KING BOXER

(Kung Min)
Not to be confused with *Five Fingers of Death,* this is a slimy modern-day thriller filmed in Thailand, with an incredibly young Meng Fei getting hacked up by twenty knife killers so Shi Tai Shan can take revenge on Shoji Karata. Almost everyone is killed just before the hero tears Shoji's heart out of his chest.

16) KUNG FU ARTS (RAGING TIGER VS. MONKEY KING)

(Lee Shi Giei)
A girl is sent adrift with a monkey. The monkey is able to cure the girl's wounds when she is accidentally injured by the hero. She has a baby boy who can communicate with monkeys. With the boy's help, the hero usurps the villain and takes over the land. A kungfu version of *Tarzan* with bad martial arts.

17) KUNG FU-RY

(Fung James)
Pretty clever title, huh? The movie matches the title in sophistication. The fight scenes are speeded up and everybody gets croaked before this grimy story of a paid assassin's comeuppance winds down.

18) LAST CHALLENGE OF THE DRAGON

(Steve Chan)
The last word in sweaty melodrama, as a kungfu master seeks to put his spoiled children right. He is constantly prevented in his goal by the evil Mr. Wong, a drug pusher and an all-around lousy guy. This film's idea of subtlety has the number-one son answer Mr. Wong's challenge by driving through his wall on a motorcycle. After that, the two groups of antagonists start shooting one another in the head.

19) THE MAGNIFICENT FIST (KUNG FU TITANS)

(Kam Aug)
The Japanese want to steal our hero's ginseng. That's right, the herb ginseng. This makes our hero into a latter-day Robin Hood—stealing from the Japanese and giving to the Chinese—until he gets a note reading "Your father has been killed and your mother is in very poor health." Our hero then kills the rest of the Japanese.

20) SEVEN BLOWS OF THE DRAGON (THE WATER MARGIN)

(Chang Cheh)
Although important historically, this sumptuous Shaw Brothers movie is badly dated, as were director Cheh's previous films, filled as they were with ripped-open stomachs and dripping intestines. Especially laughable are the "Eighteen Tumbles of Young Dragon," which are announced on screen triumphantly. Then there's a shot of David Chiang awkwardly rolling down a hill.

21) SHAOLIN DEATH SQUAD

(Joseph Kuo)
After releasing the Bruce Lee films to good sales, CBS/FOX Video insisted on finding some of the worst kungfu films imaginable and putting them on the market—erroneously thinking that any kungfu garbage they foisted on the public would work. This was their first attempt. It didn't work. They followed this up with the even more dreadful *Fight for Survival*. For the record, this has nothing to do with Shaolin.

22) STORY IN TEMPLE RED LILLY

(Pao Yung)
Understanding this film is tantamount to understanding Swahili with no lessons. Based on a famous Chinese tale that had to be more comprehensible than this, it has some bad guys attempting to usurp the throne and some good guys stopping them. People fly around on giant eagles, flame spurts from a variety of strange places, a tiny child fights with a hoop, and monks fight with iron bells.

23) STREETGANGS OF HONG KONG

(Chang Cheh)
For a man who made great superhero kungfu movies in the last seventies and early eighties, his earlier career is full of screeching clunkers, such as this one. Although Chang Cheh directed and Liu Chia Liang and Tang Chia choreographed, nothing could save this modern-day turkey in which a young man seeks vengeance for his dad, the night watchman's, death. It's one of those in which everybody swings knives around while screeching.

24) THUNDER STORM SWORD

(No director conceded)
The very hard-to-follow story concerns a magic sword that makes a waterfall go up. Unfortunately that's all it does. The martial arts in the movies consists of one guy swinging his arms into the camera.

25) THE YOUNG TIGER

(Wo Ma)
The modern-day police are so hard up that they release suspected killer Meng Fei to lead them to the real killer, mob boss Ko Tai Lung. It is hard to decide which is worse; the filmmaking or the fighting.

HONORABLE MENTION

Run screaming from these too:

26) CHALLENGE THE DRAGON—Star Tarng Long swings his arms a lot.
27) CHINESE KUNG FU AND ACUPUNCTURE—/What a combination.
28) A CITY CALLED DRAGON—The murky fights that can be seen are unwatchable.
29) DEATH COMES IN THREE—Not "threes" mind you, just three.
30) ENTER THREE DRAGONS—The worst of many awful Bruce Lee ripoffs.
31) THE FLYING GUILLOTINE—A hatbox with teeth.
32) THE FUNNY MAN AND ??? BOXING—Even the title is illegible.
33) JAWS OF THE DRAGON—Hilarious sex and violence.
34) MY KUNG FU MASTER—A woman looks for an imp.
35) RIDER OF REVENGE—A homicidal brewery owner.

ALIASES

Finding good actors and directors is hard enough without English translations of Oriental names getting in the way. The Japanese occasionally switch family and first names. In other words you might see Toshiro Mifune credited as Mifune Toshiro, but at least they don't rename him Teddy Mifune or something equally ridiculous.

Below are most of the Orient's major martial arts filmmakers. On the left, the most common or accurate use of their names. On the right, various pseudonyms and translations.

DAVID CHIANG	—	Chiang Tai Wei, Garth Lo
JACKIE CHAN	—	Jacky Chan, Chen Yuan Lung, Chen Yuan Long, Chen Long, Chen Lung, Cheng Lung
CHANG CHEH	—	Chang Chen, Zhang Che
HUANG CHENG LI	—	Wong Chung Lee, Huang Zhengli
LUI CHIA HUI	—	Gordon Lui, Liu Jiahui
LIU CHIA LIANG	—	Lou Chiana, Larry Linshire, Liu Jialiang
SHINICHI CHIBA	—	Sonny Chiba
BILLY CHONG	—	Chong Kuan Li, Zhong Quanli
KUO CHUI	—	Kuo Chue, To Lung
CARTER HUANG	—	Carter Wong, Carter Wang, Huang Ka Ta, Huang Jiada, Ca Ta Wang
SAMO HUNG	—	Hung Chin Pao, Hong Jinbao
SHIH KIEN	—	Shi Jian, Shih Chien, Shik Chien
CHEN KUAN TAI	—	Chen Guantai
BRUCE LE	—	Huang Kin Lung
BRUCE LEE	—	Lee Jun Fan, Lee Shao Lung, Li Xiaolung
LIN LEI JEI	—	Jet Lee
BRUCE LI	—	Ho Tsung Tao, Ho Tsun Tao, Li Shiao Lung, Lee Roy Lung
BRUCE LIANG	—	Bruce Leung, Leung Siu Lung
LILY LI	—	Li Lili, Lili Li
LO LIEH	—	Luo Lie
CHIA LING	—	Jia Ling
JOHN LIU	—	Liu Chung Liang, Liu Zhong Liang
TI LUNG	—	Di Long
ANGELA MAO	—	Angela Mao Ying, Mao Ying
NORA MIAO	—	Miao Ho Sau, Miao Ker Hsui
HIROYUKI SANADA	—	Henry Sanada, Duke Sanada
NG SEE YUEN	—	Ng Sze Yuen, Wu Siyuan
FU SHENG	—	Alexander Fu Sheng
ETSUKO SHIOMI	—	Sue Shiomi
CHEN SING	—	Chen Hsing, Chen Xing, Chen Shing
YANG SZE	—	Bolo
KWAN TAK HING	—	Guan Dexing
TAN TAO LIANG	—	Delon Tam
MAI TE LO	—	Mai Te Tao
LO WEI	—	Luo Wei
CASANOVA WONG	—	Ca Sa Fa
YUEN WOO PING	—	Yuan Heping
JIMMY WANG YU	—	Wong Yu
SIMON YUEN	—	Yuen Hsaio Tien, Yuan Xiaotian

It can be confusing and frustrating being a martial arts movies enthusiast. But remember, you can always talk to us. Please feel free to write with any questions or comments to Richard Meyers, in care of the publisher. Thank you.